Gurudakshina:
Facets of Indian Archaeology
(Part II)

Essays presented to Prof. V.N. Misra

SOUTH ASIAN ARCHAEOLOGY SERIES

EDITED BY ALOK K. KANUNGO   No. 8

Gurudakshina:
Facets of Indian Archaeology
(Part II)

Essays presented to Prof. V.N. Misra

Edited by

Alok Kumar Kanungo

BAR International Series 1665
2007

Published in 2019 by
BAR Publishing, Oxford

BAR International Series 1665

South Asian Archaeology Series No. 8
Series Editor: Alok K. Kanungo

Gurudakshina: *Facets of Indian Archaeology (Part II)*

ISBN 9781407300696 paperback
ISBN 9781407331393 e-book

DOI https://doi.org/10.30861/9781407300696

A catalogue record for this book is available from the British Library

This book is available at www.barpublishing.com

BAR Publishing is the trading name of British Archaeological Reports (Oxford) Ltd.
British Archaeological Reports was first incorporated in 1974 to publish the BAR
Series, International and British. In 1992 Hadrian Books Ltd became part of the BAR
group. This volume was originally published by John and Erica Hedges Ltd. in
conjunction with British Archaeological Reports (Oxford) Ltd / Hadrian Books Ltd,
the Series principal publisher, in 2007. This present volume is published by BAR
Publishing, 2019.

BAR
PUBLISHING

BAR titles are available from:

BAR Publishing
122 Banbury Rd, Oxford, OX2 7BP, UK
EMAIL   info@barpublishing.com
PHONE   +44 (0)1865 310431
FAX   +44 (0)1865 316916
www.barpublishing.com

Foreword

Alok Kumar Kanungo
Series Editor, South Asian Archaeology Series
International Series of British Reports

The International Series of British Archaeological Reports, with its 1500 titles to the present time, is undoubtedly one of the most important places of publication in the discipline of Archaeology. But it is a pity that works on the archaeology of South Asia have been less represented in the series than their interest and value deserves.

The archaeological record of South Asia (comprising India, Pakistan, Nepal, Bhutan, Bangladesh, Sri Lanka and the Maldives) is extremely rich. This wealth begins in the Lower Palaeolithic period and includes, for example, the Harappan Civilization, one of the oldest in the world (covering a very large area and having many unique features -- the most ancient known town planning, its architecture and high standards of civic hygiene, its art, iconography, paleography, numismatics and international trade). South Asia also has a large number of earlier, contemporary, and later Neolithic and Chalcolithic cultures. Moreover, what makes South Asia particularly significant for the study of past human behaviour is the survival of many traditional modes of life, like hunting-gathering, pastoralism, shifting cultivation, fishing, and fowling, the study of which throws valuable light on the reconstruction of past cultures. In the region there are a large number of government and semi-government institutions devoted to archaeological teaching and/or research in archaeology and a large and professionally trained body of researchers.

Of course, a number of universities and other institutions, in the area do have their own publication programmes and there are also reputed private publishing houses. However, British Archaeological Reports, a series of 30 years standing, has an international reputation and distribution system. In order to take advantage of the latter – to bring archaeological researches in South Asia to the notice of scholars in the western academic world – the South Asian Archaeology Series has been instituted within the International Series of British Archaeological Reports. This series (which it is hoped to associate with an institution of organization in the area) aims at publishing original research works of international interest in all branches of archaeology of South Asia.

Those wishing to submit books for inclusion in the South Asian Archaeology Series should contact the South Asian Archaeology Series Editor, who will mediate with John Hedges, one of the BAR Editors and publishers of BAR, in Oxford. The subject has to be appropriate and of the correct academic standard (*curriculum vitae* are requested and books may be referred); instructions for formatting will be given, as necessary.

Dr. Alok Kumar Kanungo
Department of Archaeology
Deccan College Post-Graduate & Research Institute
Pune 411006
INDIA
email: alok_kanungo@yahoo.com

Today Prof. V.N. Misra (Misraji) completes 70 years of his life. He is one of the most respected archaeologists of India, having a profound knowledge of archaeology, anthropology and ancient literature. In his career of nearly half a century in archaeology, he has supervised research of 25 Ph.D. students, and dissertations of a number of M.A. and M. Phil. students on diverse topics in fields like Palaeolithic, Mesolithic, Neolithic, Chalcolithic, Rock Art, Harappan Civilization, Historical archaeology, bronzes, ceramics, and ethnoarchaeology. In these days of growing narrow specialization Misraji is one of the small number of archaeologists in the country to have supervised research in such a diverse range of subjects. That prompted me to edit a volume out of Ph. D. dissertations completed under his guidance. Unfortunately, one of Misraji's students, S.C. Nanda is no more. Almost all his students are employed in different academic positions in India, Bangladesh and Nepal. This has its plus as well as minus points; the plus being that all are academically oriented and many of them are active in research; the minus points are that some have diverted themselves to research areas quite different from their Ph.D. topic, and some are fully occupied with the administration of their institutions. But then who would not like to refresh his/her memory of doctoral research? And those memories led to this volume.

The volume is purposely designed in such a way that all the papers are based on the Ph.D. dissertations of the contributors, and divided into two parts; Part I covers the gist of the thesis, and Part II covers the changes and improvements which the author would have made if he/she were to do the same research today. This part was not mandatory for scholars who got their degree in last five years[1]. I felt that a volume of this kind will probably be useful to all students of archaeology and can be widely distributed. This will also make available to scholars all the research done under Misraji in one place, and also give some idea of the kind of research that has been carried out at the Deccan College.

As regards Misraji's own publications, keeping in view their number and diversity of themes, I decided to invite two specially written papers: one an annotated bibliography of all his writings by Dr. P.P. Joglekar, and the other an evaluation of his position in the Indian archaeological context by Prof. K.K. Basa. I myself have written a piece on Misraji as an archaeologist and human being. Some overlap among these three papers is unavoidable. However, there are significant differences in our approaches. My paper basically gives a chronological account of Misraji's research career while Joglekar highlights the main points of each of his major publications. And Basa attempts an evaluation of the various aspects of Misraj's work. In all these three papers, Misraji being the core subject, justice could only be done by scholars who have not been his students but know him and his work well.

I had thought of this volume when Misraji attained the age of 65 years and I was just starting my Ph.D. but I did not dare to ask for papers from such senior people and thought I should wait until I am better equipped to edit such a volume. I started inviting the papers on *Diwali* day in November 2004. No sooner had I sent out the invitations to the potential authors, I started getting overwhelming response. This naturally reflects the regard which Misraji's students have for him. Not many people may be knowing that two of the contributors, Katy Dalal and Kurush Dalal, are mother and son. This may well be the only example anywhere that parent and child have done Ph.D. under the same teacher. Although I shared the idea of this volume only with the contributors, the word slowly got out and many of Misraji's admirers wanted to contribute to the volume. However, I explained to them that I wanted the volume to be restricted only to the contributions of Misraji's students, the exceptions being the two invited contributions and one of my own[2].

The 17 papers by Misraji's Ph.D. students cover the period from the Palaeolithic to the early historic time in India, and one paper on the early historic period of Bangladesh (Rahman). Region-wise in India, three papers are related to south (Jayaraj, Raju and Reddy); three to north

---

[1] Though some authors have finished their Ph.D. earlier than 5 years but have not written the IInd part due to various unavoidable reasons.

[2] Shaik Abdul Munaf, co-author with Jacob S. Jaya Raj is not a student of Misraji but of Jacob who did the library work for the paper.

(Ansari, Hoque and Kharakwal); one to centre (Alam); four to west (Dandekar, Kurush Dalal, Mishra and Thomas); one to northwest (Katy Dalal); and three to east (Akhilesh, Basak and Panda-Roy). Sunil Gupta's paper is not limited to a particular region. In terms of cultural periods, five papers are related to prehistory i.e. Paleolithic and Mesolithic (Akhilesh, Alam, Basak, Jayaraj, and Raju); three to Protohistory (Katy Dalal, Kharakwal and Mishra); two to Prehistory and Protohistory together (Hoque and Reddy); four to Early Historic (Kurush Dalal, Dandekar, Gupta and Rahman); one to Archaeozoology (Thomas); and one to Ethnoarchaeology (Ansari). Panda-Roy's paper covers the period from the prehistoric to the early historic.

Shafiqul Alam reports the typological, technological, functional and stylistic variability among the Palaeolithic stone tool industries of Bhimbetka in central India on the basis of a detailed metrical analysis. He also attempts to explain the formation of archaeological record at the site.

Jacob Jayaraj and Abdul Munaf discuss the cultural evolution during the Palaeolithic and Mesolithic periods in the Tirupati valley, Andhra Pradesh in the context of topographical setting, drainage pattern, raw material and other resources, and use analogies of the subsistence strategies of the Yanadi hunter-gatherers and fishermen living in the same region.

D.R. Raju's paper summarises his investigations of the rich Upper Palaeolithic sites located along permanent water pools in the Gunjana valley in Andhra Pradesh, and explains their location with the help of the use of the same water resources by the Yanadi hunter-gatherers and fishermen.

Bishnupriya Basak examines the microlithic sites in the Tarafeni valley in north-west Midnapur in West Bengal and tells us about her ongoing work in the area which focuses on prehistoric land use patterns.

Kumar Akhilesh reviews the present status of the Upper Palaeolithic 'Damin' industries of the Bansloi river basin, Jharkhand on the basis of finds from his field work. The study examines the stratigraphic context of the sites and artefacts, nature of artefact assemblages, inter-site variability of lithic technology, and prehistoric landuse patterns.

Katy Dalal's paper discusses the Early and Mature Harappan ceramics of the Ghaggar (Sarasvati) valley with special reference to the site of Binjor. She was the first person to discover Hakra Ware sherds in the Ghaggar valley.

J.S. Kharakwal summarizes the results of his discoveries of rock art, cist burials and archaeometallurgical sites in the Kumaun region of the Himalayas. He suggests that Khasas were the probable authors of these burials, and Kumaon played an important role in the diffusion of metal technology and urbanization process in the Ganga Valley.

Anup Mishra gives an account of the varied ceramics found in the Chalcolithic levels at Balathal, and discusses the changes through time.

V.R. Reddy reports his discoveries of a large number of Mesolithic, Neolithic, ashmound, and megalithic sites, and excavation of the ashmound at Palavoy in the semi-arid region of Andhra Pradesh. Palavoy has yielded a very interesting bone tool industry.

M.M. Hoque's paper gives an account of the settlement patterns during the prehistoric and protohistoric periods in the Middle and Lower Ganga Valley in the context of landscape, soils, climate, water sources, flora and fauna.

Sunil Gupta writes on the historiographical framework of the early maritime trade in the Indian Ocean. He attempts to reconstruct, primarily from archaeological evidence, aspects of sea borne commerce between India and the Roman Empire.

S.S.M. Rahman attempts a reconstruction of the cultural history and settlement patterns in the Bogra district, Bangladesh during the Early Historic and Early Medieval periods mainly on the basis of his own field work.

Kurush Dalal reports his study of the non-ceramic material remains, including two interesting terracotta sealings, from Early Historic Balathal. According to him Balathal, located on a north-south trade route, was a major centre of the production of iron objects and their trade.

Abhijit Dandekar's paper attempts to understand the local traditions of pottery shapes and technology in the Early Historic period at Balathal in Rajasthan in relation to surrounding regions.

P.K. Thomas writes on the role of faunal remains in the reconstruction of the subsistence patterns of the Mesolithic and Chalcolithic communities of western India. His study was the first in India of the total faunal remains from an archaeological site (Bagor). He also discusses the methodological advances in archaeozoological research, with special reference to work at the Deccan College.

Shahida Ansari has attempted a reconstruction of the settlement and subsistence patterns during the Mesolithic-Chalcolithic periods in the South-Central Ganga Valley on the basis of archaeological data collected by archaeologists of the Allahabad University and her own extensive field work among the primitive communities of Kols, Musahars and Mallahs of the region.

Tama Panda-Roy has attempted to trace the socio-cultural evolution in the area covered by the undivided coastal districts of Puri and Ganjam, and inland district of Sambalpur in Orissa on the basis of geographical, archaeological, historical, ethnographic, and linguistic data.

All the papers in the volume were sent to different referees and all of whom have been most cooperative. I thank Drs. Kishore K. Basa, Kuldeep K. Bhan, Ravi Korisettar, M.L.K. Murty, S.B. Ota, Vinod Nautiyal, Gautam Sengupta, V.H. Sonawane, and Rakesh Tewari for sparing their time to read the papers and give their comments. I am grateful to Ravi Misra for proof reading; Shriikant Pradhaan for making the sketches of professors K.N. Sharma, D.N. Majumdar, H.D. Sankalia and V.N. Misra; Trupti More for archival help; and Shahida Ansari for listening and discussing everyday on this volume through out the year.

I am grateful to John and Erica Hedges for agreeing to publish this volume in the BAR series and bringing it out in a short time.

Dr. Alok Kumar Kanungo
Department of Archaeology
Deccan College Post-Graduate & Research Institute
Pune – 411 006, INDIA
Email: alok_kanungo@yahoo.com
17th August 2005

Editorial (*Gurudakshina* Part II)

As mentioned in the editorial of the first part of Gurudakshina published in 2005 in this series, 25 students completed their Ph.D. under Prof. V.N. Misra's guidance. Papers of 17 of these students covering the period from the Palaeolithic to the early historic in India, and one paper on the early historic period of Bangladesh; were published. All the papers were sent to different referees and papers were finalised on the basis of their suggestions. Mr. Ravi Misra helped in the editing of the language. That the book was well appreciated by students and scholars is evident from the reviews by Prof. D.P. Agrawal in *Man and Environment* 31(1), 2006, Prof. S.P. Gupta in *Puratattva* 36, 2006; and Prof. J.N. Pal in *The Eastern Anthropologist* 60(2), 2007.

When the volume went to press, I was contemplating the idea of getting the remaining eight students also to write their papers so that the volume is complete. I also thought of bringing out an Indian edition which would reach most of the readers in South Asia. And if anyone other than my wife Shahida was aware of my unhappiness for not being able to get all the work done under Prof. Misra at one place, despite the grand success of the volume, he was Mr. Ravi Misra (Chunnu Bhai), on whose shoulders rested the responsibility for the flawless language. Unfortunately Chunnu Bhai left us exactly a year ago on 20th May 2006. I was one of the saddest persons when on reaching the hospital I found he was no more. At that very moment I promised myself that I will see the original objective realized as soon as possible as an expression of my gratitude to Chunnu Bhai's contribution to the first part. It took me some time to get over the shock of losing such a trusted friend and brother. Chunnu Bhai, born on 8th August 1963, was an exceptionally bright child and a voracious reader. He also had a fairly good knowledge of archaeology both from regular use of his father's rich library and from participation in the excavations at Bhimbetka and Samnapur. He worked for sometime in the editorial department of *Maharashtra Herald*, an English daily of Pune. Among Chunnu Bhai's many quality was his highly respectful attitude to elders and his deep devotion to his mother. I take a sigh of relief today that on his first death anniversary we are ready with the second part of *Gurudakshina*, which completes my original objective.

This part of the volume has five (remaining three papers never came) papers by Misraji's Ph.D. students covering the period from prehistory to history in India, and one paper (Mala's) on the historic period of Nepal. Region-wise, of the Indian papers, one is related to south (Hari Shankar); one to central (Mathpal); and two to east (Nanda-Ota and Tripathy). In terms of cultural periods one paper each relate to Palaeolithic (Nanda-Ota); Rock Art (Mathpal); Megalithic (Hari Shankar); Early Historic (Tripathy); and one to Bronzes of Nepal (Mala).

[3]Nanda-Ota's paper deals with the upper Paleolithic and Mesolithic cultures of the Indravati valley in Koraput district. Mathpal's paper is based on his study of rock paintings of Bhimbetka, the first through documentation of rock art at any site in India. Harishankar's paper is devoted to Megalithic monuments of south Kerala. Tripathy discusses emergence of urbanization in central and western Orissa and the coastal-hinterland trade network. Mala discusses a rich bronze work of Nepal during the medieval period and her documentation of the various processes involved in the production of bronzes today.

All the papers in the volume were sent to different referees and all of whom have been most cooperative. I thank Drs. H. P. Ray, S.P. Gupta, and K. Mankodi for sparing their time to read the papers and give their comments.

I am grateful to John and Erica Hedges for agreeing to publish this part of the volume too in the BAR series and bringing it out in a short time.

Dr. Alok Kumar Kanungo
Deccan College Post-Graduate & Research Institute
Pune – 411 006, INDIA
Email: alok_kanungo@yahoo.com
20th May 2007

---

[3] As Nanda is no more the paper has been written by S.B. Ota who knew his work very closely.

List of Contributors (*Gurudakshina* Part I)

1. Alok Kumar Kanungo
    Dept. of Archaeology
    Deccan College Post-Graduate & Research Institute
    Pune 411 006, INDIA
    alok_kanungo@yahoo.com

2. Kishor K. Basa
    Indira Gandhi Rashtriya Manav Sangrahalaya
    Shamla Hills, Bhopal 462 013, INDIA
    homosapien@sancharnet.in

3. Pramod P. Joglekar
    Dept. of Archaeology
    Deccan College Post-Graduate & Research Institute
    Pune 411 006, INDIA
    prmjog@yahoo.co.in

4. Md. Shafiqul Alam
    Dept. of Archaeology
    22/1, Block-B, Babar Road
    Mohammedpur, Dhaka-1207
    BANGLADESH
    archaeology@agnionline.com

5. Jacob S. Jaya Raj
    Dept. of Anthropology
    Sri Venkateswara University
    Tirupati 517 502, INDIA
    jacobsj@yahoo.co.in

6. Shaik Abdul Munaf
    Dept. of Anthropology
    University of Hyderabad
    Hyderabad 500 046, INDIA
    samunaf28@yahoo.co.in

7. D. R. Raju
    Dept. of Archaeology and Architecture
    P.S. Telugu University
    Srisailam 518 101, Andhra Pradesh, INDIA
    drrajutu@rediffmail.com

8. Bishnupriya Basak
    Dept. of Archaeology, Calcutta University
    C/o A. Gupta, 228 Kendua Main Road
    F1 402, Kolkata 700 084, INDIA
    mun2000@vsnl.net

9. Kumar Akhilesh
    Dept. of Archaeology
    Deccan College Post-Graduate & Research Institute
    Pune 411 006, INDIA

10. Katy Feroze Dalal (nee Katy Nariman Frenchman)
    2nd floor, Mangalam House
    38, Walchand Hirachand Marg
    Mumbai 400 001, INDIA
    kaetayun@rediffmail.com

11.   Jeewan S. Kharakwal
        Institute of Rajasthan Studies
        Rajasthan Vidyapeeth
        Udaipur 313 001, INDIA
        kharakwal@rediffmail.com

12.   Anup Mishra
        Dept. of Ancient History and Culture
        M.J.P. Rohilkhand University, Bareilly 243 006, U.P., INDIA
        mishraanup@rediffmail.com

13.   V. Rami Reddy
        Dept. of Anthropology
        C/o House No. 980, Alipore Road
        NGOs Colony, Tirupati 517 507, INDIA
        vramireddy@hotmail.com

14.   M.M. Hoque
        Dept. of Archaeology, Jahangirnagar University
        Savar, Dhaka 1342, BANGLADESH
        pawankarju@yahoo.com

15.   Sunil Gupta
        Allahabad Museum, Allahabad 211 002, INDIA
        sunilcharu@hotmail.com

16.   Shah S. Mostafizur Rahman
        Dept. of Archaeology, Jahangirnagar University
        Savar, Dhaka 1342, BANGLADESH
        rahmanl@dhaka.net

17.   Kurush Feroze Dalal
        Dept. of Heritage Studies, K.C. College
        C/o Mangalam House, 2nd Floor
        38, Walchand Hirachand Marg
        Mumbai 400 001, INDIA
        kurushdalal@gmail.com

18.   Abhijit Dandekar
        Dept. of Archaeology
        Deccan College Post-Graduate & Research Institute
        Pune 411 006, INDIA
        ar_dandekar@rediffmail.com

19.   P.K. Thomas
        Dept. of Archaeology
        Deccan College Post-Graduate & Research Institute
        Pune 411 006, INDIA
        deccancollege@vsnl.com

20.   Shahida Ansari
        Dept. of Archaeology
        Deccan College Post-Graduate & Research Institute
        Pune 411 006, INDIA
        shahi_ansari@hotmail.com

21.   Tama Panda Roy
        Dept. of Archaeology
        Deccan College Post-Graduate & Research Institute
        C/o AC 82, Salt Lake City
        Kolkata 700064, INDIA
        tamatama@rediffmail.com

List of Contributors (*Gurudakshina* Part II)

22.   Siba Charan Nanda
        C/o Seema Nanada
        Anant Niwas
        Gautam Nagar
        Bhubaneswar, Orissa, INDIA

23.   Simadri B. Ota
        National Mission on Monuments and Antiquities
        Archaeological Survey of India
        24, Tilak Marg
        New Delhi-110 001, INDIA
        simadriota@gmail.com

24.   Yashadhar Mathpal
        Post Box No. 14, Geetadham
        Bhimtal, 263136
        Uttaranchal, INDIA

25.   B.S. Harishankar
        Sree Sailam, PLRA –12
        Panachamood Lane
        Pattom, Thiruvananthapuram-695004
        Kerala, INDIA
        bsharishankar@yahoo.com

26.   Balaram Tripathy
        Orissan Institute of Maritime and South East Asian Studies
        State Museum Building
        Bhubaneswar- 751 014, INDIA
        drbalaram2002@yahoo.co.in

27.   Mala Malla
        Post Box No. 13266
        Kathmandu, NEPAL
        mala_malla@yahoo.co.in

VIII

Contents (*Gurudakshina* Part I)

Contents (*Gurudakshina* Part II)

Stone Age Cultures of Indravati Basin, District Koraput, Orissa

Siba Charan Nanda & Simadri B. Ota

Background of the Article

In 2005 Dr. Alok Kumar Kanungo brought out a publication entitled *Gurudakshina: Facets of Indian Archaeology* (Part I) which was a tribute to Prof. V.N. Misra, from his Ph.D. students. The volume, besides carrying three articles about Prof. Misra's career and contribution to archaeology, contained 17 articles from his Ph.D. students summarising their doctoral dissertations and adding what they would have done if they had to carry out the same piece of research today. Unfortunately the volume could not include the paper of Dr. S.C. Nanda as he had passed away in 2002. Dr. Kanungo therefore requested me (Ota) to write for Dr. Nanda on his dissertation on the prehistory of the Indravati basin. The present article represents the synthesis of Nanda's work on Indravati basin.

In fact, it is felt since long that his thesis needs to be published, so that scholars working in Eastern India, particularly in Orissa get benefited. Unfortunately it could not happen and with the present volume I think my dream along with others will come true when this is published. Since the present paper is the synthesis of Nanda's work, it would not be out of place to make him as co-author. In fact, I feel privileged to be associated with Nanda's work through this article. One way it would be my tribute to him who died at an early age.

My association with S.C. Nanda goes back to 1981 when I just began to understand the fundamentals of lithic artefact typology. This was the time when typological study was very popular in Indian Prehistory. Being trained under Prof. V.N. Misra, S.C. Nanda was one, from whom many scholars learnt the stone artefact typology. I owe my knowledge on lithic artefact typology to him.

The Area

The district Koraput lies in the northern most part of the Eastern Ghats. Its southeastern boundary is almost parallel to the seacoast and shortest aerial distance from the sea is 67 km. The topography of the area is characterized by open upland plateaux, fringed by forested hills with an average elevation of 1000 metres. The southern extremity of the region has the tropical moist deciduous forest which occurs in combination with a semi-evergreen type. The western portion has a dry deciduous forest (Nanda 1985: 159).

The river Indravati originates from the forest of Thooamulrampur Block of Kalahandi district near Madriguda village. Further downstream it receives a number of hill streams and enters Koraput district near the Gaurakurumuli village of Tentulikhunti tehsil. It flows through Kashipur, Nawrangpur and Kotpad tehsils of Koraput district, and then meet the Godavari in Bastar district of Madhya Pradesh. Its total length is 410 km, of which 95 km lies within Koraput.

Three-quarters of the total population in the district are Scheduled Castes and Tribes. The main tribal communities include Paraja, Gadaba, Koya, Bonda, Bhotra, Saora, Konda and Gond. The subsistence pattern of some of these communities is based on shifting cultivation, hunting and gathering.

Present Investigation

Since the first discovery of Palaeolithic artefacts in Orissa more than a century ago by V. Ball (1876), a number of stray finds are reported from time to time from various regions of Orissa. However, the first systematic investigation to the prehistory of Orissa began around 1940 with the work by Bose and Sen (1948, 1958) in Mayurbhanj district. Subsequently, G.C. Mohapatra (1962) carried out the investigations covering almost the entire Orissa which established for the first time a general stone age cultural pattern for Orissa. Again during late 50's and early 60's quite a few isolated discoveries have been made from various areas of the state (Basa 1994).

The work of Tripathy (1972, 1980) during the early 70's gave a footing to the Mesolithic cultural research in southwestern Orissa. Following Tripathy, is the investigation by S.C. Nanda (1982-83, 1983, 1985 and 2000). Nanda's investigation is a landmark in the history of prehistoric research in Orissa for the following reasons:

1. It is the first intensive investigation of any area in Orissa.
2. Investigation is confined to a smaller area confiding to a single geographical unit.
3. It is an early example of investigations of primary sites, avoiding the earlier strategy of looking into the river stratigraphy for understanding culture and cultural succession.
4. It is an excellent example of lithic typological study.
5. It established for the first time the existence of Upper Palaeolithic industry as a distinct typo-technological entity in the Indravati basin.
6. It is the first work on Orissa where attempt has been made to understand the tribal communities adaptational pattern as a clue to understand the prehistoric life ways to certain extent.
7. It is a detailed ethnographic account of Gadabas and other communities particularly on subsistence strategies.

The present investigation is mainly confined to the upper Indravati basin in the undivided Koraput district of Orissa that was carried out by S.C. Nanda between 1975 and 1980. It covered an area of about 2400 sq km along river Indravati and its tributaries forming a single geographical unit.

The investigation in this area has brought to light seventeen Upper Palaeolithic sites and eighty-five Mesolithic sites (Figs. 1 & 2). Such an intensive survey of a limited geographical area and understanding the prehistoric life-ways through ethnographic approach is first of its kind in prehistoric studies of Orissa.

The investigation had two main objectives:

1. It concerned with establishing cultural chronology and for getting an insight into the living patterns of prehistoric societies and aimed at reconstructing the typo-technological evolution during the Upper Palaeolithic and Mesolithic period. The study is also aimed in delineating the pattern of prehistoric human settlements against the ecological background of the region (Nanda 2000: 153-155).

2. Attempt has also been made to reconstruct the past life ways of the region through ethnographic observations of tribes of Koraput with special reference to the tribe Gadaba, giving emphasis on their dependence on the eco-system and their subsistence and exploitation pattern.

Upper Palaeolithic Sites

Nanda's discovery of Upper Palaeolithic sites come at a time when the existence of Upper Palaeolithic culture in the country was just established and the evidences there on coming from different parts of the country were very limited. As regards the evidence of Upper Palaeolithic culture in eastern India was concerned, it was almost unknown then. However, by then Mohapatra (1962) and Tripathy (1972, 1980) had reported few blades in the Middle Palaeolithic collections. This was the time when Murty's (1979) evidence from the limestone caves of Kurnool established the existence of Upper Palaeolithic culture beyond doubt and delineated for the first time the nature of industry which is associated with Upper Palaeolithic culture. Based on the typo-technology, Murty grouped the Upper Palaeolithic industry into (1) flake-blade industry, (2) blade tool industry, and (3) blade and burin industry.

Nanda being a scholar of Deccan College was also influenced and exposed to the study of Upper Palaeolithic culture by Murty. He writes ' . . . Dr. M.L.K. Murty, who was very kind in granting me sometime to discuss various problems connected with Upper Palaeolithic culture which forms a major part in my thesis' (Nanda 1983: acknowledgement). Therefore, Nanda tried to analyse his evidences in the light of Murty's classification and writes that the Upper Palaeolithic industry from Koraput region falls into the 'flake-blade' group with minor variation (Nanda 1983: 99).

Nanda has reported seventeen Upper Palaeolithic sites from his study area in erstwhile Koraput district of Orissa and established for the first time the existence of this industry in this part of the country. Of these, sixteen sites are located on small isolated hillocks, hill slopes, foot-hills and low plateaux, and one site is located in village Paidapali on the bank of the stream called Bhaskel. Interestingly, all these sites are located in the vicinity of present day tribal settlements. The artefacts bearing horizon is the lateritic soil or red soil and the extension of the artefactual scatter varies between 40 sq m to 1200 sq m. All these sites are surface sites and no organic remain has been noticed from any of these sites during investigation.

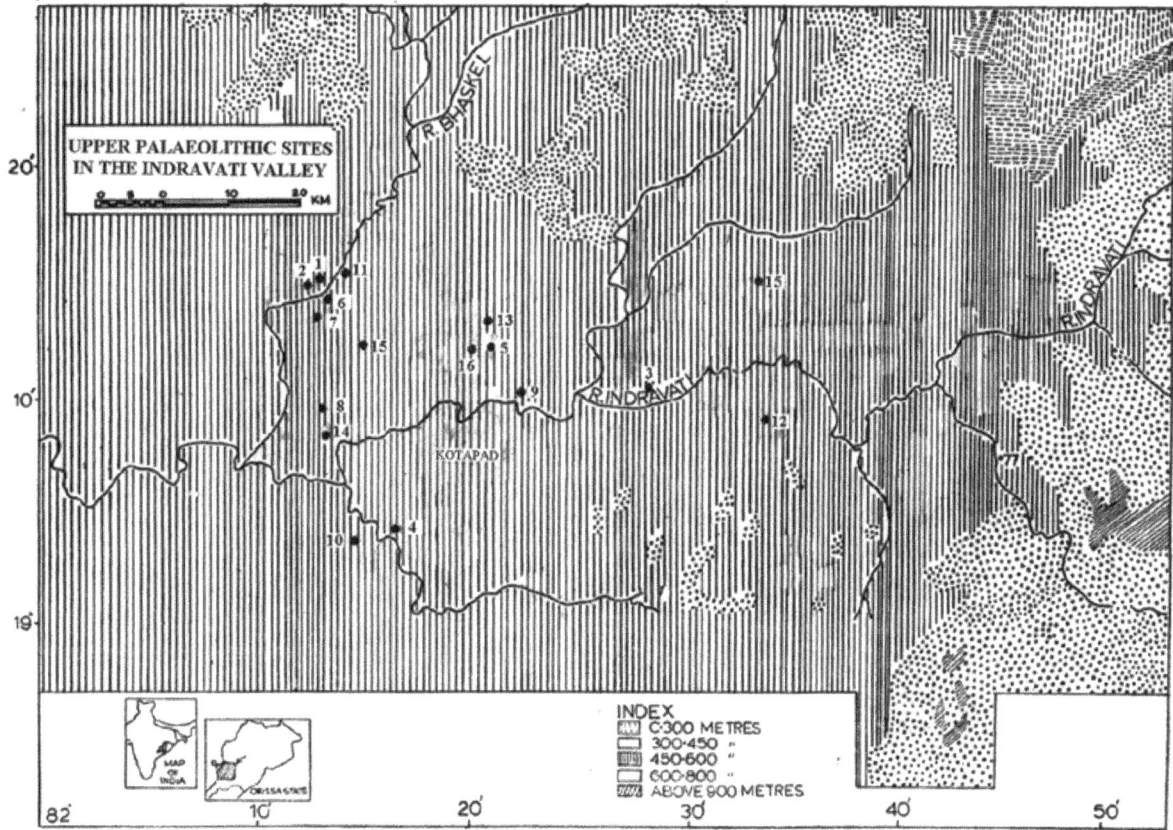

Figure 1: Upper Palaeolithic sites in the Indravati valley

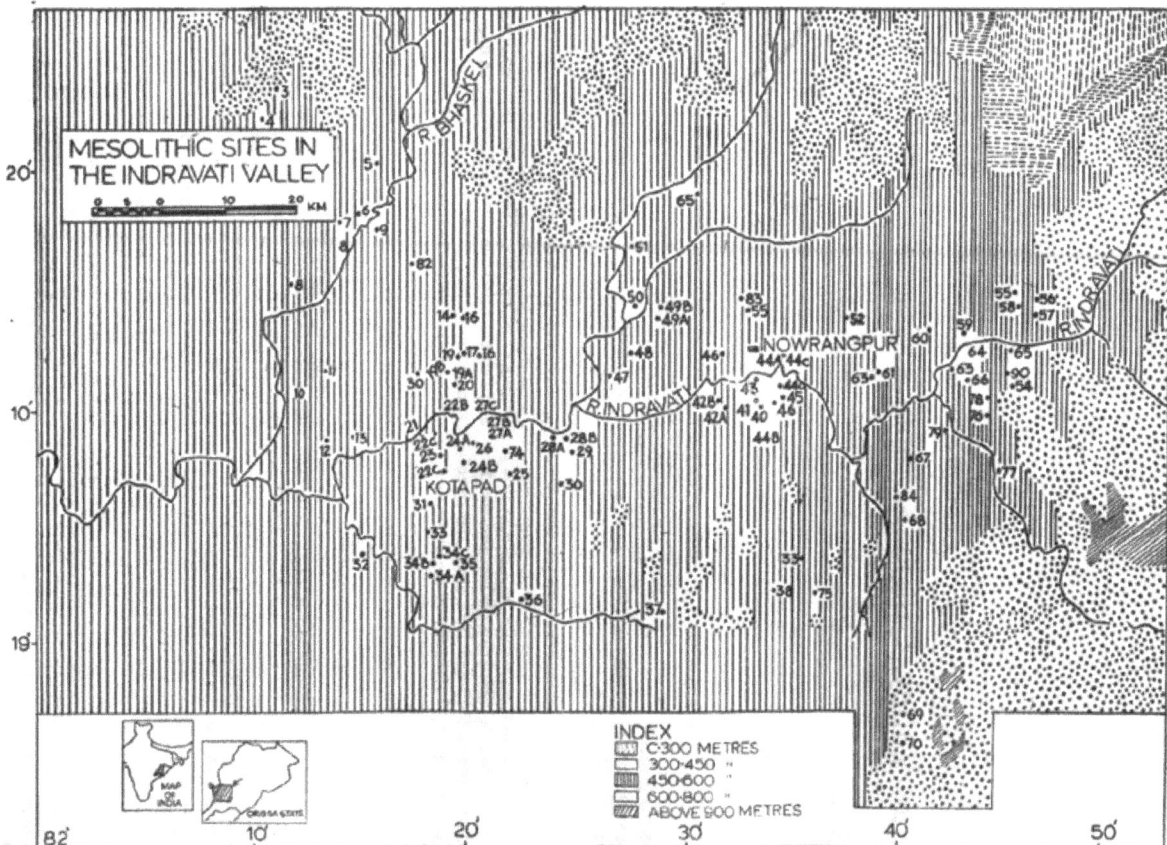

Figure 2: Mesolithic sites in the Indravati valley

3

Following Upper Palaeolithic sites are reported by Nanda (1983: 51-57):

1. Paidapali – A (19°16' : 82 °13'30'')
The village Paidapali is located 12 km to the southwest of the town of Kodinga, about 2 km from the river Bhaskel, near a small stream. The artifacts were found scattered over a chert bed covering an approximate area of 1200 sq m. One hundred thirty eight artifacts mostly on whitish colour chert were identified. All are well preserved and have a fresh appearance with thin film of brownish patina.

2. Paidapali –B (19°16' : 82° 13')
This site lies 50 metres to the north of Paidapali –A. Artefacts were found scattered in an area of about 40 sq m and thirty-four artefacts collected from the site show typo-technological and morphological affinity with the assemblages from Paidapali –A. Artefacts are made on yellowish red colour chert and most of these are highly patinated.

3. Amota (19°10' : 82°27')
The site lies in Amota village which is about 15 km northeast of Kotpad town and about 3 km south of river Indravati. The artefacts were scattered over an elevated land, stretching about 0.25 km on the right side of the Kotpad-Ghotorla road. The main artefact concentration patch covers an area of only 30 sq m. Sixty-eight artefacts selected from the site are made on chert, fresh in condition and red patination noticed due to the long association with red soil.

4. Semla (19°4' : 82°18')
Semla is a small village very close to Joura stream and is located 8.5 km southwest of Kotpad. A small artefact collection of forty artifacts was made from a wasteland of about 25 sq m. The site is partially disturbed by recent cultivation. Artefacts are made on yellowish red chert and are fresh in condition.

5. Chirma (19°11' : 82°22')
The village Chirma is located approximately 6 km northwest of Kotpad town. The site is located very close to this village and is less than a kilometre to the north of Indravati. Sixty-six artefacts were collected from the surface of a hillock over an area of about 50 sq m. These artefacts are mostly made on chert and are in mint condition.

6. Kosagumura (19°16' : 82°15')
The village Kosagumura on the eastern bank of river Bhaskel is situated 15 km southwest of Kodinga town and also the block headquarter of Kodinga. The site is situated just behind the block office. One hundred eleven artefacts were found on a rocky wasteland covering an area of 150 sq m; these are made on chert and are highly patinated (Fig. 3).

Figure 3: Chert slabs at Kosagunda village

7. Majhidhanua (19°15' : 82°11')
The village Majhidhanua lies 14 km southwest of Kodinga town near the border of undivided districts of Bastar and Koraput. The site is located about 150 metres to the left side of the Kodinga-Saraladhanua-Jagdalpur road. The small stream of Bhaskel flows 0.5 km east of the site. Only thirty-six artefacts were collected from a plain wasteland of about 20 sq m. The artefacts are made on chert and are fresh in condition.

8. Ukiapali (19°10' : 82°11')
The village Ukiapali is situated about 13 km northwest of Kotpad town, on the right bank of river Bhaskel. The site is located on an elevated land that lies about 500 m north of village Ukiapali. A total number of forty-four artefacts were collected; these are made on chert and are in mint condition.

9. Chitagaon (19°8' : 82°22')
The village Chitagaon is situated about 4.5 km southeast of Kotpad and one km north of Kotpad-Vizianogaram road. The site is located about 200 metres east of the village Chitagaon where artefacts were found scattered over a plain wasteland which was covered with shrub. Altogether thirty-one artifacts found exclusively made on chert and are fresh in condition.

10. Kusumpali (19°13' : 82°15')
The village Kusumpali lies approximately 20 km north of Kotpad. The site is located 0.5 km north of village Kusumpali. The river Bhaskel flows northwest of the site at a distance of about 3.5 km. Altogether twenty-one artefacts were collected which were scattered on an elevated land. These artefacts are exclusively made on reddish yellow chert and are fresh in appearance.

11. Parajasahi (19°15' : 82°15')
The village Parajasahi lies 2 km south of Kutegura. The site is located 500 metres north of the village Parajasahi and about 3 km northwest of river Bhaskal. One hundred fifty one artefacts were selected; these are made on yellowish chert and show a thin reddish patination.

12. Majiha : (19°9' : 82°34')
The village Majiha lies 3.5 km northeast of Kotpad and nearly 1.5 km from the river Indravati. The artefacts were found scattered over an area of 800 sq m of shrub land. Seventy-two artefacts collected are exclusively made on yellowish red chert. The redness is the patination due to its long association with red soil.

13. Sitiliguda (19°12' : 82°22')
The village Sitiliguda is situated 15 km northeast of Kotpad town on the left bank of Indravati. The site is located on the left bank of Indravati about 250 metres south of this village. The artefacts were found both on the top of a hillock and also in top 2 metres of older alluvium. This site was slightly disturbed due to cultivation from where sixty-three artefacts were collected. These artefacts are in mint condition and are fabricated on chert.

14. Borogaon (19°9' : 82°11')
The village Borogaon lies one km east of river Bhaskel and 4 km northwest of Indravati. The site is situated on a rocky elevated ground to the south of the village Borogaon. Thirty-nine artefacts were collected which are slightly patinated and are made on chert.

15. Gadabaguda (19°15' : 82°34')
The village Godabaguda which is inhabited by Godabas is situated 3 km northeast of Nowrangapur. The artefacts were found scattered on a plain area of 40 sq m. The site was disturbed due to cultivation. One hundred sixty six artefacts collected are exclusively made on chert.

16. Rengiguda (19°11' : 82°20')
The village Rengiguda, a small hamlet of Chirma village lies 3.5 km north of river Indravati. The site is located at a distance of 30 metres northeast of Rengiguda. Sixty-two artefacts were collected from an undulating rocky ground; these are made on chert and fresh in appearance.

17. Chatahandi (19°11' : 82°15')
The village Chatahandi is situated 6 km northwest of Kotapad. River Indravati flows 2.5 km south and river Bhaskel flows 6 km west of this village Chatahandi. The site is located on a slightly elevated rocky wasteland on the south of this village. One hundred forty artefacts collected are made on chert and are patinated with a thin film of red colour.

The Assemblage

A total number of 1,282 artefacts were collected from 17 sites which were analysed in detail from typo-technological point of view. On the basis of type-technology, the Upper Palaeolithic industry of the area comprises both shaped and simple artefacts. Out of this total collection, 129 (10.06%) are shaped and 1,153 (89.94%) are simple artefacts. The Upper Palaeolithic industry of Indravati basin represents a single homogenous industry (Fig. 4). There is no marked difference among the assemblages from the seventeen sites in spite of their locations in varied landscape.

The shaped artefacts is represented by side (47.28%) and end scrapers (21.70%) (Figs. 5 and 6) followed by notches (14.73%), burins (4.65%) (Fig. 6), borers (2.33%), denticulates (2.33%), knives (1.55%), backed microblades (0.77%) and microblade crescents (3.10%). Whereas the simple artefact category comprise cores (11.88%), flakes (20.55%), chips (42.58%), blades (14.57%) (Fig. 7), microblades (1.90%) and worked nodules (8.49%) (Nanda 2000: 156).

Figure 4: Upper Palaeolithic artifacts: Surface collection

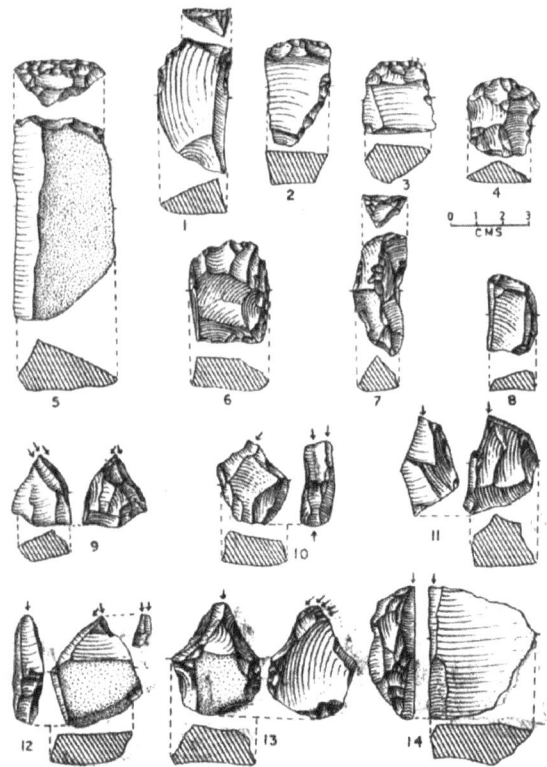
Figure 6: Upper Palaeolithic end scrapers and burins

Figure 5: Upper Palaeolithic scrapers

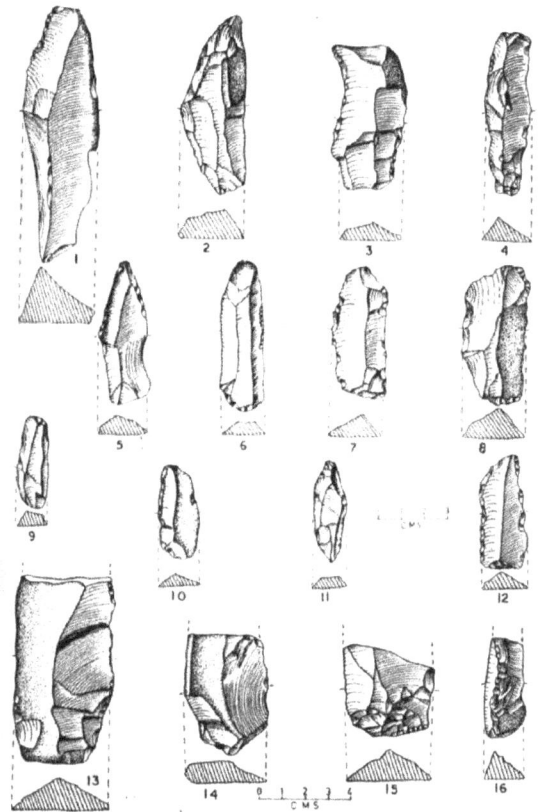
Figure 7: Upper Palaeolithic blades

The occurrence of high proportion of waste products and unfinished artefacts in all the locations suggest that artefacts must have been manufactured at the site. The site in village Parajasahi has yielded a good proportion of shaped tools vis-à-vis simple artefacts that suggests that it must have been a workshop cum camp site (Nanda 2000: 156). Chert is the main raw material that has been used for manufacturing Upper Palaeolithic Artefacts of Indravati basin.

6

One of the interesting features noticed in this assemblage is the proportion of blade cores is very small in comparison to the number of blades. Further this assemblage has 2.25 % blade cores and 4.33 % microblade cores with 14.57% blades and 1.90% microblades. Confirming to Misra's (1980) observation on the blade artefacts from the excavations at Bhimbetka, Nanda (2000: 159) states that such a less representation of the blade cores might be for the reason that they were further exploited for the removal of microblades.

The blades with plain platform and tiny prominent bulb suggest the application of indirect percussion or punch technique. There is no evidence of elaborate preparation of the platforms. In most cases, a single flake was removed on the horizontal axis. The blades are generally irregular or somewhat parallel and are comparatively thick, and some of them show use marks on the edges.

Flakes are thick, large and irregular with prominent positive or negative bulbs. These were removed with a stone hammer. The flakes are eventually finished by pressure chipping, by punch, and by soft hammer into various forms. The steep retouched scrapers possess laminar retouching. Levalloisian flakes are completely absent. One specimen shows alternate preparation of guided ridge. As a whole the industry represents a crude craftsmanship (Nanda 2000: 159).

Since blades are one of the diagnostic artefact types of both Upper Palaeolithic and Mesolithic industries, it is essential to understand in detail the characteristic features of Upper Palaeolithic blade industry that have been analysed in detail by Nanda (1983: 113-119).

Blades form second to flakes in frequency among the simple artefacts. These have been classified as simple blades and utilized blades. A total number of 186 blades have been collected from the sites.

Simple blades are the most important element of the Upper Palaeolithic industry. Out of total collection of 168 simple blades, 18 show utilization. Few of these blades have a ridge, partly or fully, in the center of the dorsal surface. Usually blades have a single ridge and in some cases double ridges. Of the total collection of simple blades, 44 specimens are complete that have been analysed in detail for

understanding the nature of blade industry in Upper Palaeolithic assemblage of Indravati basin. These are classified as regular blades, divergent blades, convergent blades and irregular blades. There are 112 (66.66%) specimens with triangular cross section, 34 (20.24%) with trapezoidal cross section, 13 (7.74%) with plano-convex cross section, and 9 (5.35%) with irregular cross section. In case of plano-convex cross section, the blades are comparatively thin, whereas blades with irregular cross section do not have any fixed number of ridges. The scars on the dorsal surface are parallel to the longer axis, or perpendicular to longer axis, or irregular in orientation. The dorsal surface has two flake scars (77 : 45.83%), three flake scars (50 : 29.76%), four flake scars (5 : 2.97%), and in a few cases with cortex (28 : 16.66%). Four specimens (2.38%) retain cortex on the whole of dorsal surface.

As regards striking platform is concerned, 7 (4.17%) specimens contain cortex, 74 (44.05%) have plain platform and 2 (1.19%) have dihedral platforms. In 77 (45.83%) cases the platform is broken and in 8 (4.76%) specimens it is not clear. A significant percentage i.e. 22.72% of the blades fall in the length range of 46-55 mm, 43.18% of the blades fall in the breadth range of 12-17 mm and 50% of the blades fall in the thickness range of 4-9 mm (Fig. 8).

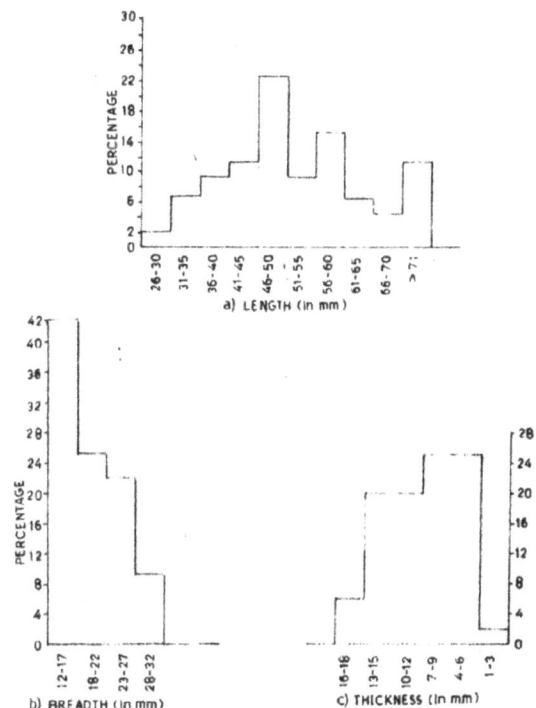

Figure 8: Frequency distribution of Length, Breadth and Thickness of Upper Palaeolithic blades

Mesolithic Sites

Besides the stray reporting of Mesolithic sites and microliths from different parts of Orissa since 1950s (Nanda 1985: 159), K.C. Tripathy (1972) for the first time reported 27 sites spreading over erstwhile Kalahandi, Sambalpur and Bolangir districts of Orissa.

Subsequently Nanda's work (1983, 1985) that was confined to Indravati basin in district Koraput brought to light a large concentration of 85 Mesolithic sites within an area of about 2400 sq km for the first time in Orissa.

A total of 85 microlithic sites were located in association with various landscapes such as foot hill, hill slope, hill top, hill top and slope, elevated rocky waste land, plain wasteland, cultivated land and cave. These are all open-air sites except one i.e. Khirki which is a cave site. Further with the exception of the site in village Girla, no other site shows any indication of an occupational deposit.

Most of the sites occur within 7 km from the banks of river Indravati. The average distance between two sites is about 2.5 km. The area of artefacts scatter in the sites very between 8 to 1,250 sq m. The hillocks on which sites are located vary in heights from 20 to 250 metres above the surrounding ground level. Most of the sites are located in the vicinities of present day tribal settlements. The artefacts from all these 85 sites show a homogeneity character. Therefore, they are treated as a single cultural entity.

The Mesolithic sites in the area is found in the context of foothill, hill slope, hilltop and hill slope, elevated rocky wasteland, plain wasteland, cultivated land and cave. Accordingly, the sites are classified below (Nanda 1983: 57-93):

Foot Hill Sites

1. Asanga (19°11' : 82°20')
The village Asanga lies 5.5 km north of Kotpad. The site is located on the right side of the Asanga-Kokdi road at a distance of about 0.5 km from the village Asanga. Two hundred twenty one artifacts were collected from the foot of a hillock. These artefacts are made on chert and are fresh with red stain due to its long association with red soil.

2. Hirlidanguri (19°13'30" : 82°32')
Hirlidanguri is a hill with an approximate elevation of 350 metre lies behind the weekly market of Nowrangpur town. The river Indravati flows at a distance of about 4 km north of the hill. Artefacts were thinly scattered at the fort of this hill covering an area of about 750 sq m. From here forty-two artefacts were collected.

3. Paljur (19°35' : 82°56')
Paljur is a small village of Thuamulrampur tehsil of Kalahandi district. This village lies 7 km east of the Thuamulrampur on the left side of the Thuamulrampur-Bhabamipatna road. The river Indravati flows further east of the site at an approximate distance of 4 km. Here the river flows through a narrow channel with alluvium of 5 metres height on both the banks. Fifty-three artefacts made mainly on chert were collected from the foot of a hill.

4. Dakutha – A (19°37' : 82°59')
It is a small tribal village in the hilly forested land of Thuamulrampur tehsil. The site is about 2.5 km from Paljur site along the Thuamulrampur-Bhabanipatna road. Twenty-four artefacts mainly of quartz were collected from a scatter at the foot of a hillock. Besides quartz, the assemblage also constitutes some artefacts on chert, chalcedony and jasper.

5. Dakutha – B (19°33' : 82°58')
The site is located just at the left bank of the river Indravati at a distance of 1.5 km from the previous Dakutha-A site. Only seventeen artefacts were collected from an area of eight sq m and are mainly made on chert and in mint condition.

Hill Slope Sites

6. Binjili (19°9' : 82°14')
The village Binjili is about 9 km northwest of Kotpad town and 0.5 km north of the river Indravati. The site is located on the slope of a hillock that lies north of the village Binjili at a distance of 30 metres. One hundred thirty seven artefacts collected are fresh. The predominant raw material used is yellow chert. The artefacts show a reddish patination due to long association with red soil.

7. Asanga –A (19°11' : 82°20')
The village Asanga is situated 5.5 km north of Kotpad. The site is located to north of the village Asanga, about 0.25 km on the left side

of Asanga-Kokdi road. River Indravati flows at a distance of about 3 km south of the site. Three hundred twenty seven artefacts collected from an area of 40 sq m on a hill slope are made on chert and are slightly patinated.

8. Kokdi-A (19°11' : 82°19'30")
The village Kokdi is about 2 km west of village Asanga. The site is located on a hillock slope at a distance of 100 metres northeast of village Kokdi. This spot has yielded hundred one artefacts.

Another locality, labelled as Kodki-B, about 150 metres to the north of Kokdi-A was located. Artefacts thirty-eight in numbers were collected from here in an area of about 20 sq m. Artefacts collected from both Kokdi A & B sites are made on chert.

9. Photaguda (19°14' : 82°46'30")
The Village Photaguda is situated southeast of village Lambtaguda at a distance of approximately 1.5 km. The site is located on the left bank of the river Indravati. The distance between the village Photaguda and Lambtaguda is about 2.5 km. One hundred thirty eight artefacts collected from the slope of a hillock are made on chert.

Hill Top Sites

10. Umarkot-A (19°40'30" : 82°11')
The village Umarkot is situated about 60 km north of Nowrangpur on Jeypore-Raipur road. The site on the top of a hillock. This hillock is of about 30 metres in height in village Umarkot located on the left side of the Raipur-Jeypore road at a distance of one km from Umarkot bus stand. Fifty-four well preserved artefacts made on chert and quartz were collected from an area of 25 sq m.

11. Umarkot-B (19°40' : 82°11')
The site Umarkot-B is located one km north of Umarkot bus stand and 2 km from Umarkot-A site. Fresh artefacts of chert and quartz were found scattered over a rocky surface of about 36 sq m on a top of hillock which is about 35 metre high from surrounding level. Altogether two hundred fifty three artefacts were collected from this site.

12. Keragaon (19°22' : 82°11')
The village Keragaon is situated 7 km northwest of village Balenga. The site in village Keragaon is located on the side of Motigaon-Keragaon road and less than one km from Keragaon. A small stream flows 0.5 km west of the site. Thirty-three artefacts made on chert were collected from an area of about 24 sq m.

13. Churchunda (19°13' : 82°18')
Village churchunda is situated 7 km southwest of Kodinga town and is connected by road with Kodinga, Kotpad and Kosagumura. The site is located to the north of the village Churchunda about 0.25 km from Kotpad-Kosagumura road. One hundred thirty three artefacts of chert were collected from an area of 150 sq m.

14. Girla (19°10' : 82°23')
The village Girla is situated 8 km northeast of Kotpad town, on the left bank of Indravati. The topography of the area is characterized by extensive cultivated land with isolated low hills covered with shrubs and a few trees. There are three hillocks around this village that contains artefacts scatter. The richest artefact scatter (Girla-a) was located on the top of a hillock which is about 12 metre high from the ground level and lies on the right side of the Kotpad-Girla road and about one km south of village Girla. Four hundred fifty-five artefacts were collected from an area of 420 sq m. These artefacts are made on chert of yellowish red colour, highly patinated but fresh.

The other two localities (Girla-b and Girla-c) are located southwest of the site Girla-a at a distance of about 0.25 km. The distance between Girla-b and Girla-c localities is about 150 metres. Forty-two and thirty-eight artefacts were collected from Girla-b and c respectively. These artefacts come from rocky wasteland, and are exclusively made on chert and are highly patinated.

15. Phupugaon (19°3' : 82°23')
The village Phupugaon is situated about 13 km southeast of Kotpad town. The site is located on the right side of the Kotpad-Kundra road, on a hillock that is approximately 8 metres in height from surrounding ground level. Forty artefacts collected from here are mostly made on chert.

16. Sargiguda-A (19°3' : 82°35')
The site in village Sargiguda is located at a distance of 2 km from the left side of the Borigum-Sargiguda road. It is one of the few sites which is located away from tribal settlement. The artefacts are found scattered over a small hill with a few isolated big boulders of granite and patches of wild shrubs.

The artefacts mainly on quartz are found in clusters at the edges of these boulders, suggesting that these might have been fabricated on the boulders and subsequently rolled down. Altogether fifty-six artefacts mainly made on quartz were collected from this site.

17. Rangapiajaguda (19°14' : 82°39')
The village Rangapiajaguda lies on the east of Nowrangpur town at a distance of 12 km southeast of village Sagarmunda. The site in village Rangapiajaguda lies on the outcrop of granitic boulders located on the right side of Nowrangpur-Sagarmunda road. A total number of forty-two artefacts mainly made on quartz were collected from the site. A large number of nodular pieces of quartz as raw material are also noticed around the site.

18. Ekamba-A (19°12' : 82°39'30")
The village Ekamba lies nearly 12 km southeast of Nowrangpura town. The site is located on the top of a hill at a distance of one kilometre west of the village. The hill on which the site is located is about 75 metres in height and about 250 metres (north-south) and 150 metres (east-west) approximately. The plains and hill slopes are extensively cultivated. One hundred twenty nine artefacts were collected from this site are made on chert, quartz and jasper.

19. Ekamba-B (19°12' : 82°39')
This site on a hill is about one km from Ekamba-A. The approximate height of the hill is 80 metres from plain agricultural land and it extends about 200 metres (north-south) and 175 metres (east-west). The artefacts were found scattered in clusters covering an area of about 1500 sq m. Two hundred sixty two artefacts collected from this locality are mostly made on chert followed by quartz and are fresh with few specimen on chert show staining.

20. Bairagiguda (19°13' : 82°42')
The village Bairagiguda lies on the right bank of river Indravati, about 4 km northeast of Ekamba village. The site is located 0.25 km east of village Bairagiguda on a hillock of approximately 40 metres high from the river bed that flows touching the foot hill. Two hundred twenty four artefacts collected from this site are fresh and are made on quartz.

21. Phupugaon (19°14' : 82°45')
The village Phupugaon lies at a distance of 7 km south of Tentulikhunti town. The river Indravati flows north of the village. The site is located about 1.5 km east of the village. Artefacts were found scattered over three hillocks adjacent to each other and surrounded by cultivated fields, on the right side of Lambtaguda-Phupugaon road. One hundred two artefacts collected from this locality are fresh and mainly on quartz.

22. Muchagaon (19°13' : 82°46')
The village Muchagaon is situated about 4 km southeast of Tentulikhunti town. The site is located 0.5 km east of the village. The river Indravati flows very close to the hillock where artefacts were found scattered on the top of granitic surface covering an area of 168 sq m. One hundred twenty-eight artefacts collected are mainly on quartz.

23. Kumuli (19°7' : 82°41')
Kumuli is a big village of Bhairab Singpur Police Station; from the southwest it is connected by a road to Boriguma and from the south to Bhairab Singpur. From Kumuli, Narigaon village is about 3 km by Kumuli-Bhairab Singpur road. The site is located on left side of Kumuli-Narigaon road at a distance of about 0.5 km. Artefacts mainly on chert were found scattered over a hillock. Altogether forty-eight artefacts were collected from this site.

24. Dangarkarchi (18°59' : 82°40'30")
The village Dangarkarchi is situated to the south of Bhairab Singpur at a distance of about 8 km. The site is on the top of a hillock which is about 0.5 km to the north of the village. Thirty artefacts collected from this site are made on quartz and are in mint condition.

25. Nagalatal (19°10' : 82°44')
The village Nagalatal in Tentulikhunti tehsil is approached by road from Bhairab Singpur to Munja and then to Chopadi, and from Chopadi to Ghatlguda which is separated from Nagalatal by Muran, one of the largest tributary of Indravati. The site is located on a big hill locally known as Badaraja. The average height of these hills that surrounded the village Nagalatal varies between 800 to 1400 metres and are covered with dense forest. Besides lithic artefacts, this site has yielded a fragment and one complete bead of jasper, two hammer stones and four pieces of ground red ochre. One hundred two artefacts collected are made on quartz and chert.

26. Lauguda (19°12' : 82°45')

The village Lauguda is about 4 km southeast of river Indravati and 12 km from the town Tentulikhunti. The site is located on the left side of the Jaganathpur-Berapadar road in village Lauguda. Fresh artefacts on quartz numbering one hundred were found scattered on a top of a hillock which is about 45 metres in height.

27. Kamata (19°75' : 82°39')

The village Kamata lies 3 km south-west of village Kumuli on Kumuli-Boriguma road. The village Ratali is about 3.5 km North of Kamata. The river Tellingiri, a tributary of the Indravati flows at a distance of 0.5 km south of Kamata. The site is located on a barren hillock that is one km north of village Kamata on the left side of Kamata-Ratali road. Twenty-two artefacts collected from the site are predominantly made on chert and quartz.

Hill Top and Hill Slope Sites

28. Komtabadi (19°8' : 82°18')

The site is located on the top as well as on the slope of two hillocks that are located 2 km northwest of Kotpad High School in village Komtabadi. River Indravati flows northwest of the site at a distance of about 2 km. The distance between two hillocks is about 60 metres and therefore artefacts collected from this site are labelled as Komtabadi 'A' and Komtabadi 'B'. A total number of three hundred twenty and thirty-five artefacts were collected from Komtabadi 'A' and Komtabadi 'B' respectively; these are made on chert and in mint condition.

29. Batra Dhargudi (19°7': 82°16')

The site is located southwest of Kotpad town at a distance of 8 km on Kotpad-Jagdalpur highway no. 43, near to the village Batra Dhargudi. The artefacts were found on the top as well as slope of a hillock, cut by the highway and ia approximately 3.5 metre in height from the road level. The site has yielded one hundred twenty five artefacts mostly made on chert.

30. Boragaon (19°11' : 82°34')

The village Boragaon lies on the right side of the Boragaon-Nowrangpur road at a distance of about 18 km northwest of Boriguma. There is an adjoining village called Anuli. There is a big hill to the north of village Boragaon with an elevation of about 300 metres from the river bed of Indravati that flows on the north of the village forming a boundary. Close to this hill, there are a few hillocks and the artefacts were found in five scatters on these hillocks. The average distance between two scatters varies between 30 and 150 metres.

The five scatters are named as Boragaon A, B, C, D and E and have yielded 71, 180, 49, 53 and 31 artefacts respectively. These artefacts are made on chert and are highly patinated.

Elevated Rocky Waste Land Sites

31. Motigaon (19°11' : 82°12')

The village Motigaon is located on a rocky elevated land and lies approximately 18 km northwest of Kodinga. The site is located at an approximate distance of 1.5 km northwest of the village Motigaon and about 0.5 km from the nearest stream, a feeder of the river Bhaskel. The artefacts were found scattered over an elevated rocky land. Sixty-eight artefacts collected are mostly made on chert and are in mint condition.

32. Churahandi (19°18' : 82°14'30")

Churahandi is a small village, located about 9 km west of Kodinga town and 6 km north of Kosagumura. The site is located on an elevated rocky land lies at a distance of about 400 metres north of the village. The eastern part of the village boundary is demarcated by the river Bhaskel and the southern part by a small *nullah* of the Bhaskel. Twenty-six artefacts collected from an area of 96 sq m are made on chert except a few which are on quartz.

33. Neigaon (19°9' : 82°15')

Village Neigaon lies to east of Binjili. The site is located at a distance of one km to the east of the village. The artefacts were scattered over an elevated land, located north of the river Indravati. Two hundred five artefacts collected are in mint condition and are made on chert.

34. Asanga – B (19°12' : 82°21')

The village Asanga lies 5.5 km north of Kotpad town. The site is located about 1.5 km north of the village. Artefacts exclusively made on chert were scattered covering an area of 60 sq m on a slightly elevated rocky land. A total number of eighty-four artefacts were collected from this site.

35. Nuagaon (19°35' : 82°20')

The Nuagaon village lies about 10 km south of Kotpad on Kotpad-Kundra road. River

Indravati flows to north of the village at a distance of 12.5 km. Joura, a tributary of Indravati flows at a distance of about 3.5 km south of the site. Chert artefacts were found scattered over an elevated rocky wasteland with bushes and a few isolated trees covering an area of 12 sq m. Sixty-one artefacts were collected from this site.

36. Bandiguda (19°10' : 82°37')
Bandiguda is a small village, about 9.5 km northeast of Boriguma town and 1.5 km from the right bank of Indravati. The site is located in village Bandiguda at a distance of about 0.5 km southwest of the Indravati. Thirty-six chert and quartz artefacts were collected from an elevated rocky land covering an area of 60 sq m.

37. Kumutitarai (19°6' : 82°19')
The site in village Kumutitarai is 6.5 km southeast of Kotpad town, near the village Sarigaon. Forty-four chert and few quartz artefacts in fresh condition were collected from a scatter on an elevated rocky wasteland covering an area of 12 sq m.

38. Ghotorla (19°10' : 82°25')
The village Ghotorla lies on the right bank of Indravati, about 7.5 km northeast of Kotpad town. The village is well connected with Kotpad and Nowrangpur by Kotpad-Saragiguda-Ghotorla road and Ghotorla-Nowrangpur road respectively. Two sites are located to the east of the village at a distance of 150 metres between them. A total number of two hundred seventy and thirty-four artefacts made on chert and few specimens on quartz in mint condition were collected separately from these two localities, called as Ghotorla-A and Ghotorla-B respectively.

39. Miriguda (19°7' : 82°24')
This small village of Miriguda comes under Kotpad tehsil and is connected by national highway no. 43 with Kotpad and Boriguma. The site in village Miriguda is located at a distance of 6 km towards east by road from Kotpad. Artefacts were found scattered on an elevated land covered with bushes. Fifty-two artefacts in fresh condition made on mostly quartz and chert were collected from an area of 56 sq m.

40. 5.5 km from Boriguma towards Bhairab Singpur (19°1' : 82°36')
There is no village close to this site. Artefacts were found scattered in the site which is located on the left side of the road on an elevated land extending over an area of about 150 sq m. Seventy-eight artefacts mainly made on quartz with few pieces on chert were collected.

41. Khandiguda (19°10' : 82°35')
The village Khandiguda lies about 10 km north of Boriguma town. The river Indravati flows at a distance of approximately 2 km north of the village. Collections of sixty-two artefacts in mint condition were made from an elevated rocky land of 240 sq m.

42. Deula (19°15' : 82°29')
The village Deula lies about 6.5 km northwest of Nowrangpur town. The site is located at a distance of less than one km south of village. Artefacts were found scattered in two localities over an elevated rocky ground. The first locality termed as Deula-A is about 30 sq m, whereas locality Deula-B is about 18 sq m. Deula-B lies 0.5 km to north of Deula-A. Chert is the most popular raw material in both the collection. A total number of fifty-five and thirty-five artefacts were collected from Deula-A and Deula-B respectively.

43. Bentaguda (19°9' : 82°23')
The site is located 70 metres southwest of village Bentaguda which is a small hamlet and lies at a distance of about 5 km northeast of Kotpad town and just before the village Dhanpur. A collection of one hundred ten artefacts of chert was made from an area of 102 sq m.

44. Bejuguda (19°16' : 82°46')
The village of Bejuguda is situated 2 km west of the main road Tentulikhunti-Patradora. A small collection of twenty-one artefacts was made from an elevated rocky ground located at a distance of nearly 300 metres north of the village. Artefacts are made on quartz and chert, and are in mint condition.

45. Gatiput (19°15' : 82°45')
The village Gatiput comes under Tentulikhunti Police station and lies 3 km north of Patradora dam on Indravati. The site is located in village Gatiput on the left side of Gatiput-Patradora road at a distance of 2 km from the dam site. The surrounding area of the site is hilly and thickly forested. Twenty artefacts collected from an area of 72 sq m are mostly made on quartz except a few specimens on chert. The chert pieces are slightly patinated.

46. Six km from Bhairab Singpur towards Boriguma (19°8' : 82°41')

The site is located on the left side of the Bhairab Singpur-Boriguma main road at a distance of 6 km from Bhairab Singpur. There is an elevated land extending about 0.5 km which was partially under cultivation. In the central part of the land are a few isolated granitic boulders. Forty-six artefacts collected from near the boulders are mostly made on quartz and in mint condition.

47. Bentaguda (19°32' : 83°1')

The site lies in village Bentaguda, located at a distance of approximately 6 km south of village Dakutha. Artefacts on chert and quartz were found sparsely scattered on a rocky elevated wasteland covering an area of 40 sq m. A total number of twenty artefacts were collected from this site.

48. Sargiguda (19°3' : 82°36')

The village Sargiguda lies about 6 km east of Boriguma town. The site lies on an elevated wasteland, as one approaches the village. Twenty-six artefacts mainly made on chert were collected from an area of 15 sq m are in mint condition.

49. Jagnathpur (19°12' : 82°44')

The village Jagnathpur is about 9.5 km southeast of Tentulikhunti town. About 1.5 km north of village Jagnathpur is a small stream joining Indravati at about 4 km further north of the village. The site is located on an elevated rocky land, one km to the north of the village. Eighty-nine artefacts collected are mostly made on chert with a few specimens on quartz. These are fresh with a thin film of red patina.

50. Patiaguda (19°00' : 82°40')

The village Patiaguda lies about 6 km south of Bhairab Singpur. The site lies on elevated rocky lands which are located on the left side close to the Bhairab Singpur-Kotpad road. A collection of twenty-nine artefacts made on quartz and chert was made from this area covering an area of about 180 sq m.

51. Limbata (19°11' : 82°17')

The village Limbata lies 8 km northeast of Kotpad town. The site lies very close to this village and about 1.5 km northwest of village Karla. The Indravati flows at a distance of 2.5 km south of the site. One hundred ninety artefacts collected from an area of 45 sq m are

exclusively made on yellowish red chert and have thin red patina.

Plain Waste Land Sites

52. Balenga (19°12' : 82°15')

The village Balenga is located on the left bank of the river Bhaskel which forms the eastern boundary of the village. To the northwest of Balenga at a distance of 6 km lies the town of Kodinga. The site lies 0.5 km west of the river Bhaskel. Seventy-six artefacts made on chert and quartz in mint condition were collected from an area of 12 sq m wasteland.

53. Temra (19°18' : 82°14')

The village Temra is situated at a distance of about 3.5 km southwest of the village Balenga. The site is located on a plain wasteland to the left of Kosagumuda-Temra road which is of 5 km stretch. A small stream flows approximately 0.5 km southwest, whereas the river Bhaskel flows one km southeast of the site. Forty-five artefacts in mint condition collected are mainly made on chert with a few pieces on quartz.

54. Saraladhanua (19°15' : 82°12')

The village Saraladhanua is situated approximately 5 km southwest of Kosangumuda. The site lies on a plain bushy land very close to the left side of Kosangumuda-Saraladhanua road. The river Bhaskel flows at a distance of 0.5 km northeast of the site. Forty-four artefacts collected from an area of about 200 sq m are mostly made on chert and fresh in appearance.

55. Bajagar (19°12'30" : 82°16')

Village Bajagar is situated at a distance of about 6 km northeast of Kosangumuda and about 9 km west of Kodinga town. The site is located nearly 200 m north of the village. The river Bhaskel flows at a distance of 1.5 km northwest of the site. Fifty-three artefacts mostly on yellowish chert were found spread over an area of about 60 sq m. These are in mint condition and have a thin red patina.

56. Duragaon (19°11' : 82°11')

The village Durgaon is approximately 13 km to the northwest of Kotpad town. The river Bhaskel flows at the periphery of the village and form the border with Bastar district. The site is located on a plain lateritic surface on the left side of the Ukipali-Duragaon road. Seventy-one artefacts made on chert and in mint condition were collected from the site.

57. Bamuni (19°12' : 82°15')
The village Bamuni lies about 10 km northwest of Kotpad town. The site is located very close to the village Bamuni on the right side of Kotpad-Kodinga road. The Indravati flows 7 km south of the site. One hundred eighteen artefacts mostly made on chert except a few pieces on quartz were collected from an area of 180 sq m.

58. Rajoragaon (19°14' : 82°16'30")
The village Rajoragaon is about 11 km southwest of Kodinga. The site lies to the right side of Kodinga-Rajoragaon road at a distance of about 800 metres from the village. Fifty-eight highly patinated chert artefacts were collected from a plain land covering an area of about 60 sq m.

59. Churahandi (19°12' : 82°21'30")
The village Churahandi lies about 5.5 km northeast of Kotpad town and 2 km east of Asanga site. The site is located to the left of Kotpad-Kodinga road. Twenty-seven chert artefacts were collected from an area of approximately 35 sq m.

60. Kotpad-A (19°8' : 82°19')
Kotpad is situated northwest of Jeypore at a distance of 40 km on national highway no. 43. The site Kotpad-A lies to the northeast of Kotpad high school and one km away from Kotpad police station. Only thirty-four chert artefacts in mint condition were collected from plain wasteland covering an area of 50 sq m.

The site Kotpad-B is only 70 metres from Kotpad-A. Hundred thirty-three artefacts exclusively made on chert were found scattered on the lateritic surface.

The site Kotpad-C is about 1.5 km northwest of Kotpad police station and just behind the inspection bungalow. River Indravati lies 2.5 km from the site. Eighty artefacts mostly made on chert were collected from the site covering an area of approximately 210 sq m.

61. Five km from Kotpad towards Boriguma on NH 43 (19°8' : 82°23')
The site is on the left side of national highway no. 43 and is 5 km away from Kotpad towards Boriguma town. Due to thick vegetation at the site, the extent of artefactual scatter could not be determined. Twenty artefacts collected from the site are all made on chert and are in mint condition.

62. Bathasana (19°9' : 82°24')
The village Bathasana lies east of Kotpad town at a distance of 8 km by road and about 2 km south of village Ghotorla. The site is located on the left side of Kotpad-Bathasana-Ghotorla road. Twenty-three artefacts mostly made on chert were found scattered on a plain wasteland covering an area of 600 sq m and lies at a distance of 0.5 km to the south in Bathasana village.

63. Amlabhata (19°7' : 82°19')
The village Amlabhata lies at a distance of about 4 km by road on south of Kotpad town. The present site is located to north of the village. One hundred thirty seven artefacts made on yellow chert with reddish patina were collected from a lateritic land covering an area of 80 sq m.

64. Narahandi (19°6' : 82°18')
The site in village Narahandi is located southeast of the site Amlabhata, at a distance of 3 km from Narahandi on Kotpad-Mundaguda road. Twenty-two artefacts found over a rocky wasteland covering an area of 45 sq m are exclusively made on chert and are highly patinated were.

65. Sandhagaon (19°4' : 82°19')
This village is about seven km southeast of Kotpad on the Kotpad-Mundaguda road. The artefacts numbering 69, 30 and 31 were found in three clusters i.e. A, B and C respectively on undisturbed wasteland within a distance of one km. Artefacts from all these clusters are exclusively made on chert with red stain due to long association with red soil.

66. Parsola (19°11' : 82°32')
The village Parsola lies in Boriguma tehsil and is bout 19 km north of Boriguma. There were two clusters i.e. A and B yielding 177 and 53 artefacts respectively scatter at a distance of 40 metres from each other located close to Parsola village. The artefacts are mostly made on chert and are in mint condition.

67. Anuli (19°11' : 82°33')
The village Anuli lies east of Parsola and 18 km north of Boriguma. The Indravati flows at a distance of one kilometre north of the village. Twenty-nine chert and quartz artefacts in fresh condition were found on a plain wasteland covering an area of 50 sq m, just on the left side of the Boriguma-Anuli road.

68. Mahulpadar (19°13' : 82°28')

The village Mahulpadar lies 2 km southeast of village Siuni. Forty artefacts of chert and quartz were found scattered over a plain undisturbed land covering an area of approximately 70 sq m to the north of the village Mahulpadar. The chert artefacts are patinated.

69. Bikrampur (19°15'30" : 82°27')

The village Bikrampur is the adjacent village of Deula. Both these villages are separated by Turi *nullah*. The site lies very close to the village settlement of Bikrampur. Fifty-three artefacts made on chert and quartz in mint condition were found in an area of 150 sq m on a plain wasteland that was covered with patches of wild bushes.

70. Teliguda (19°16'30" : 82°27')

The village Teliguda lies nearly 2 km south of the village Bikrampur. The site is located about 0.25 km north of village Teliguda. Forty-two artefacts mainly made on chert and a few specimens on quartz were found on the left side of the Teliguda-Bikrampur road.

71. Rangamatiguda (19°14'30" : 82°34')

The site is located at a distance of about 500 metres southwest of the village Rangamatiguda and about three km northeast of Nowrangapur town, just on the right side of Nowrangapur-Ekamba road. The river Indravati flows 5 km north of the site. One hundred ninety five artefacts were found scattered on red soil covering an area of about 725 meters which was partly disturbed due to cultivation. Artefacts chiefly on quartz with few pieces of chert, jasper and chalcedony were collected from an area of 40 sq m. Artefacts are in mint condition and those which are made of chert are highly patinated.

72. Bairagiguda to Ekamba (19°13' : 82°14')

Bairagiguda is a small village, about 0.5 km north of the village Ushuripadar. The site is located on the right side of the Ushuripadar-Bairagiguda-Ekamba road. Artefacts were found on a plain land of red soil from where one hundred nine cherts with a few pieces of quartz artefacts were collected from an area of 150 sq m. The chert artefacts are slightly patinated.

73. Kutiguda (19°15' : 82°17')

The village Kutiguda lies nearly seven km southwest of Kodinga town. The site is located about 150 metres to the south of the village.

Sixty-six chert artefacts collected are fresh with a thin film of red patina.

74. Majhiguda (19°17' : 82°15'30")

The village Majhiguda is the neighbouring village of Kosagamura and lies eight km southwest of the Kodinga town. The site is located on the right side of the Kosagumura-Temra road at a distance of 150 metres from the village Majhiguda. Fifty-two artefacts collected from a rocky plain land covering an area of 35 sq m are exclusively made on chert and patinated.

Cultivated Sites

75. Boriaguda (19°10' : 82°18')

The village Boriaguda is situated about 3 km northwest of Kotpad town. River Indravati flows northwest of this village. The site was slightly disturbed due to cultivation that lies on the left side of Kotpad-Boriaguda road. Forty-one artefacts mostly made on chert with few on quartz in mint condition were collected from this site covering an area of 140 sq m.

76. Dhanpur (19°9' : 82°22')

The village Dhanpur lies seven km northeast of the Kotpad town. The site is located just opposite the village Dhanpur on the right side of Kotpad-Girla road. Indravati flows about 3 km north of the site. Sixty-three artefacts were found scattered over an elevated land which was disturbed due to shifting cultivation. All the artefacts collected from an area of 250 sq m are made on chert except one specimen on quartz and are fresh; few pieces that show slight rolling.

77. Siuni (19°14' : 82°27')

The site is about 0.5 km to the north of village Siuni, which lies 4 km south of Bikrampur and one km southeast of Turi *nullah*. Forty-one chert artefacts were collected from 35 sq m of disturbed area.

78. Lambtaguda (19°15' : 82°46')

Lambtaguda is a large village in Nowrangpur tehsil which is connected by two straight roads with Nowrangpur and Tentulikhunti towns. The site is located on a hill slope that lies 3.5 km east of the Indravati and about one km south of the village Lambtaguda. The height of this hillock is about 40 meters from the surrounding ground level. The site was disturbed due to cultivation. One hundred seventeen artefacts collected from this site are made on chert and are in mint condition.

79. Panaspadar (19°15' : 82°44')
The village Panaspadar lies 8.5 km south of Tentulikhunti. The site is one km away from the road, located near Baghadori *nullah* that flows to the south of Panaspadar. Fifty-nine quartz artefacts were collected from the site which was an agricultural field.

80. Antasar (19°14' : 82°42')
The village Antasar lies at a distance of 2 km east of village Panaspadar. Indravati flows about one km east of the village. The site is located just near the village, on the right side of the Dahana-Antasar road. Only nineteen quartz artefacts in mint condition were collected from an area of 20 sq m.

81. Munja to Kumuli (19°9' : 82°41'30")
The village Munja lies at a distance of 15 km by road from Bhairab Singpur and 5 km from village Kumuli. The site is about 2 km to the south of the village on an elevated land with a rock exposure at the centre on the right side of the Munja-Kumuli road. Eighty artefacts mostly of chert with red stain were collected from an area of about 75 sq m confiding to the rock exposure and nearby area which had been brought under cultivation.

82. Berapadar (19°12' : 82°46')
The village Berapadar in Tentulikhunti tehsil, lies 5.5 km south of Tentulikhunti. The site is located on the left side of the Jaganathpur-Berapadar road. Thirty-nine artefacts collected from this site are mostly made on chert.

83. Five km from Nowrangpur towards Boriguma (82°33'30" : 19°9'30")
The site is located five km from Nowrangpur on the left side (200 metres away) of the Nowrangpur-Boriguma main road. Artefacts were found over a vast area with very poor concentration. Thirty-seven artefacts mostly made on chert were collected from a single spot.

84. Six km from Nowrangpur towards Boriguma (82°34' : 19°9')
The site lies on the right side of Nowrangpur-Boriguma road at a distance of 6 km from Nowrangpur. The landscape is characterized by low hillocks with a height rages between 30 and 50 metres from the surrounding ground level. Most of the hillocks are brought under cultivation during the rainy season. Two hundred thirty six artefacts mainly made on chert with a few specimens on quartz were collected from an elevated land which was disturbed due to cultivation. Artefacts are fresh, with a thin film of red patina on chert specimens.

Rock Shelter

85. Kharki (82°30' : 19°19')
The village Kharki comes within the area of Pappadahandi police station. Pappadahandi is situated south of Nowrangpur at a distance of 12 km by state highway no. 2 and Kharki is about 10 km by road from Pappadahandi in northeast direction. Behind the Kharki village, there is a hill range which extend for about one km in length and 0.75 km in breadth. It is largely a barren hill with a few patches of vegetation.

There are about 30 rock shelters in this hill range. The size of the shelters varies between two and five metres in length and less than one to six metres in breadth. The height of these shelters varies from 0.5 to two metres. On the ceiling of one of the shelters, there are some paintings in red colour belonging to historical period. Outside the shelters, large number of microliths was noticed on the surface. One hundred forty three artefacts of chert and quartz in mint condition were collected from one of the scatters in front of the shelter.

Assemblage

Like Upper Palaeolithic assemblage, Nanda (1983) has studied the Mesolithic assemblage in detail from typological point of view. The following are the observations made by Nanda that high light the nature of Mesolithic assemblage in the area:

1. A total collection of 8709 artefacts from 85 sites have been analysed in detail, of which 844 (9.69%) are shaped artefacts and 7865 (90.32%) are simple artefacts.
2. Out of total 844 shaped artefacts, 220 (26.07%) comprise microliths (Fig. 9) and 624 (73.93%) are flake tools (Figs. 10, 11, 12 and 13). The detail tool types in each category are given in tables 1 and 2. Among the flake tools varieties of side scrapers together forms the major chunk, while backed blade variants and crescents

16

predominate amongst the microliths (Nanda 1985: 162).

Table 1. Indravati Valley: Flake tools from surface collections

Tool Types	No.	Percentage
Straight side scrapers	92	14.7
Convex side scrapers	113	18.1
Concave side scrapers	71	11.4
Side scrapers with steep retouch	19	3.1
Side scrapers with ventral retouch	9	1.4
Double side scrapers	32	5.1
Denticulates	29	4.6
End Scrapers	118	18.9
End scraper + side scraper	10	1.6
Dejete	3	0.5
Notch	66	10.6
Point on flake	38	6.1
Borer	13	2.1
Burin	2	0.4
Knife	9	1.4
Total	624	100

Table 2. Indravati Valley: Microlithic Tools from surface collections

Tool Types	No.	Percentage
Retouched blade, one margin	39	17.4
Retouched blade, two margins	6	2.8
Transverse truncated blade	7	3.1
Oblique truncated blade	2	0.9
Blunted-back blade one margin	64	29.1
Blunted-back blade two margins	2	0.9
Blunted-back blade with margin retouched	3	1.4
Blunted-back blade with oblique truncation at one end	2	0.9
Rectilinear point with retouch on one margin	22	10.0
Curvilinear point with retouch on one margin	6	2.8
Point with retouch on two margins	1	0.5
Long Crescent	18	8.2
Short crescent	41	18.7
Triangle	6	2.8
Trapeze	1	0.5
Total	220	100

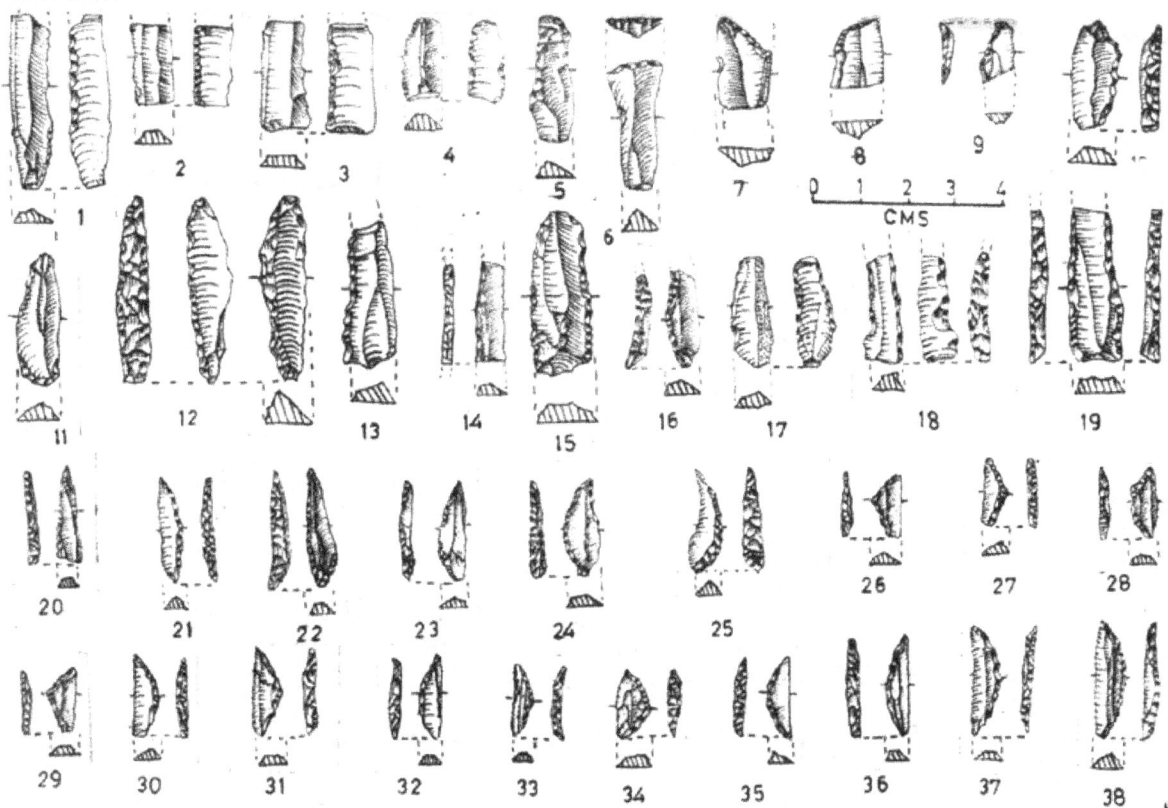

Figure 9: Surface microliths from Indravati valley

17

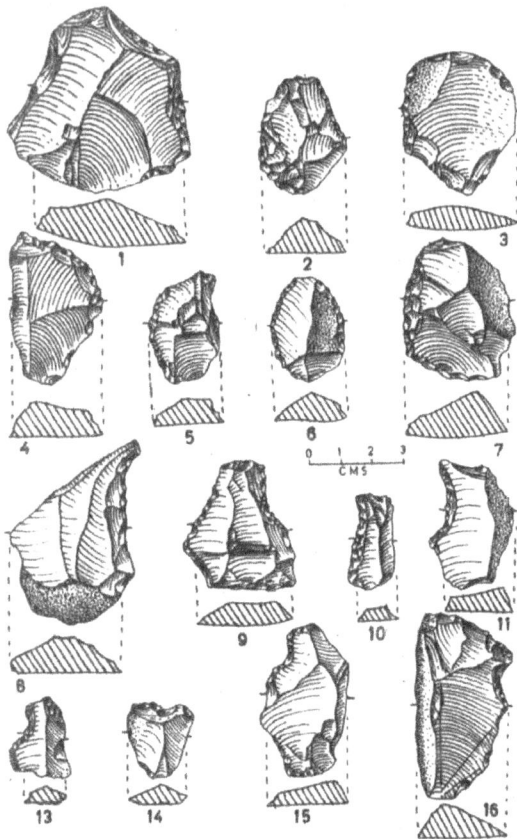
Figure 10: Surface Mesolithic scrapers and notches

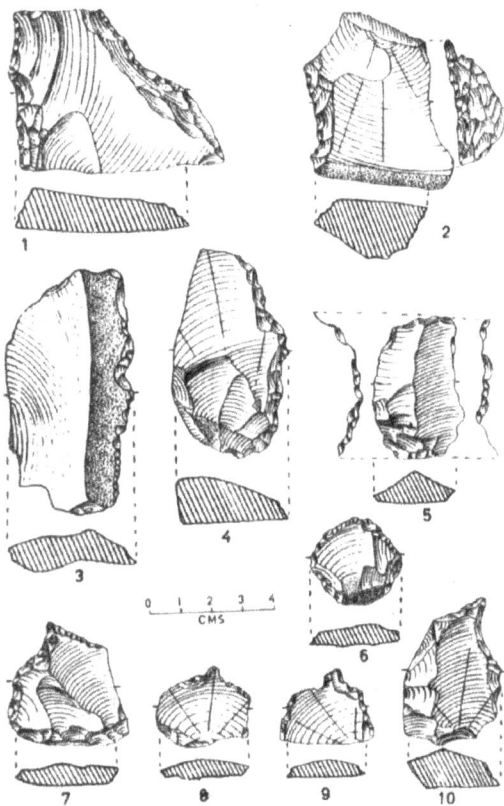
Figure 12: Surface Mesolithic end scrapers, points and knife

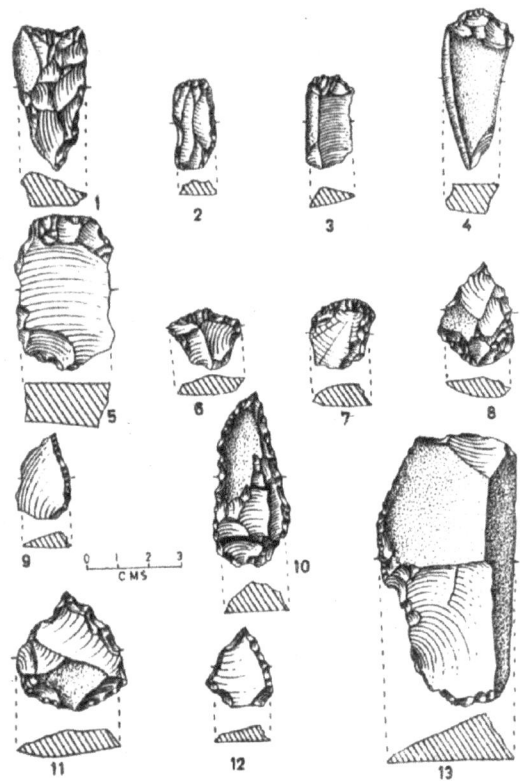
Figure 11: Surface Mesolithic scrapers

Figure 13: Mesolithic artifacts: Flakes tools

3. The simple artefacts (Figs. 14 and 15) that accounts for 7865 specimens comprise cores 1323 (16.92%), flakes 1367 chips 3067 (38.99%), worked (17.38%), blades 1338 (17.01%), nodules 761 (9.67%) and microburins 9 (0.14%) (table 3). Only five per cent of the microblades show signs of utilization, and the ratio between microblade cores and microblades is virtually 1:1.

18

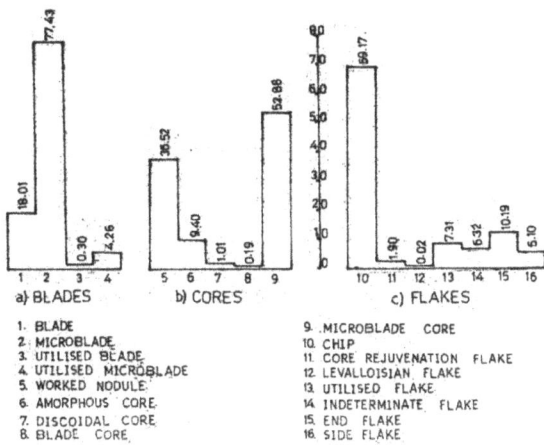

a) BLADES   b) CORES   c) FLAKES

1. BLADE
2. MICROBLADE
3. UTILISED BLADE
4. UTILISED MICROBLADE
5. WORKED NODULE
6. AMORPHOUS CORE
7. DISCOIDAL CORE
8. BLADE CORE
9. MICROBLADE CORE
10. CHIP
11. CORE REJUVENATION FLAKE
12. LEVALLOISIAN FLAKE
13. UTILISED FLAKE
14. INDETERMINATE FLAKE
15. END FLAKE
16. SIDE FLAKE

Figure 14: Frequency distribution of simple Mesolithic artifacts (Surface)

Figure 15: Mesolithic artifacts: Flakes and cores

Table 3. Indravati Valley: Simple Artefacts from Surface Collection

S. No.	Artefact Types	No.	Percentage
1	Cores	**1323**	**16.92**
	(a) Flake core	217	16.40
	(b) Blade core	4	0.30
	(c) Microblade core	1102	83.29
	(i) Single directional	1027	93.19
	(ii) Double directional	74	6.71
	(iii) Tridirectional	1	0.09
2	Flakes	**1367**	**17.38**
	(a) Side flake	226	16.53
	(b) End flake	452	33.06
	(c) Indeterminate flake	280	20.48
	(d) Utilised flake	324	23.70
	(e) Levallois type flake	1	0.07
	(f) Core rejuvenation flake	84	6.14
3	Blades	**1338**	**17.01**
	(a) Simple blades	245	18.31
	(b) Microblades	1093	81.68
4	Chips	**3067**	**38.99**
5	Worked nodule	**761**	**9.67**
6	Microburin	**9**	**0.11**
	Total	**7865**	

4. The metrical values of blades (Fig. 16) show that the distribution of the breadth frequency of blades from the Mesolithic sites fall in high proportion within the class group of 12-14 mm, while the blades from Upper Palaeolithic sites fall in high proportion within the class group of 18-20 mm. The thickness of blades from both Mesolithic and Upper Palaeolithic sites fall in high frequency within the class group of 7-9 mm (Fig. 17). The high frequency of blades in respect of length from Mesolithic sites fall within 36-40 mm, whereas blades from Upper Palaeolithic sites fall in high frequency within the class group of 41-45 mm (Fig. 18). This show the gradual reduction in length and breadth of blades from Upper Palaeolithic culture to Mesolithic culture.

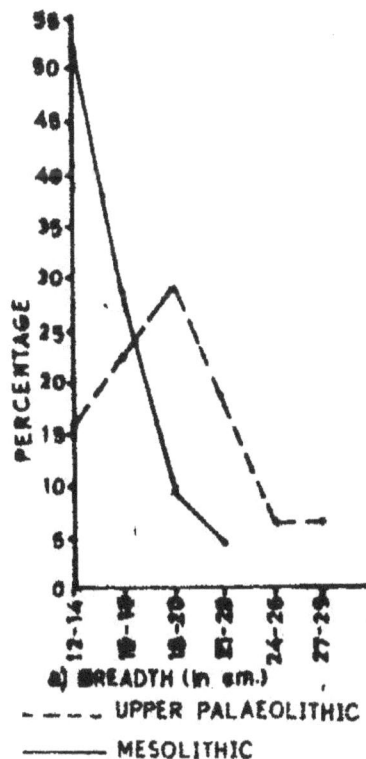

a) BREADTH (in mm.)

- - - - UPPER PALAEOLITHIC
———— MESOLITHIC

Figure 16: Frequency distribution of breadth

19

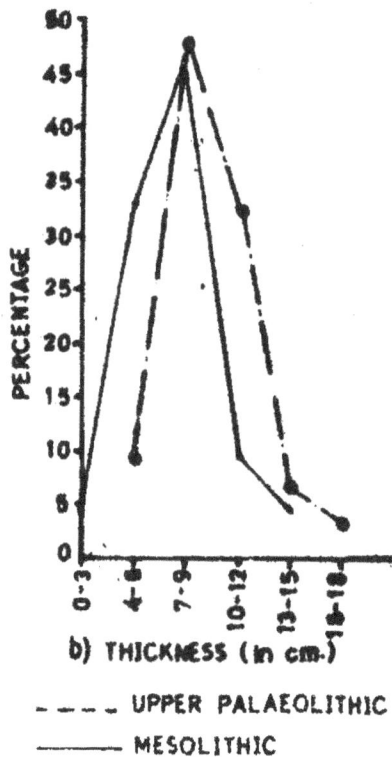

b) THICKNESS (in cm.)

‒ ‒ ‒ ‒ UPPER PALAEOLITHIC
———— MESOLITHIC

Figure 17: Frequency distribution of thickness

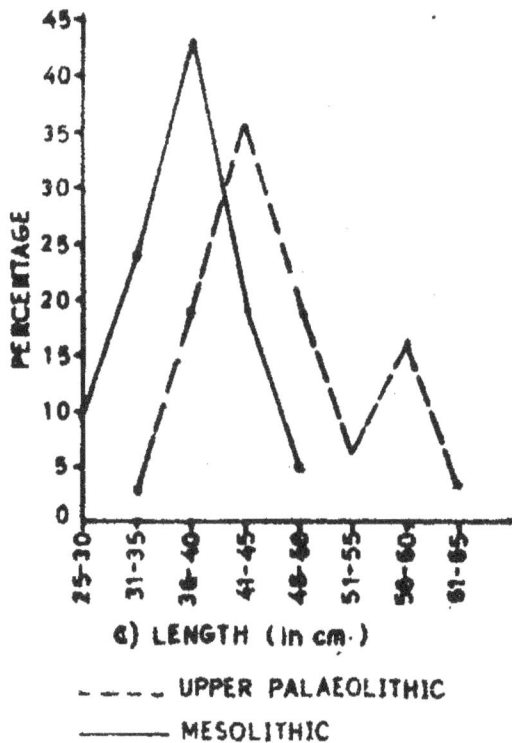

c) LENGTH (in cm.)

‒ ‒ ‒ ‒ UPPER PALAEOLITHIC
———— MESOLITHIC

Figure 18: Frequency distribution of length

5. The other lithic materials (Fig. 19) include four hammer stones, one fragment of ring stone, two rubber stones and two jasper beads (Fig. 20). The stone hammers are of quartz pebbles of size varying from 3.4 to 5.2 cm on length, 2.4 to 3.9 cm in breadth and 1.3 to 2.2 cm in thickness. All these hammer specimens show battering marks on

the surface that is suitable for hammering. The ring stone fragment is of basalt having a thickness of 2.1 cm. The two rubber stones are of 4.5 x 2.1 x 4.0 cm and - x 3.8 x 1.7 cm (broken) in dimension. The two red jasper bead pieces measures 2.0 x 1.5 x 0.4 cm and 1.9 x 1.4 x 0.2 cm in dimension. Besides the above mentioned material rubbed haematite pieces have also been collected from four sites.

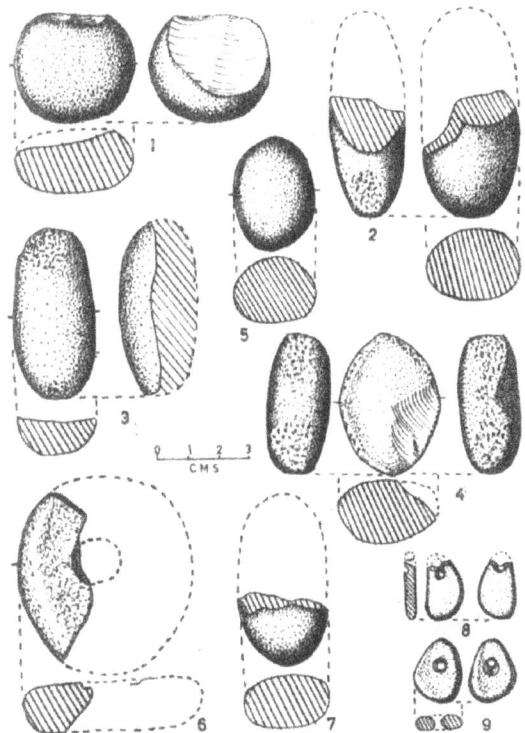

Figure 19: Surface Mesolithic grinding stones, hammer stones and beads

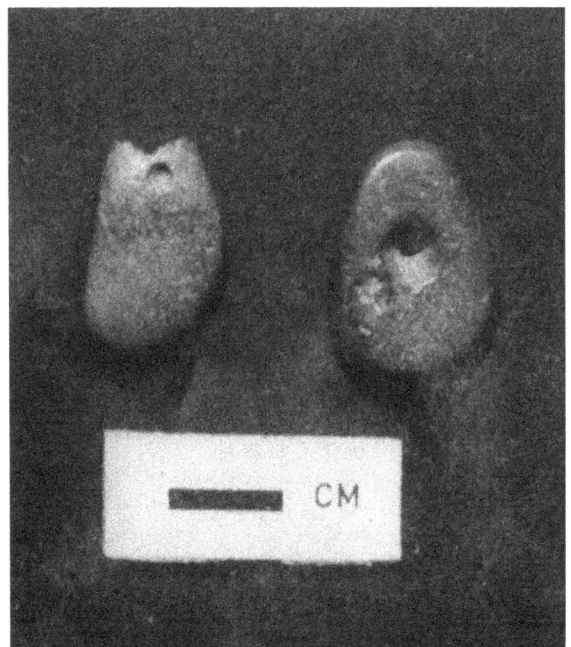

Figure 20: Mesolithic jasper beads

20

6. Chert (71.03%) is the most common raw material used for fabricating lithic artefacts. Other materials used are quartz (27.68%), chalcedony (0.77%), granite (0.29%), and jasper (0.23%). Seven sites are exclusively of chert industry, at 54 sites chert is more common and at 24 sites quartz is more common. Cherts in various shades as raw material occur in slab form at the site or within a range of one to two kilometres from the site. The chert implements are highly patinated with a reddish stain because of long association with red soil and lateritic soil. The shaped artefacts are mainly on chert with an insignificant proportion of quartz and chalcedony.

The quartz dominant sites are near the granitic out crops or on granitic hillocks. The both crystal and milky quartz found in nodular and chunk form of different sizes. The quartz dominant sites have a low proportion of shaped artefacts and a high proportion of chips and nodules. The flakes from these sites are smaller in size. There is no patination on any of these artefacts.

The artefacts made on granite are mostly worked nodules and chips only. None of the shaped artefacts are of granite. The same is in the case with jasper.

7. Until 1970 the microlithic industry of Orissa was considered to be purely non-geometric, but Nanda (1985: 163) shows the presence of geometric element.

Trial Excavation at Girla

Occurrence of large number of microliths on the surface of Girla-A site from where a total number of 455 artefacts were collected from an area of 42 sq m prompted Nanda to carry out a trial excavation at the site with a view to determine the stratigraphic position of the artefact horizon and understand the nature of industry. A trench measuring 2 x 2 m divided into 4 squares were dug (Fig. 21) up to a depth of 75 cm. The entire content of each square from each dig of five cm were sieved and the archaeological materials were collected.

The excavation has yielded a total cultural deposit of 0.5 m, in which artefacts are mostly confined to the upper 35 cm. The deposit has shown three layers. The layer 1 is of five cm thick and is slightly loose in composition,

yellowish to reddish in colour. The colour of the sediment slowly darkens towards the base. The underlying layer 2 is 30 cm in thick, reddish in colour which is slightly darker in shade than layer 1. Layer 2 is the main artefactual horizon and the nature of assemblage does not differ from that of Layer 1. The layer 3 is of 40 cm thick, dark red in colour, more compact than previous layers, sticky with moisture and with a few angular debris. The upper 15 cm of the layer 3 is associated with cultural material and the remaining part is sterile.

Figure 21: View of excavation at Girla

Based on detailed typological analysis (Fig. 22) the assemblage can be summarized as below:

1. The assemblage is characterized by the occurrence of microblades. The excavated squares A1, A2, B1 and B2 have yielded 1070, 794, 926 and 560 artefacts respectively. Out of total collection of 3350 artefacts, 338 (10.1%) are shaped and 3012 (89.9%) are simple artefacts.

2. Besides the above mentioned artefacts the excavation has yielded three pieces of hammer stones, a fragment of ring stone, two pieces of rubber stone and 22 pieces of rubbed iron oxide.

3. Of the shaped artefacts the proportion of microliths and flake tools are 279 (82.54%) and 59 (17.45%) respectively.

4. The microliths variety (Figs. 23 and 24) include one margin retouched microblades 20 (7.17%), oblique truncated microblades 21(7.53%) and transverse truncated microblades 2 (0.72%), backed microblades one margin 44 (15.77%), backed microblades with oblique truncation 5 (1.79%), points 32 (11.47%), crescents 146 (52.32%), triangles 6 (2.15%) and trapezes 3 (1.08%).

5. The flake tool component includes notches 19 (32.20%), scrapers 16 (27.11%), side scrapers 14 (23.72%), points on flakes 4 (6.78%), denticulates 3 (5.08%), burins 2 (3.39%) and borer 1 (1.69%). Distribution of tool types is not uniform in all squares.

6. The simple artefact category (Figs. 25 and 26) comprise microblade cores 86 (2.86%), flake cores 8 (0.27%), worked nodules 45 (1.49%), microblades 1194 (39.64%), blades 11 (0.36%), utilized microblades 36 (1.20%), utilized blade 1 (0.03%), flake 99 (3.29%), chips 1480 (49.14%) and microburins 33 (1.10%).

7. The proportion of microblades to microblade cores is roughly 13.1.

8. The raw material used for manufacturing artefacts include yellowish, reddish and greenish colour chert (79.58%), quartz (18.18%), chalcedony (1.67%), granite (0.53%) and agate (0.03%).

a) DISTRIBUTION OF RAW MATERIAL

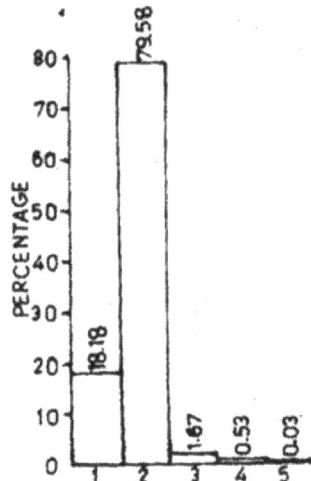

b) DISTRIBUTION OF FINISHED FLAKE TOOLS

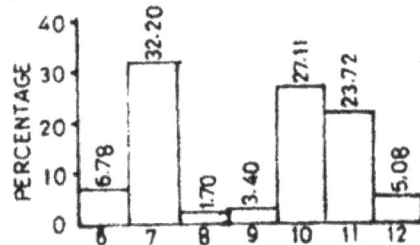

c) DISTRIBUTION OF MICROLITHS & OTHER FINISHED TOOLS

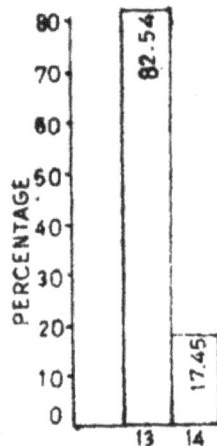

d) DISTRIBUTION OF MICROLITHS

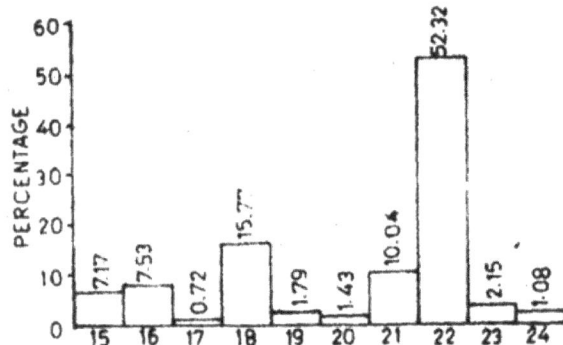

1. QUARTZ	10. END SCRAPER	
2. CHERT	11. SIDE SCRAPER	20. CURVE POINT
3. CHALCEDONY	12. DENTICULATE	21. STRAIGHT POINT
4. GRANITE	13. MICROLITH	22. CRESCENT
5. AGATE	14. OTHER FINISHED TOOL	23. TRIANGLE
6. POINT ON FLAKE	15. RETOUH BLADE - 1 MARGIN	24. TRAPEZE
7. NOTCH	16. TRUNCATED BLADE OBLIQUE	
8. BORER	18. BACK BLADE - 1 MARGIN	
9. BURIN	19. OBLIQUELY TRUNCATED BACK BLADE	
	17. TRUNCATED BLADE - TRANSVERSE	

Figure 22: Girla excavation

The assemblage that has been recovered from the excavations at Girla is characterized by high proportion of microliths made on microblades, low percentage of flake tools, complete absence of core tools and well developed blunted back technique. The retouched tools are a few in numbers. Crescent is the predominant type among the microliths. Triangle and trapezes occur in a considerable proportion. The use of microburin technique is very clear. Notch and end scrapers are the two predominant types among the flake tools. The assemblage is a geometric form of microlithic industry fabricated on microblades with skilful workmanship (Nanda 1983: 198).

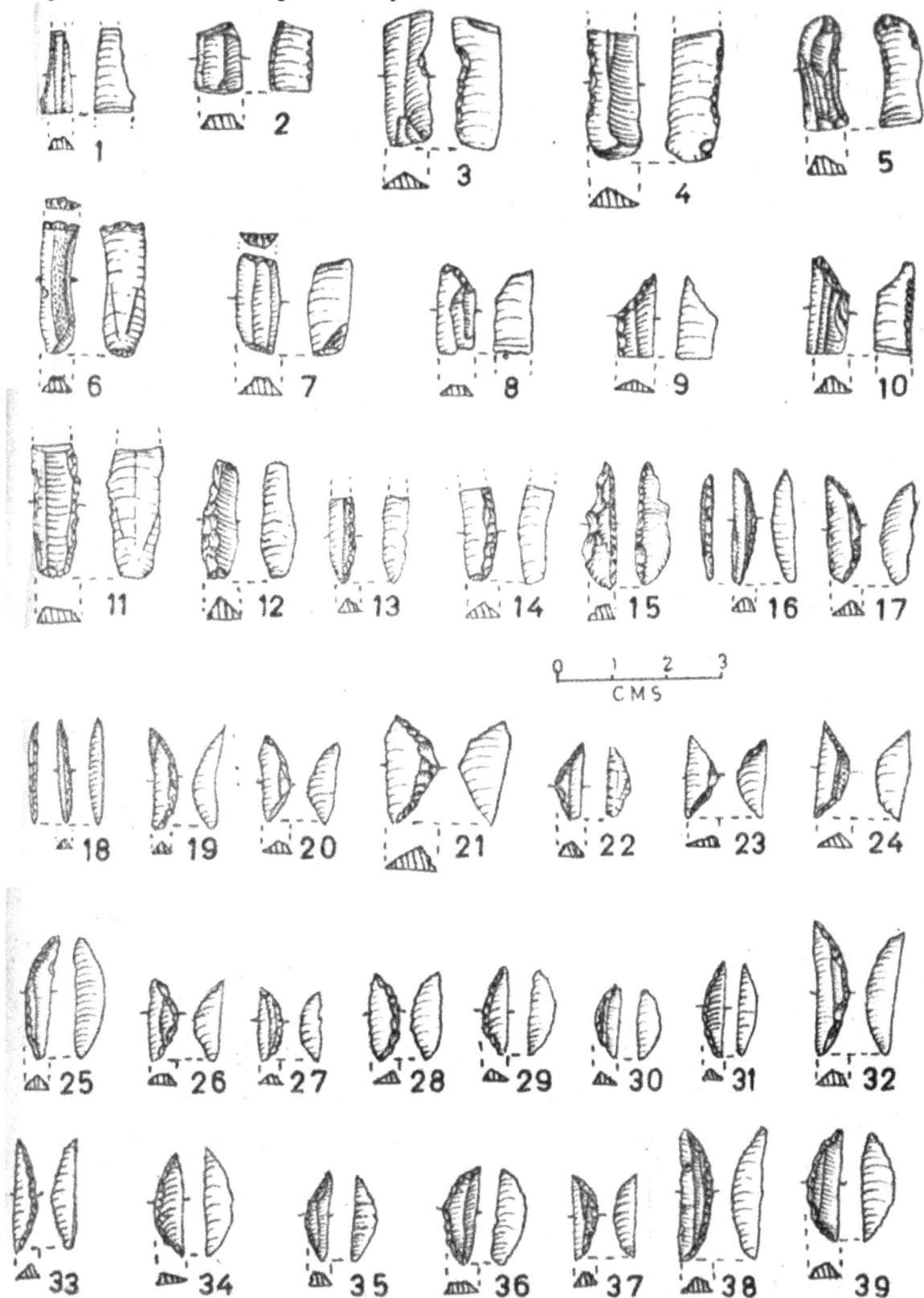

Figure 23: Excavated Mesolithic microliths

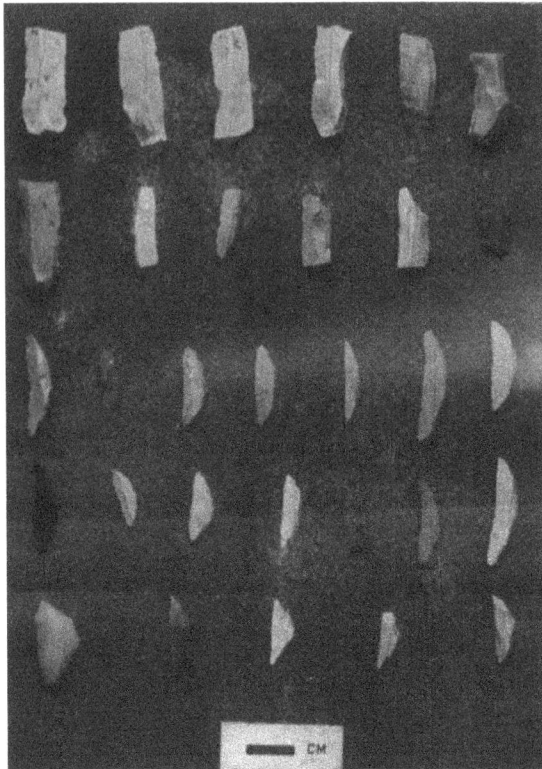

Figure 24: Mesolithic artifacts from excavation at Girla: Microliths

Figure 26: Mesolithic artifacts from excavation at Girla: Flakes, cores and flake tools

Figure 25: Excavated Mesolithic cores and flakes

With the view to understand the compositional difference between the artefactual assemblages of the surface and excavated, Nanda (1983: 198-202) has done a typological comparative study (Fig. 27) of the assemblages from Girla-A. From this study he has derived the following inferences (Nanda 2000: 167-169).

1. There is no significant difference in the proportion of artefacts and the use of varieties of raw material in both collections.
2. The proportion between finished artefacts and simple artefacts remains very similar in both the collections.
3. The density of flake artefacts is much higher in the surface collection than the excavated collection.
4. The microliths in the excavated collection is much higher than in the surface collection.
5. The collection from the excavation is characterized by a lower percentage of flake cores and microblade cores, while the surface collection consists of a high percentage of flake cores and blade cores.
6. Microburins are more common in the excavated collection than in the surface collection.
7. Among the flake tools, side scraper is the dominant type in surface collection, while end scraper is the dominant variety in excavated collection.
8. Knife is absent in the excavated collection, but it occurs in a significant proportion in the surface collection.
9. Triangle and trapeze are more significant in excavated material than in the surface collection.
10. Crescents dominate the microliths in the excavated collection, while the backed

blade is the dominant type in the surface collection.

11. Though technology remains same, the typological and morphological variations are very much distinct in the two collections.

Ethnographic Observations

Besides the study of lithic industries in the area, Nanda also carried out extensive ethnographic study of the local communities in general and Gadaba community in particular. The objective of ethnographic study in the area was to understand the probable way of life of prehistoric man through ethnographic analogies. To understand the subsistence strategies of prehistoric human, few local tribes, specially Gadabas (Fig. 28) has been studied. Besides, the other communities inhabiting the Indravati basin are Paraja, Bondo (Fig. 29), Bhatra etc. who are still practicing some sort of primitive way of life and economy (Figs. 30 and 31). The subsistence pattern is based on shifting cultivation, hunting, fishing and gathering. These are the communities who have not been culturally transformed much. It is so much so that many of the archaeological traditions in these societies continue even today.

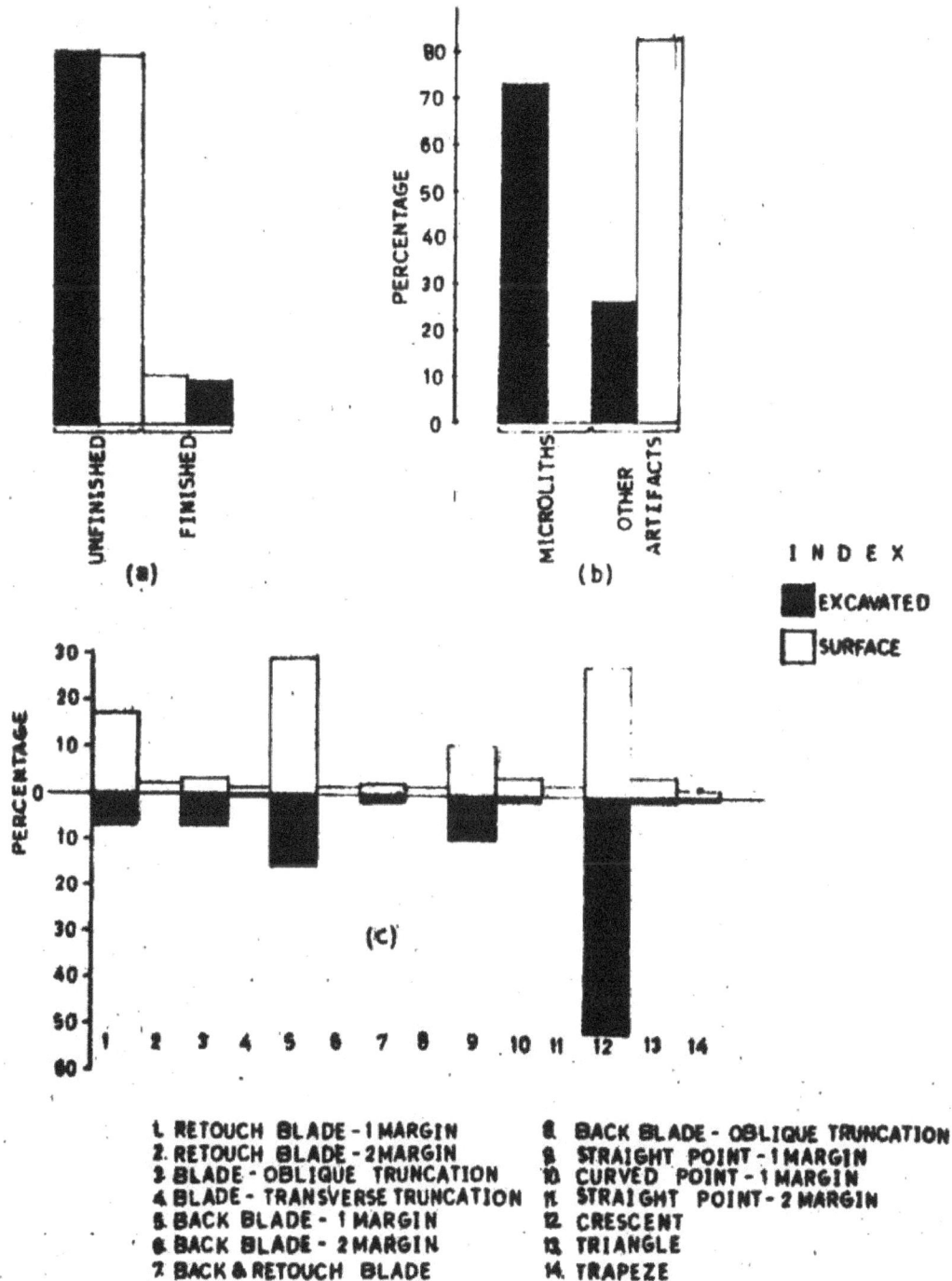

INDEX

■ EXCAVATED
□ SURFACE

1. RETOUCH BLADE - 1 MARGIN
2. RETOUCH BLADE - 2 MARGIN
3. BLADE - OBLIQUE TRUNCATION
4. BLADE - TRANSVERSE TRUNCATION
5. BACK BLADE - 1 MARGIN
6. BACK BLADE - 2 MARGIN
7. BACK & RETOUCH BLADE
8. BACK BLADE - OBLIQUE TRUNCATION
9. STRAIGHT POINT - 1 MARGIN
10. CURVED POINT - 1 MARGIN
11. STRAIGHT POINT - 2 MARGIN
12. CRESCENT
13. TRIANGLE
14. TRAPEZE

Figure 27: Comparative distribution of Mesolithic artifacts from surface & excavation

Figure 28: A Gadaba woman

Figure 29: A Bonda girl extracting fibers from a palm trunk

Nanda's ethnographic observations in the area is one of the earliest attempts of such studies in understanding of the subsistence and cultural patterns of the stone age systems and their relationship with the existing ethnographic reality. The main problem that concerns Nanda is the effectiveness of the methodology of understanding archaeological reality through ethnographic study and its continuity to the present day (Nanda 2000: 169). Such a system may establish a model and then be used to draw general implication for comparisons with archaeological records.

Figure 30: Two Gadaba men catching rats

Figure 31: A Gadaba boy with three rats

Acknowledgement

I am thankful to Ms. Sandhya Dabral for typing the manuscript. Besides many of the illustrations that have been used from S.C. Nanda's original thesis are duly acknowledged.

26

References:

Ball, V. 1876. On Stone Implements Found in the Tributary States of Orissan. *Proceedings of the Asiatic Society of Bengal*, pp. 122-23.

Basa, K. K. 1994. *Problems and Perspectives in Archaeology of Orissa, India*. Occasional Paper 4. Bhubaneswar: Utkal University.

Bose, N.K. and D. Sen 1948. *Excavations in Mayurbhanj*. Calcutta: Calcutta University.

Bose, N.K., D. Sen and G.S. Ray 1958. Geological and Cultural Evidences of the Stone Age in Mayurbhanj, *Man in India* 38: 49-55.

Misra, V.N. 1980. Evolution of the Blade Element in the Stone Age Industries of Rock-shelter III F. 23, Bhimbetka. Paper presented at the *XI Annual Congress of the ISPCES*, Bhopal.

Mohapatra, G.C. 1962. *The Stone Age Cultures of Orissa*. Poona: Deccan College.

Murty, M.L.K. 1979. Recent Research on the Upper Palaeolithic Phase in India, *Journal of Field Archaeology* 6(3): 301-320.

Nanda, S.C. 1982-83. A Note on Stone Age Succession of Indravati Valley, Koraput District, Orissa, *Manav* 1(1): 83-85.

Nanda, S.C. 1983. *Stone Age Cultures of the Indravati Basin, Koraput District, Orissa*. Unpublished Ph.D. Thesis. Pune: University of Poona.

Nanda, S.C. 1985. The Mesolithic Culture of the Indravati Valley, District Koraput, Orissa, in *Recent Advances in Indo-Pacific Prehistory* (V.N. Misra and P. Bellwood Eds.), pp. 159-163. New Delhi: Oxford & IBH Publishing Co.

Nanda, S.C. 2000. The Upper Palaeolithic and Mesolithic Cultures of the Indravati Valley, South Orissa: An Ethnoarchaeological study, in *Archaeology of Orissa* (K.K. Basa and P.K. Mohanty Eds.), pp.153-172. New Delhi: Pratibha Publications.

Tripathy, K.C. 1972. *Lithic Industries of South Western Orissa*. Unpublished Ph.D. Thesis. Bhubaneswar: Utkal University.

Tripathy, K.C. 1980. *Lithic Industries in India: A study of South Western Orissa*. New Delhi: Inter India Publication.

Prehistoric Rock Paintings of Bhimbetka, Central India

Yashodhar Mathpal

Bhimbetka (22° 55' and 22° 56' N 77° 36 and 77° 37' E) is the name of a hill in the western Vindhyas, 45 kilometres southwest of Bhopal in Central India. The hill is two kilometres away from the tribal hamlet of Bhiyanpur in Raisen district of Madhya Pradesh. Bhiyanpur lies between Ubaidullahganj and Barkhera stations on the Mumbai-Delhi line of Central Railway. The Bhopal-Itarasi highway runs parallel to the railway line. From Bhiyanpur one can either trek to the top of the hill or reach by a vehicle. The northeast-southwest oriented hill is 600 metres high from sea level and 100 metres from the surrounding ground. It has an equal length and breadth of about two kilometres, the northern and western faces having gentle slopes and the eastern and southern ones steep slopes. The hill is surmounted by a flat topped ridge 25 metres high and running east-west. It is broken up into a series of tall blocks by weathering through geological time. There are caves and shelters at the bottom of these blocks. The sandstone of the lower Vindhyan system forming the Bhimbetka group of hills has suffered extensive erosion. The weathering agents like sun, rain, wind and changing temperature and the vegetational growth, have all contributed to the loosening and break up of rocks and formation of weird shaped structures. Thus the ridge from a distance gives the impression of a medieval fort and is an easy guide for locating Bhimbetka. The climate of the area is tropical monsoon, and the hills are covered with thick deciduous vegetation enriched with a large variety of wildlife and food plants. Bhimbetka provides all resources for satisfying the three primary needs of man – food, water and shelter. It is therefore, not surprising that man occupied the area for more than a hundred thousand years.

The antiquity of man's occupation of Bhimbetka is well attested by archaeological and historical sources. Excavations in a number of shelters have revealed the occupational history of man here from late Acheulian to the beginning of historical times. Artificially made stone floors are found in all phases of the occupation. The largest number of caves were occupied during the Mesolithic period. In this period we also find organic remains - animal bones and human burials, and ground pieces of colour nodules. The earliest paintings in the shelters also belong to this period. They are found on the walls and ceilings of shelters, on vertical cliff faces and in small hollows formed by natural weathering. There are 243 shelters on Bhimbetka hill of which 133 have paintings. Sometimes broad and even surfaces are left unpainted while uneven surfaces and corners are chosen. Paintings are often located at considerable heights and in inconvenient places. Though caves inhabited by man over varying lengths of time contain paintings, they are nearly always poor in number. Indeed, some shelters which have thick habitation deposits have no paintings at all. On the other hand, shelters with no evidence of habitation have not only the largest number of paintings, but also the oldest, aesthetically most pleasing and visually most impressive paintings. Most of the paintings are located in shelters which are well lit and get direct sunlight from the rising or setting sun. A number of shelters rich in paintings are located on ground higher than the surrounding land surface. Later artists have often painted over existing paintings and several superimpositions of figures are found (Fig. 1). Some shelters contain only a few figures while others have several hundred of them.

The paintings of Bhimbetka may be classified broadly in two groups, one depicting wild animals, and scenes of hunting and food gathering and the other of fighters riding on horses and elephants and using metal weapons. The first are considered prehistoric while the second are certainly of the historic period. On the basis of superimposition and style, the prehistoric paintings are divided into five phases (A, B, C, D and E) and the historic into three (G, H and I). Between these two broad periods there are some more figures which show domesticated and tamed animals and are grouped in a third phase – transitional (phase F). The most common subjects of prehistoric paintings are animals (Figs. 2, 3 & 4). Among them the chital is commonest. We usually see large herds of chital, both stags and does. In some instances only one species is repeated while in others boar, buffalo, cow, gaur, nilgai, monkey and langur are found interspersed among the herds. These drawings are very

Figure 1: Ten superimpositions: a jumble of figures (III C-50).

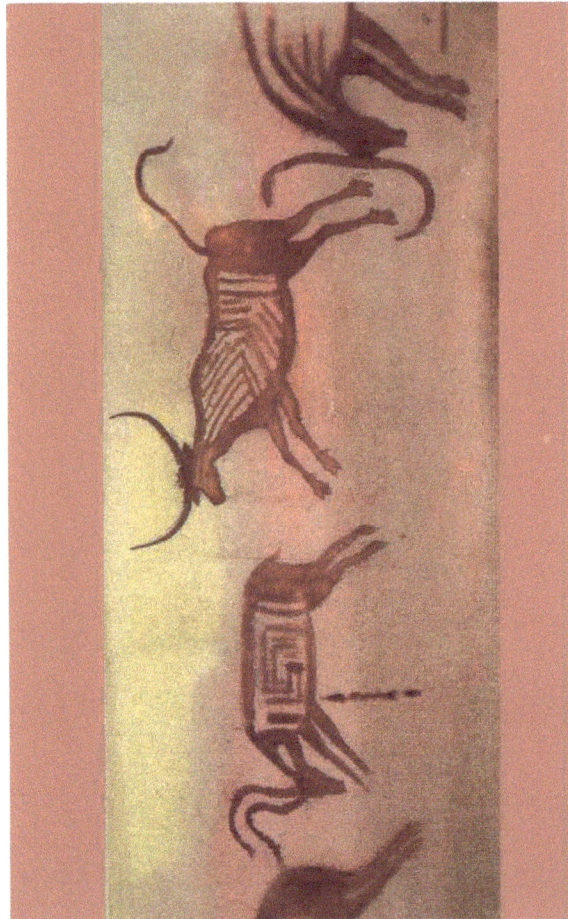
Figure 3: A Chinkara (Mesolithic)

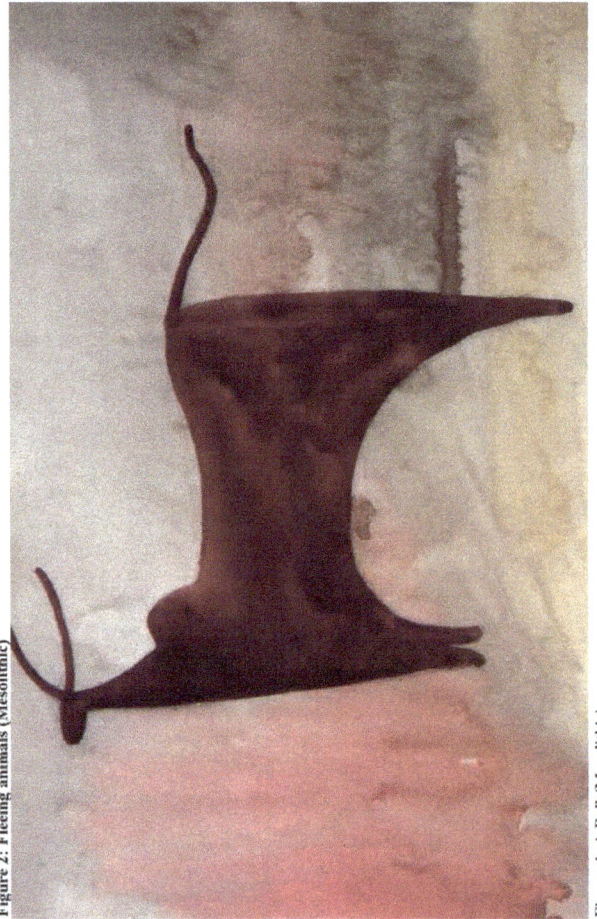
Figure 5: A Chase (Mesolithic)

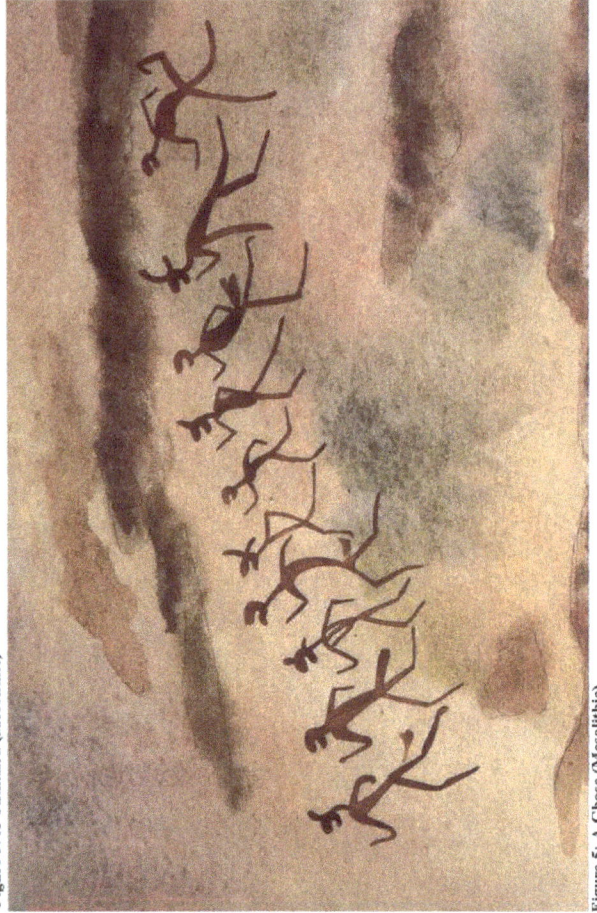
Figure 2: Fleeing animals (Mesolithic)

Figure 4: A Bull (Mesolithic)

30

Figure 6: Human figures in different styles at Bhimbetka

realistically executed and show animals in various postures and modes, standing, walking, running, leaping, looking back, up or down or grazing. Among the most beautiful drawings at Bhimbetka are backward looking fawns and frightened gaurs. The gaurs are easily identified because of their massive shoulder ridges. As many as 29 animal species are portrayed in the paintings. These cover big cats, bovids, rhinoceros, elephant, deer, antelope and

31

rodents. Besides, there are fish, frog, crab, lizard, scorpion and small centipede like-creature. Six varieties of birds are shown perching on trees, swimming or floating on water and occasionally flying. Some animal images are as big as life size while some are medium sized. But the bulk are micrographic; only a few centimetres long. Next to animals, hunting scenes are the most common subjects. In many cases hunters are shown in small groups. They camouflage themselves with masks crowned with horns or antlers. In some paintings they are shown accompanied by dogs and armed with sticks, bows and arrows, stone-tipped spears, snares and broom-shaped traps. They face large animals like wild buffalo and rhinoceros. Some hunters are chased and tossed by charging animals.

Human figures account for more than a third of the total figures (Figs. 5 & 6). They represent ages from new born babies to old men, from young women to those with bent backs. In several instances women are shown pregnant. Boys are always shown playing, running and jumping. A variety of cultural, religious and domestic and economic activities are shown in paintings of earlier phases. There are scenes of collecting honey and food. Dancers are shown dancing arm in arm and accompanied by drummers. In one instance a man is drinking from a pitcher.

Drawings of historic phases show bands of soldiers marching or engaged in battle, cavaliers and elephants riders. There are royal processions and royal personages standing under canopies. It is very clear that these paintings do not depict the life of cave dwellers; instead they appear to have been inspired by scenes cave dwellers saw in valleys and cities of the plains. The subject matter of Bhimbetka paintings also includes a large number of prints of hand, fist and fingers, symbols and signs, mythical creatures, trees bushes, flowers, decorative designs and inscriptions. Drawings are executed in 16 colours. The main colours are white and light red. Blue has never been used. The style of figures ranges from very naturalistic to very abstract. Twelve styles of execution are recorded. Rock paintings are found faded, partially obliterated and fragmented condition, sometimes covered with a thin coat of calcium or moss. They are in different stages of preservation according to location in shelters and exposure to sunlight, wind and rain.

There is no ethnographic record of any tribal painting in the shelters. Although all the rock art sites are located in tribal areas, the tribal people do not accept any direct or indirect relation with these paintings. They regard the paintings as the work of evil spirits. Unlike tribal and folk art, these paintings do not show any object of the last two or three centuries-such as bicycle, motor-car, aeroplane or rifle. The uppermost figures in the paintings of phases G, H and I are older than the inscriptions overlapping them.

These inscriptions are found in Shankha, Gupta Brahmi and Asokan Brami scripts. This evidence shows that the major figurative artistic activity in the shelters is at least 1500 years old. Soldiers and cavaliers look contemporary to the Shunga and Kushana periods by their dresses and weapons. Urban life was established around Bhimbetka as early as 600 B.C. Thus the paintings of phases G, H and I can be dated between 600 B.C. and 600 A.D. The drawings of phase F are close to those of the south Indian Neolithic period and the Chalcolithic period. These drawings may be placed between 2500 B.C. and 600 B.C. The paintings of the earlier phases (A-E) belong to the Mesolithic or even Upper Palaeolithic stage. The oldest of them may be dated to 10,000 B.C. or even earlier. The motivations behind the paintings of Bhimbetka seem to be the expression of aesthetic pleasure, representation of mythology, pictorial narratives of some major events and decoration of dwellings.

Written in the universal language of drawings, the rock paintings are as vibrant as they had been at the time of their execution by the stone age artists. They are a mine of archaeological information about the prehistoric man and his society. A great variety of evidence, especially that based on organic materials, has vanished from man's habitation sites, but it is preserved in the paintings. We can learn from the paintings about contemporary fauna, methods of hunting and gathering, vegetable foods, hafting of stone implements and crafts like basketry, rope making, trapping etc. We can also get an insight into the social, religious and ritual aspects of ancient man's life. We know about the dresses, masks, headgears and other material culture developed by those people. The Bhimbetkians of the Mesolithic period were using masks of different shapes-bird headed, rhinoceros-headed and C-shaped, during hunting and dancing. They were fond of decorating their bodies with ornaments. They wore necklaces, pendants, bracelets, elbow-bands, wristbands, bangles, knee bands and anklets, sometimes with long tassels. Men wore long loose hair and the women braids. They used sticks, slings, spear, bows and arrows, traps and snares for hunting. Their arrows and spears were barbed with microliths. In the absence of pottery these folk used dry gourds and leather bags as water bottles. Kanwars and bucket-shaped baskets were used to transport articles of animal and vegetable food. This information about their society and environment left by Stone Age artists has come down to us without any contamination and can be understood easily. So far prehistorians in India have concentrated mainly on the study of stone industries and their stratigraphic settings. They have largely neglected the study of rock art. It is hoped that in the years to come prehistorians will pay greater attention to this rich source of knowledge about prehistoric man.

The earliest mention of Bhimbetka is found in a paper published by W. Kincaid in 1888. For the purpose of reconstructing the history of Bhojpur lake, Kincaid collected information from the native tribal people. He mentions Bhimbet hill on the opposite end of the lake as a Buddhist site. As there is no other place known as Bhimbet or Bhimbetka on the boundary of the ancient lake, Kincaid could have been referring only to Bhimbetka. No archaeologist seems to have visited the site until 1957 (*IAR* 1956-57: 79). V.S. Wakankar rediscovered it in that year, but no research was done at the site for the next 14 years. In 1971-72 K.D. Bajpai and S.K. Pandey of Saugor University dug a small trench in shelter IIIF-13 and discovered a thin Mesolithic deposit (*IAR* 1971-72: 30) although they have mentioned the name of the nearby village of Barkhera as the site name. In 1972 Wakankar (1973a, 1973b, 1973c, 1975a, 1975b) on behalf of Vikram University, Ujjain excavated two trenches in shelter IIIF-24 and IIB-33 and discovered Acheulian and Mesolithic deposits, respectively. In 1976-77 Wakankar (1985) excavated eight more shelters of which two yielded Acheulian and later remains while others yielded only Middle Palaeolithic and Mesolithic materials. In 1973 V.N. Misra of Deccan College initiated excavations in shelter IIIF-23 and brought to light a continuous sequence of stone age cultures from the late Acheulian culture to the late Mesolithic during the course of four seasons of excavations (Misra 1976, 1980). In 1976-77 Misra excavated shelters IIIF-13 and IIB-33, both of which produced evidence of the evolution of Mesolithic culture (Misra 1978, 1982, 1985; Kennedy, Lukacs and Misra 2002). Miss Susan Haas of the Museum fur Volkerkunde, Basle excavated three shelters which yielded only Mesolithic remains.

Wakankar also copied the paintings in black and white off and on. He has published several papers on the paintings and also included them in his Ph.D. thesis (1975) and in his book on stone age paintings written jointly with R.R.R. Brooks. Erwin Neumayer (1983, 1993), an enthusiastic amateur from Austria, has been photographing and sketching selected paintings on Bhimbetka and other hills from the point of view of reconstructing the cultural history of the stone age. In 1973 news of the discovery of a large gallery of prehistoric paintings at Bhimbetka was widely reported in the Indian and international press. Several popular articles on the paintings and Stone Age remains from excavations were published by V.N. Misra (1973a, 1973b) and V.S. Wakankar (1975a).

In 1971 I got my Master's degree in Drawing and Painting, and was invited by the State Lalit Kala Academy, Lucknow for a one-man-show of my paintings. Among the exhibits there was a painting showing a stone age artist painting in a cave. K.S. Mathur, then head of the department of Anthropology, Lucknow University was so impressed with the painting that he advised me for higher study in prehistoric art. After the exhibition I wrote to several eminent scholars like V.S. Upadhyaya of Ujjain and H.D. Sankalia of Deccan College, Pune requesting them to accept me as a Ph.D. student in prehistoric art. Sankaliaji replied to me that I might go to Deccan College and work under Dr. V.N. Misra but with my own financial resources as there was no guarantee of any immediate scholarship. Receiving the response, I resigned from my teaching job of an Inter College, and rushed to Deccan College with a meagre saving of 1400 rupees. It was also the year when I lost my father and I was taking only self-cooked food. During the whole journey from Almora to Pune, I did not purchase any foodstuff and so I was hungry and weak. On reaching Deccan College I met Dr. Misra who took me to Sankalia's residence. For the first time I saw and bent before that tiny angel clad in a *kurta* and *dhoti*. He looked at me from head to feet and knowing that I had come to work on Bhimbetka paintings, asked me to draw a portrait for which he would sit as a model for me. I humbly accepted his offer. Next day and the day after I painted Sankalia in his office. He was pleased with the portrait and asked me about the cost of drawing material. It was rupees 25 only but he gave me rupees 125 along with his blessings to work on Bhimbetka rock art. I was advised to apply for a hostel room. I did so, but knowing that cooking was not allowed in the room, I met him again. Sankaliaji allotted me a barrack-room now, and also got me a scholarship of rupees 200 per month. After a few months I went to Bhimbetka with excavation team of Deccan College, and started my fieldwork of manually recording of rock paintings. Seeing the handprint of a boy in the Auditorium Rock I went in a state of trance finding myself amidst the prehistoric artists. On another occasion I could identify the images drawn by me in my previous birth in shelter IIIC-48. Several times Misraji and I moved in the area exploring hardly approachable shelters. One day while crawling through a narrow passage on a steep rock in the nearby Bhonrawali hill, he had to stop me for my over-enthusiasm saying, 'Panditji, please take care of yourself. No body is going to shed a tear if we die in this wilderness'. In fact, I completely forgot that I was the oldest student in Deccan College, had a family responsibility, and, above all, had very limited time and resources to complete my research work. It took me over 12 months during four seasons' stay at Bhimbetka from 1973-1976 for faithful recording of 6214 figures from 133 shelters. In the words of Prof. Sankalia, 'Each figure has been studied according to subject, colour, style, technique, phase and location. All the figures are drawn in original colour, to scale and on the spot. This is a unique feature of the work not attempted before by any scholar. Generally, students of Indian rock art have attached very little importance to faithful recording of paintings. They have used the free-hand sketching method and ignored the size, colour and location of a figure. Only well preserved and sharply visible drawings have been copied. Neither the stratigraphy of the paintings nor the whole composition have been recorded. Dr. Mathpal has spent nearly one year copying the drawings and four years in their analysis. So far nobody in India has attempted to reproduce the cave paintings in such faithful detail'. D.J. Mulvaney, Professor of Prehistory in the Australian National University, Canberra was an external referee for evaluation of my work. He wrote, 'This detailed study of the rock art of Bhimbetka by Yashodhar Mathpal represents one of the most significant attempts to record India's prehistoric heritage of art for posterity. I believe that no scholar has attempted a more detailed and exact record, and it will prove an invaluable source of information not only for Indian scholars but for students of prehistoric art around the world. I have visited Bhimbetka and I was impressed by the accuracy of Mathpal's record including comprehensiveness, colouration and scale'.

Out of over 400 compositions of Bhimbetka rock art, 36 small-sized reproductions were displayed at Southampton during the First World Archaeological Congress. Commenting on these copies editors of Congress Souvenir say, '... Originally conceived as a project to produce accurate recordings of the cave art of this region, these watercolours have themselves become works of art. The startling colours of the paintings leave a haunting image in the mind, and the delicate recording techniques have resulted in water colours of remarkable quality ... Bhimbetka art is more than just an exhibition of modern-day art: it is an important attempt to record India's prehistoric art heritage for prosperity...'.

At Bhimbetka, I had to pay rupees ten every day to my local guide and helper, and rupees four for my meals to the camp mess. Thus I required some 1500 rupees on every trip of my field work, while I was getting rupees 180 per month as scholarship after deduction of room rent of rupees twenty. After the first trip, I went to my village and brought my family to Pune, as my eldest son needed admission in school. For drawing material too I was spending 500 rupees on each trip. I had a very ordinary camera which was not suitable for research work. To meet my expenses I worked as a commercial artist for the Tribal Research Institute, Anthropological Museum and Central School at Pune, and for other museums outside Pune.

I tried my best to make good use the rich library of Deccan College, and went through the maximum possible books and journals on archaeology, prehistory, geology, rock art and wildlife, as I had literally no knowledge of these subjects. Moreover, I had been a mediocre student with least command on English language. I never wrote any research article prior to my arrival in Pune. For my thesis I prepared all the section-drawings of 133 caves, maps, charts and diagrams, myself. Dr. Misra brought for me a portable typewriter from England on which I typed 1300 odd pages of my thesis and all research articles, and which I am still using. Computer was not in use then, and I could not afford a calculator also, so all the calculations were done by me manually. During his visit to Pune in 1978, Prof. Mulvaney had lunch at my residence. He was shocked by the wretched living condition of a research scholar. After returning to Canberra he sent an aerogramme to Dr. Misra with the following comments, '... Mathpal impressed me as a man of character and great honesty and dedication. Students like that are rare out here ... Please let me know if I can assist him in any way ...'.

The Deccan College scholarship was only for one year. The U.G.C. denied me the Junior Fellowship due to age factor. Next year, I got a fellowship of rupees 300/- on the basis of a strong recommendation from Dr. Sankalia. It took me six years to complete my dissertation. After two years I applied to Deccan College for a Senior Fellowship of rupees 400/- per month. There were five successful candidates for four fellowships. One of them, Shri Subrata Chakrabarti, refused to accept his fellowship saying that Mathpal was a more deserving candidate as he had to support a five-member family. I got the fellowship and remained grateful to my friend Chakrabarti.

Finally, I must confess that I was fortunate not to have been required to face a viva-voce test. My both referees (Prof. Mulvaney and Prof. B.B. Lal) mentioned clearly in their evaluation reports that they did not consider it necessary to hold viva-voce test in my case.

I got my Ph. D. degree on the thesis, *Prehistoric Rock Paintings of Bhimbetka, Central India*, from Pune University in 1978, and it was published as a book under the same title in 1985. I have also published over two hundred papers and 22 books on rock art, folk art, wood craft and Indian culture. A few of them are enlisted in Mathpal 1976-77, 1977, 1984; Misra and Mathpal 1979. Even 30 years after the completion of my thesis I do not find anything more to be included in the dissertation, except a few good photographs, contour map of the area and 'more accurate' section-drawings of painted shelters, prepared by a draftsman.

Acknowledgement

I am extremely thankful to Prof. V.N. Misra, my research guide, for transforming me from a rustic into an internationally acknowledged rock art researcher. I am equally grateful to Dr. Statira Wadia, who read almost the entire Ph.D. manuscript of nearly 1300 pages, improved its language, and reduced it to 500 pages.

References

Brooks, R.R.R. and V.S. Wakankar 1976. *Stone Age Paintings in India*. Bombay: Taraporewala and Sons.

IAR, Indian Archaeology – a Review, Annual publication of the Archaeological Survey of India, New Delhi

Kennedy, K.A.R., J.R. Lukacs, and V.N. Misra. 2002. *The Biological Anthropology of Human Skeletal Remains from Bhimbetka, Central India*: Pune: Indian Society for Prehistoric and Quaternary Studies.

Kincaid, W. 1888. Rambles among Ruins in Central India, *The Indian Antiquary* 17: 348-52.

Mathpal, Y. 1976-77. Further evidence of giraffe-like long-necked animals in the rock paintings of India, *Bulletin of the Deccan College Research Institute* 36(1-4): 110-14, VII.

Mathpal, Y. 1977. Rock art of Bhimbetka, in, V.N. Misra, Y. Mathpal and M. Nagar (1977). *Prehistoric Man and His Art at Bhimbetka, Central India*, pp. 17-22. Pune: Exhibition Souvenir Committee.

Mathpal, Y. 1978. *Prehistoric Rock Paintings of Bhimbetka, Central India*, Ph.D. Thesis. University of Poona.

Mathpal, Y. 1984. Newly discovered rock paintings in central India showing honey collection, *Bee World*, 65(3); 121-126.

Mathpal, Y. 1985. *Prehistoric Rock Paintings of Bhimbetka, Central India*, New Delhi: Abhinav Prakashan.

Misra, V.N. 1973a. Life in India a hundred thousand years ago, *Sunday Standard Magazine*, Indian Express 16th September 1973.

Misra, V.N. 1973b. Art in Prehistoric India, *Sunday Standard Magazine*, Indian Express 23rd September 1973.

Misra, V.N. 1976. The Acheulian Industry of Rock-shelter III F-23 at Bhimbetka, Central India, *Puratattva* 8: 13-36.

Misra, V.N. 1978. Acheulian Industry of Bhimbetka, Central Inida, *Bulletin of the Indo-Pacific Prehistory Association* 1: 130-73.

Misra, V.N. 1980. The Acheulian Industry of Rock-Shelter III F-23 at Bhimbetka, Central India – A Preliminary Study, *Australian Archaeology*.

Misra, V.N. 1982. The Evolution of Blade Element in the Stone Industries of Bhimbetka, Central India, in *Indian Archaeology: New Perspective* (R.K. Sharma Ed.), pp. 7-13. Delhi: Agam Prakashan.

Misra, V.N. 1985. The Acheulian Succession at Bhimbetka, Central India, in *Recent Advances in Indo-Pacific Prehistory* (V.N. Misra and P. Bellwood Eds.), pp. 35-47. New Delhi: Oxford-IBH.

Misra, V.N. and Y. Mathpal. 1979. Rock art of Bhimbetka region, central India, *Man and Environment* 3: 27-33.

Neumayer, E. 1983. *Prehistoric Indian Rock Paintings*. New Delhi: Oxford University Press.

Neumayer, E. 1993. *Lines on Stone: The Prehistoric Rock of India*. New Delhi: Manohar Publishers.

Wakankar, V.S. 1973a. *Prehistoric Rock Shelters of Central India*, Ph.D. Thesis. University of Poona.

Wakankar, V.S. 1973b. Bhimbetka excavation, *Journal of Indian History*, 51(1): 23-33.

Wakankar, V.S. 1973c. Bharteeya Shailashrayeed Chitrakala aur Usaka Kal Nirnaya, *Manav* 1(1): 38-51.

Wakankar, V.S. 1975a. Bhimbetka, *Marg,* 28(4): 2-34.

Wakankar, V.S. 1975b. Bhimbetka – The Prehistoric Paradise, *Prachya Pratibha* 3(2): 7-29.

Wakankar, V.S. 1985. Bhimbetka: The Stone Tool Industries and Rock Paintings, in, V.N. Misra and Peter Bellwood (Eds.). *Recent Advances in Indo-Pacific Prehistory*, pp. 175-176. New Delhi: Oxford-IBH.

Prehistory and Early History of South Kerala with Special Reference to District Kollam

B.S. Harishankar

Introduction

South Kerala, juxtaposed with southeast Tamil Nadu, extends between 10º 15' north latitude and 77º 05' east longitude and is located between Upper Periyar and Neyyar river basins (Fig. 1). It is bound by Western Ghats on the east and Lakshadweep Sea on the west. Covering six districts, with focus on Kollam, the study aimed to reconstruct the Iron Age/Megalithic Period and the Early Historical Period of the region, spanning the time bracket between 300 B.C. and 900 A.D.

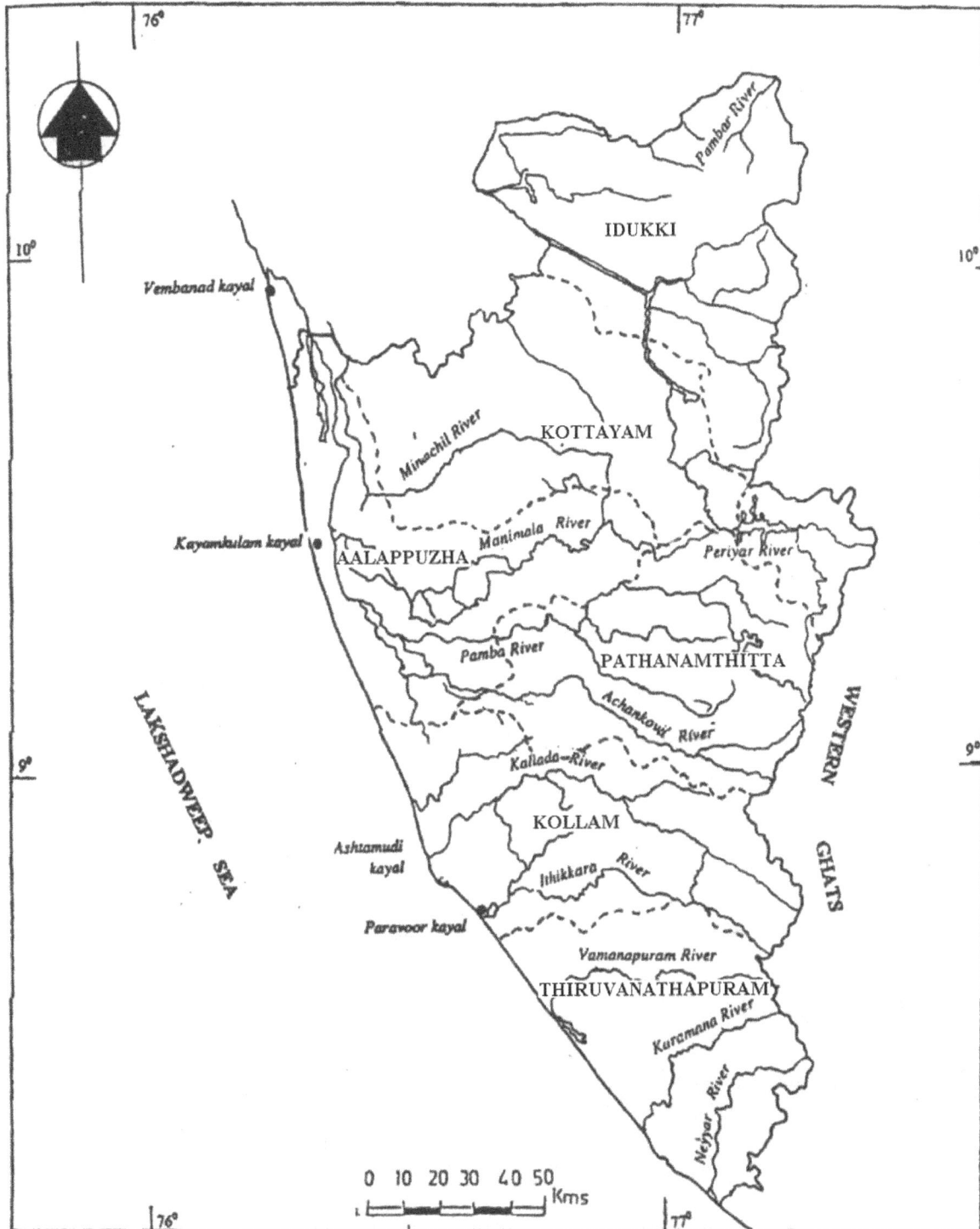

Figure 1: Map of south Kerala with its drainage system (modified *after* Gupta 1984)

Pre-Megalithic

Prehistory of Kerala has been a subject of controversy among the archaeologists. Till 1970s most of the scholars were of the opinion that Kerala didn't have any of the Stone Age cultures. Robert Bruce Foote (1916: 47-48), attributed this to the geographical factors; he cited two reasons, first, the lack of proper raw material, and second, the area was impenetrable due to the dense forests. H.D. Sankalia (1974: 233), made similar kinds of observation while describing the Mesolithic cultures of India but cautioned that this assumption might be due to absence of systematic exploration in Kerala.

However, lately a good number of prehistoric sites have been discovered from various parts of Kerala. Evidences of these have come from surface, stratified context and rock shelters. The stone tool industries of the region mainly show characteristics of two groups of cultures, viz., Lower Palaeolithic and Mesolithic. A few celts testify the existence of Neolithic whereas there is complete absence of other cultures.

Evidence of Palaeolithic is noticed in seven sites confined to the northern part (Rajendran 1989). The tools are represented by chopper-scraper-flake assemblage which show typological affinity with the Lower Palaeolithic industries from the west coast. The industry is devoid of standardized tool types such as hand axes or cleavers and as such it contrast strongly with the nearby well known Tamilnadu hand axe-Cleaver industry.

Among the 26 known Mesolithic sites, 23 are in north Kerala and only three in south Kerala. Of the 10 rock shelters, four are in north Kerala and only three in south Kerala.

K.R.U. Todd reported Microliths from Chevayur, Kozhikode district during 1902 (Todd 1950). Excavation in Tenmalai rock shelter, district Kollam yielded Mesolithic tools and wood charcoal in primary context. The three wood charcoals dates from the site are 5120±120, 5120±110 and 4420±110 B.P. Human and animal figures have been engraved in other rock shelters. The tools were made exclusively on quartz. The Mesolithic site discovered at Maraiyur in Idukky district seems to be of later date (Tampi 1976: 137-144). The tools are very small (2cm) in length and are found made on quartz and chert in equal proportion. Triangles and trapezes are absent in Kerala microlithic industry.

Neolithic celts are reported by Colin Mackenzie in 1890 (cited in Mathpal 1998: 45) from his Kuppamudi estate at Wayanad, Philip Lake in 1891 from Kanjikodu near Palaghat, Fawcett in 1896 from Edakkal cave, Commaiade in 1930 from Kathiroor in Kozhikode district, from the Periyar river bed in the Alwaye taluk of Ernakulam district (*The Hindu*, 21.01.1971, Madurai edition), local people from Pulpally and Kalpetta of Wayanad (John 1975), K.J. John (1975) from Cinnari, and recently Malat (2007) during his MA dissertation fieldwork identified two celts displayed in the Ambalawayal Museum. These Celts were found during construction activity in Karachal, Murani east of Ambalawayal district Wayanad. But none of these celts are found either from south Kerala or from stratified context; without any excavation of Neolithic site nothing more can be presumed about its existence in time and space.

In short, the cultural sequence of south Kerala consists of Mesolithic, Iron Age/Megalithic and Early Historical periods. The explored and excavated Megalithic and Early Historical sites constitute the major archaeological wealth of Kerala. Hence the work is restricted more to Megalithic phase of south Kerala.

Megalithic Period

It is widely believed that the first Megalithic site in India was discovered in 1819 at Bungala Motta Paramba, in Chirakkal taluk of Kanannore district of north Kerala by Babington (1823)[1]. Since then there have been reports of 335 Megalithic sites in Kerala (Mathpal 1998: 54-58). In 1950, B.K. Thapar at Porkalam, district Thrissur did first systematic excavation of a Megalithic pot burial site. Three important works of 1970s on south India Megaliths including that of Kerala which set the trend of systematic research are that of S.P. Gupta in 1972, B.K. Gururaja Rao again in 1972 and L.S. Leshnik in 1974. Out of 65 reported Megalithic sites in south Kerala 26 are excavated.

---

[1] However, Paddayya (2006: 17-18) claims that Colonel Colin Mackenzie had discovered megalithic monuments comprising stone circles and dolmens at various places in the region of Coimbatore, Chittor, Hyderabad and Amaravati before Babington in beginning years of the 19th century.

Typology & Distribution

The Megalithic types in south Kerala are broadly classified into Chambered and Un-chambered megaliths. Chambered types include cists (Fig. 2), dolmens (Fig. 3), dolmenoid-cists (Fig. 4) and subterranean rock-cut tombs. Unlike subterranean rock-cut tombs, which are very few in this region, other chambered types have a significant presence in south Kerala. The un-chambered tombs, on the other hand, include menhirs (Fig. 5), barrows, stone-circles and urn-burials or tombs (Fig. 6). Unlike other un-chambered types, barrows and stone-circles have an uneven distribution in south Kerala.

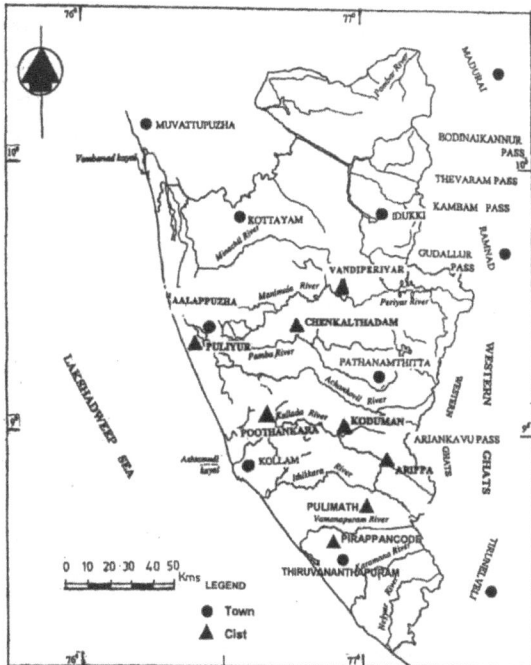

Figure 2: Distribution of Cist in south Kerala

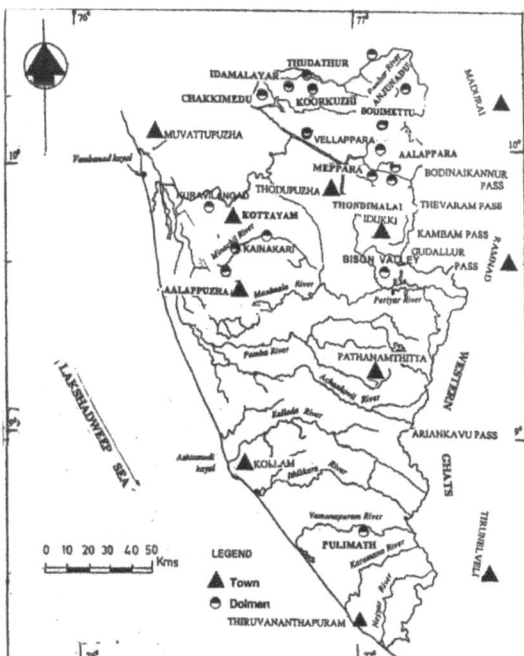

Figure 3: Distribution of Dolmens in south Kerala

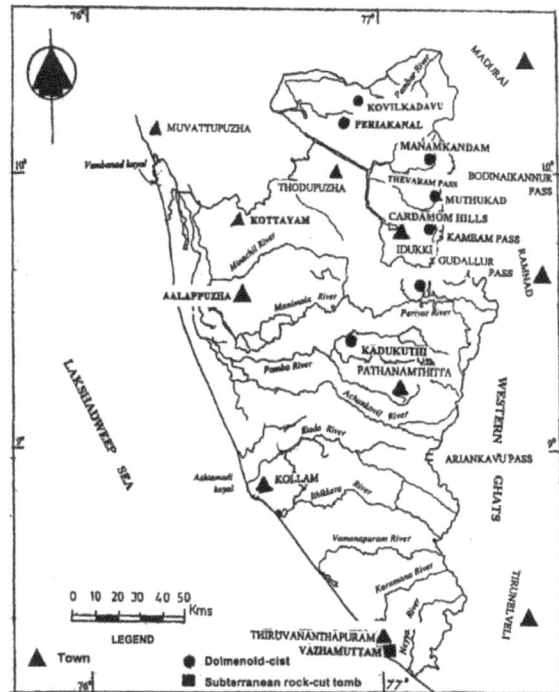

Figure 4: Distribution of Dolmenoid-cist in south Kerala

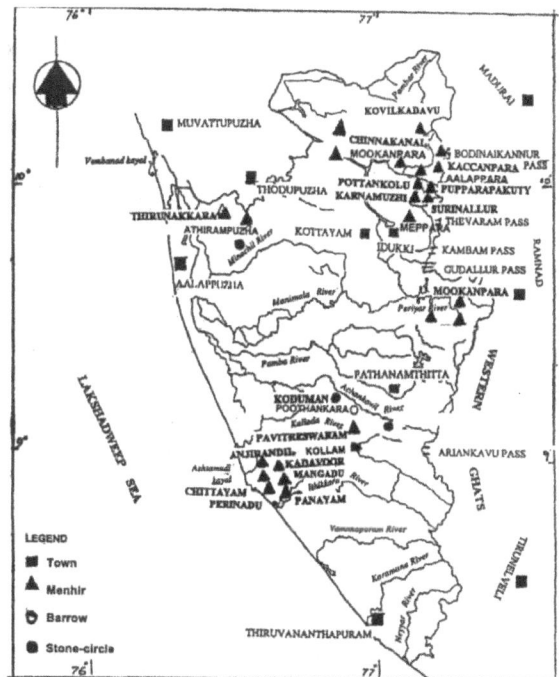

Figure 5: Distribution of Menhirs in south Kerala

The distribution of megalithic types is, to a large extent, determined by environmental matrices. The menhirs and dolmens are largely concentrated in the south Periyar basin, where the presence of charnockite rock, which is best suited for erecting megaliths, is available (Fig. 7). The Khondalite rock found in the midlands is least suitable for erecting memorial stones, and hence this region has comparatively few Megalithic tombs. Access to drainage seems to have been a major consideration in the selection of sites. In the midlands and lowlands which

39

have well knit hydraulic system, and where no cooperative effort is needed for cultivation, the Megalithic sites are widely dispersed. In the highlands there is a conglomeration of sites due to the absence of a well-knit drainage network. Another major factor that was instrumental in the development of the Megalithic culture in south Kerala, is the existence of a number of natural passes which served as exchange routes to southeast Tamil Nadu.

burials, cists and menhirs. The absence of well-knit drainage network nowadays certainly demands cooperative efforts for cultivation. However, such regions, especially in the midlands, have in concentration of megaliths. Due to the presence of lakes and estuaries, the lowlands, which are more vulnerable to heavy rains and floods, have understandably a dispersed presence of megaliths.

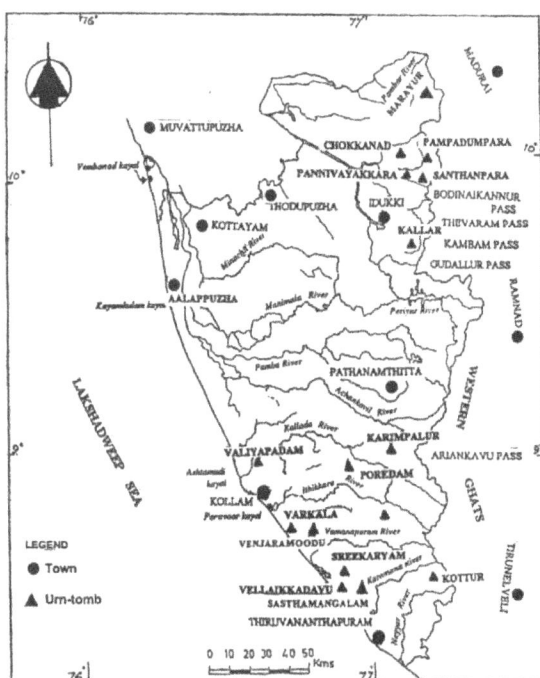

Figure 6: Distribution of Urn-tombs in south Kerala

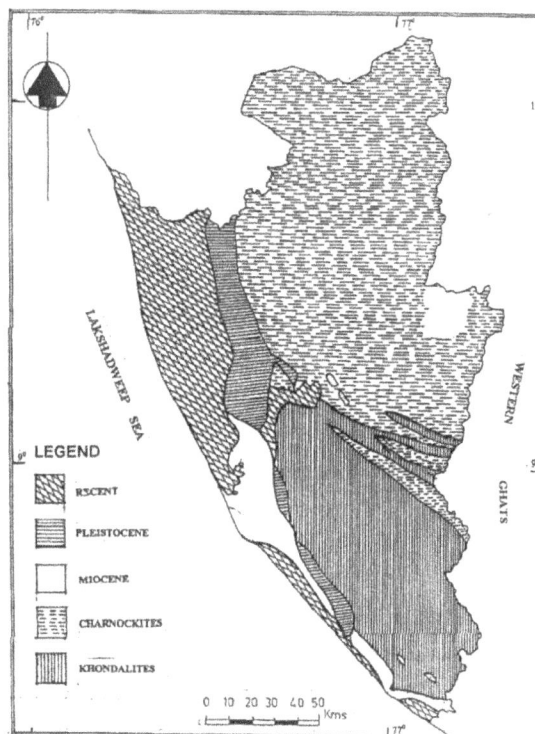

Figure 7: Geology map of south Kerala (*After* Gupta 1984)

The well-drained laterite soil, which is useful for cultivation in the supply of calcium and iron to the crops, has a large concentration of urn-

List of Megalithic sites in South Kerala

Types	Site	Location	District	Reference
Chambered Megalithic Sites				
Cist	Pirappancode	8°30' : 76°50'	Thiruvananthapuram	Joseph (1928-30: 53)
	Pulimath	8°30' : 70°00'	Thiruvananthapuram	Joseph (1928-30: 53)
	Vandiperiyar	9°30' : 77°00'	Idukki	Poduval (1936-37: 7-10)
	Koduman	9°10' : 76°50'	Pathanamthitta	Chandrasekharan (IAR 1961-62: 21)
	Poothankara	9°10' : 76°40'	Pathanamthitta	Chandrasekharan (IAR 1961-62: 21)
	Chenkaltadam	9°20' : 76°50'	Pathanamthitta	Rajendran (IAR 1990-91: 33)
	Puliyar	9°20' : 76°15'	Aalappuzha	Satyamurthy (1992: 25)
	Arippa	9°00' : 77°00'	Thiruvananthapuram	Rajendran and Iyer (1997: 61-65)
Dolmens	Thondimalai	9°55' : 76°55'	Idukki	Saunders (1928)
	Pulimath	8°30' : 77°00'	Thiruvananthapuram	Joseph (1928-30: 53)
	Bison Valley	9°30' : 77°05'	Idukki	Poduval (1938-39: 3-15)
	Bodimettu	10°05' : 77°05'	Idukki	Poduval (1938-39: 8-15)
	Aalappara	10°00' : 77°05'	Idukki	Poduval (1939-40: 14-17)
	Anjunadu	10°15' : 77°05'	Idukki	Poduval (1946-47: 1-3)
	Kainukari	9°40' : 76°40'	Kottayam	Menon (IAR 1963-64: 13)
	Kuravilangad	9°50' : 76°30'	Kottayam	Menon (IAR 1963-64: 13)

	Chakkimedu	10°15' : 76°40'	Idukki	Namboodri (IAR 1977-78: 30)
	Idamalayar	10°15' : 76°45'	Idukki	Namboodri (IAR 1977-78: 30)
	Koorkuzhi	10°15' : 76°50'	Idukki	Namboodri (IAR 1977-78: 30)
	Thudathur	10°20' : 76°45'	Idukki	Namboodri (IAR 1977-78: 30)
	Meppara	9°55' : 77°00'	Idukki	Namboodri (IAR 1981-82: 27)
	Vellappara	10°05' : 76°45'	Idukki	Namboodri (IAR 1981-82: 27)
Dolmenoid-Cist	Cardamom hills	9°50' : 77°10'	Idukki	Ward and Conner 1863 (cited in Iyer 1929-30: 124)
	Anjunadu	10°15' : 77°15'	Idukki	Poduval (1946-47: 1-3)
	Muthukad	9°45' : 77°00'	Idukki	Poduval (1938-39: 3-15)
	Perikanal	10°10' : 76°50'	Idukki	Poduval (1938-39: 3-15)
	Kadukuthi	9°20' : 76°50'	Pathanamthitta	Iyer (1941: 53-54)
	Manamkandam	10°00' : 77°15'	Idukki	Menon (IAR 1965-66: 21)
Subterranean Rock-cut Tomb	Vazhamuttam	8°10' : 77°05'	Thiruvananthapuram	Harishankar (1995-96: 93-95)
Un-chambered Megalithic Tombs				
Menhirs	Kaccanpara	10°00' : 77°15'	Idukki	Anglade and Newton (1928: 1-18)
	Pottankolu	9°05' : 77°00'	Idukki	Anglade and Newton (1928: 1-18)
	Pupparapakuty	10°00' : 77°15'	Idukki	Anglade and Newton (1928: 1-18)
	Aalappara	10°00' : 77°05'	Idukki	Poduval (1939-40: 14-17)
	Tirunakkara	9°50' : 76°30'	Kottayam	Menon (IAR 1963-64: 13)
	Athirampuzha	9°50' : 76°40'	Kottayam	Menon (IAR 1963-64: 13)
	Chinnakanal	10°15' : 76°50'	Idukki	Menon (IAR 1965-66: 21)
	Karnamuzhi	9°55' : 77°05'	Idukki	Namboodri (IAR 1977-78: 30, 1982-83: 36)
	Meppara	9°55' : 77°00'	Idukki	Namboodri (IAR 1981-82: 27)
	Mookanpara	10°00' : 76°50'	Idukki	Namboodri (IAR 1981-82: 27)
	Surinallur	9°55' : 77°10'	Idukki	Namboodri (IAR 1977-78: 30, 1982-83: 36)
	Mangadu	9°00' : 76°45'	Kollam	Satyamurthy (1992: 25)
	Anjirandil	9°00' : 76°40'	Kollam	Satyamurthy (1992: 25)
	Chittayam	8°55' : 76°40'	Kollam	Satyamurthy (1992: 25)
	Kadavoor	9°00' : 76°45'	Kollam	Satyamurthy (1992: 25)
	Panayam	8°50' : 76°45'	Kollam	Satyamurthy (1992: 25)
	Perinadu	8°50' : 76°40'	Kollam	Satyamurthy (1992: 25)
	Pavitreswaram	9°10' : 76°55'	Kollam	Satyamurthy (1992: 25)
	Kovilkadavu	10°15' : 77°15'	Iddukki	Harishankar (1999: 85)
Barrow	Poothankara	9°10' : 76°40'	Pathanamthitta	Chandrasekharan (IAR 1961-62: 21)
Stone Circles	Koduman	9°10' : 76°50'	Pathanamthitta	Chandrasekharan (IAR 1961-62: 21)
	Athirampuzha	9°40' : 76°40'	Kottayam	Menon (IAR 1963-64: 13)
Urn Tombs	Chokkanad	10°00' : 77°05'	Idukki	Iyer (1929-30: 116)
	Varkala	8°40' : 76°45'	Thiruvananthapuram	Iyer (1929-30: 116)
	Marayur	10°15' : 77°15'	Idukki	Menon (IAR 1965-66: 21)
	Pampadumpara	10°00' : 77°15'	Idukki	Menon (IAR 1965-66: 21)
	Pannivayakkara	9°55' : 77°10'	Idukki	Menon (IAR 1965-66: 21)
	Santhanpara	9°55' : 77°15'	Idukki	Menon (IAR 1965-66: 21)
	Sreekaryam	8°40' : 76°50'	Thiruvananthapuram	IAR 1967-68: 66
	Sasthamangalam	8°35' : 77°00'	Thiruvananthapuram	Tampi (1983: 379-84)
	Valiyadadam	8°35' : 76°55'	Kollam	Rajendran (IAR 1989-90: 45)
	Poredam	9°00' : 76°55'	Kollam	Rajendran (IAR 1989-90: 45)
	Karlmpalur	9°00' : 77°05'	Kollam	Rajendran (IAR 1991-92: 126)
	Kottur	8°35' : 77°15'	Thiruvananthapuram	Satyamurthy (1992: 25)
	Venjaramoodu	8°45' : 76°45'	Thiruvananthapuram	Satyamurthy (1992: 25)
	Vellaikkadava	8°35' : 76°50'	Thiruvananthapuram	Satyamurthy (1992: 25)

Conventional or internal reciprocity

Unlike north Kerala, sources the metal and mineral in south Kerala are comparatively very few. The acquisition of iron technology seems to have been the result of a trans-regional interaction. The iron tools obtained from Megalithic tombs show that the Megalithic folk had a rudimentary-sedentary base. These tools can be broadly classified into tools for subsistence and for encounter and resistance.

Agricultural and domestic tools, such as axes, sickles, chisels, blades and knives have been recovered in impressive numbers from megalithic tombs along midlands and lowlands. Such tools were found at Chenkalthadam, Puliyur, Arippa, Thondimalai, Bison Valley, Mangadu, Poredam, Sasthamangalam, Vallyadam and Karimpalur. The presence of hunting and killing tools, such as spearheads, swords and daggers are found in the graves located in thickly vegetated highlands and a few sites along midlands, indicates the kind of life they lived – killing big games as well as spreading in the forest areas with swords in hands. Hunting tools were found at Pulimath, Pirappancode and Thondimalai, and tools of offence and defense were found at Arippa, Pirappancode, Periakanal, Thondimalai, Anjunadu and Valiyapadam. The tools, used in everyday life, it has been noted, have much resemblance in typology to those recovered from Adicanallur in Tirunelveli district, Taranatmand and Illava Kunde Hills in the Nilgiris, Kil Mondambadi in Salem district, Sanur in Chingleput district, all in Tamil Nadu, Brahmagiri in Chitradurg district, Jala near Bangalore, both in Karnataka, and Ramapuram in Kurnool district of Andhra Pradesh indicating their commonality and cultural-sharing. Iron is abundant in north Kerala, hence there is strong possibility of their manufacture in this region and import from south Kerala there. However, in south Kerala as well as south Tamil Nadu metallurgy was practiced in those days, which has better proximity in terms of ore locations and their exploitation than Karnataka and Tamil Nadu ore areas.

As usual with most of the megaliths in south India vases, cups, lids, bowls, ring stands, small pots and jars made of Black-and-Red ware, red ware and black ware constitute the major ceramic types. However, kaolin, fire clay, ball clay, bauxite, titanium oxide and porcelain, available in the region, were extensively used for ceramic-manufacture.

Symmetrical or external reciprocity

The presence of gold, copper and bronze ornaments, from at least three sites, viz., Puliyur, Arippa and Pulimath suggests external reciprocity, since such raw materials and alloys do not have their fair presence in the region.

Beads of agate, feldspar, and carnelian, both etched and un-etched, have been obtained from a few sites. Carnelian is abundantly reported from the Deccan trap region. Kodumanal, near the Palakkad Gap, linking Coimbatore and Kerala, has been a major manufacturing centre for beads during the Megalithic period. Such beads have been transported from neighbouring regions of Madurai, Thirunelvelly and Coimbatore in later times also.

South Kerala has a good number of internal and external passes in the hills, such as Edagrarnam, Anchugramam, Aramboli, Ariankavu, Gudallur, Kambam, Thevaram and Bodinaikannur, linking the Vaigai and Kaveri basins in Tamil Nadu. Hence, it was not an isolated region.

Economy and Society

Palaeobotanical evidence of rice comes from at least two sites, viz., Arippa in Kollam district and Chokkanad in Idukki district. The tropical vegetation of the region has, however, made it a resourceful terrain for hunting wild animals as well. Heavy monsoons and tropical biota have kept pastoralism and nomadism alien to the region. In fact, Megalithism in south India was based upon agriculture, particularly the tank-water irrigated fields with intensive rice plantation, a practice still in vogue. Unlike other megalithic tombs in south India, the absence of animal bones in the megalithic burials of this region also highlights the absence of pastoralism, which, of course, does not mean that there was no domestication of animals and consumption of animal products; these were very much there since at other places we have the evidence for this.

The recovery of fragmented human skeletal remains, burnt and unburnt, from eight megalithic tombs viz., Arppa, Anjunadu, Thondimalai, Mangadu, Sreekaryam, Varakala, Poredam and Chenkalthadam, suggests that the people followed the practice of secondary burial as well as post-cremation burial.

Ethno-archaeological studies show that the mode of secondary burial is still practiced by a few hunting-gathering groups like Malapantaram, while post-cremation burial is pursued by agricultural communities like Kanikkar, Lzhava, Nadar and Namboodri. However, an interesting homogeneity between both the groups is the ongoing tradition of 'ancestor worship' by erecting memorials, often associated with violent death, such as suicide, murder and encounter. In the post-Megalithic period it has resulted in the emergence of a rich oral tradition based on heroism, devotion and martyrdom. Panayannarkkavu in south Kerala is an interesting site where perhaps human sacrifice was also conducted in the ritual context.

Early Historical Period

There are no excavated sites belonging to the post-Megalithic phase i.e., after 2nd century A.D., to show the transition to the early historical period. There are however, four rock-cut cave temples in south Kerala (Sewell 1882, Sarkar 1978; Harishakar 1996-97). They are Vizhinjam and Ayiroorpara temples in Thiruvanthapuruam district, Kottukal temple in Pathanamthitta district and Kaviyur temple in Aalappuzha district. These rock-cut cave temples have been dated to the 7th century A.D.

Roman coins have been reported from Kottayam district (Turner 1983), Idamakuduru and Poonjar in Idukki district (Shashibhooshan 1987; Gupta 1991) and Kadakkavur in Thiruvanthapuram district (Satyamurthy 1992). Roman contact is substantiated with copper plate inscription of Rajasekhara of the Thiruvarruvay chiefdom, dated to 9th century A.D., which mentions Roman *denari*. However, there is no excavated site in south Kerala to substantiate the issue of Roman trade.

The explored early historic sites of the author

Site	Location/district	Findings	Reference
Vizhinjam	8°22' : 77°00' Thiruvananthapuram	Two inscriptions recording encounter between the Cheras and the Ays	Sircar 1958-59: 71; Rao 1908: 134-35; Ayyar 1924: 14; Sarkar 1978; Harishankar 1996-97: 59
Narayanapuram	8°25' : 76°05' Thiruvananthapuram	A circular temple, an inscribed *balipitha* in vattezhuthu script.	Poduval 1939
Neendakara	8°55' : 76°40' Kollam	Image of Buddha.	Harishankar 1999: 144

Rock-cut temples

The following rock-cut temples are classified in accordance with the development in architectural style. The *ardhamandapa* is a common feature in these temples, while *dwarapalakas* are reliefs of gods appear at a later stage.

List of rock-cut temples in south Kerala

Temple	Village Town/District	Finds
Ayiroorpara	Sree Karayaam Thiruvananthapuram	The pillars are square sectioned with bevelled ends. The figures of Vishnu and Ganesha are in ruined state.
Kottukal	Anchal Pathanamthitta	There are two entrances to this temple. The reliefs of a seated Ganesha and Hanuman are seen.
Thirunandikkara	Thakkalai Kanyakumari	The pillars are square sectioned with bevelled ends. This is the only cave temple with inscriptions. The script is in Vattezhuthu.
Kaviyur	Thiruvalla Aalappuzha	It has the reliefs of a bearded *rishi* and *dwarapalakas*.
Vizhinjam	Vizhinjam Thiruvananthapuram	It has the reliefs of Siva as *Kiratamurti* and dancing Siva-Parvati outside the wall.

Altogether eight Early Historical sites have been reported from south Kerala. Early Historical copper-plates, belonging to the Ay chiefdom at Vizhinjam (800 A.D.), provide evidence on agriculture and cultivated products which include rice, vegetables and cash crops. Other evidences, such as rock-cut cave temples and Saptamatrika images, belong to the Shaiva pantheon. A few images of Buddha and Vishnu have, however, also been found which shows pluralism and religious harmony amongst the people.

Realm of the study -Scope and Prospects

The span of the study-area and theme would have been much wider and appealing if it had included Malabar region in north Kerala and dealt explicitly with the introduction of iron and beginnings of reciprocity, the change to redistribution and transition to trade in the Early Historical Period.

The megaliths in Malabar spread over one hundred and eighty sites. Hinterland routes link the Deccan and Coromandal with Malabar, especially through the Palakkad Gap. The Palakkad Gap region has to its credit nearly eighty-five megalithic sites. Such sites in the past were not isolated staging-points but had links with cultivators and hunting-gathering communities along the route.

Further, Malabar has a number of natural ports and monsoon-fed mud banks which gave a leverage to sea-trade with West Asia as well as

Far East. The presence of land routes linking Kaveri delta, Deccan and Andhra are also numerous. Kodungallur or Muziris was a major centre of maritime trade with West Asia, as Greco-Roman literature, and now archaeology seem to prove through the discovery of a variety of Red wares, glazed wares and porcelains along the Kerala coast. Although convincing archaeological evidence is yet to come from Kodungallur, which can come only from proper excavations, yet on its links with Kaveri delta, under the Cholas at least, has often been visualised by historians. However, there are a considerable number of Jaina sites linking Kodungallur-Palakkad Gap with Kaveri delta, Deccan, Andhra and Eastern coast. Evidence on maritime trade and movement of people come from Roman and Ummayad coins, papyrus documents, Jewish settlements and Chinese ceramics. An approach incorporating the Malabar region and its wider corpus of archaeological data would enhance the understanding of the Iron Age/Megalithic, and Historical Period of Kerala which extends up to almost 13th century, if not still beyond.

Reference

Anglade, A. and L.V. Newton 1928. The Dolmens of Pulney, *Memoirs of the Archaeological Survey of India* 36, pp. 1-18.

Ayyar, R.A.S. 1924. *Travancore Archaeological Series*, Vol. 3, Part 3, Thiruvanthapuram: Department of Cultural Relation.

Babington, J. 1823. Description of the Pandoo Coolies in Malabar, *Transactions of Literary Society of Bombay* 3: 324-30.

Cammiade, L.A. 1930. Urn Burials in Wynad, south India, *Man* 20(135): 183-86.

Fawcett, F. 1901. Notes on the Rock Carvings of Edakkal Wayanad. *The Indian Antiquary* 30: 409-21.

Foote, R. B. 1916. *The Foote Collection of Indian Prehistoric and Protohistoric Antiquities*. Madras: Government Press.

Gupta, H. K. 1984. *Resource Atlas of Kerala*. Trivandrum: Centre for Earth Science Studies.

Gupta, S.P. 1972. *Disposal of the Dead and Physical Types in Ancient India*. Delhi: Oriental Publishers.

Harishankar, B.S. 1995-96. Mesolithic Rock Shelter and Megalithic Rock-cut caves in Kerala, *Puratattva* 26: 93-95.

Harishankar, B.S. 1996-97. Saivaite Art and Thought, in the Literature of Kerala: A Survey, *Puratattva* 27: 57-61.

Harishankar, B.S. 1999. *Prehistory and Early History of South Kerala with Special Reference to District Kollam*, unpublished Ph.D. Thesis. Pune: Deccan College.

IAR. *Indian Archaeology A Review*. New Delhi: Archaeological Survey of India.

Iyer, L.A. Krishna 1929-30. Prehistoric Archaeology of Kerala, *Quarterly Journal of Mythic Society* 20: 115-26.

Iyer, L.A. Krishna 1941. Megalithic Monuments, *The Travancore Tribes and Castes*, Vol. 3, pp. 115-26. Bangalore.

John, K.J. 1975. Early Man in Wynad, *Journal of Kerala Studies* 2(2): 129-35.

Joseph, T.K. 1928-30. *Kerala Society Papers*, Vol. 1, pp. 52-56.

Lake, P. 1891. The Geology of South Malabar between the Beypore and Ponnani rivers, *Memoirs of the Geological Survey of India* 24(3): 221-37.

Leshnik, L.S. 1974. *South Indian Megalithic Burials-The Pandukal Complex*. Wiesbaden.

Malat, Arun P. 2007. *A Study of Edakkal Caves*, unpublished MA dissertation. Pune: Deccan College.

Mathpal, Y. 1998. *Rock Art in Kerala*. New Delhi: Aryan Books International.

Nair, A. K. K. R. 1986. *Gazetteer of India: Kerala State Gazetteer* (Ed.), Vol. I & II.

Paddayya, K.P. 2006. Colonel Colin Mackenzie and the Discovery of Iron Age Megalithic Tombs in South India, *AdhAram* 1: 17-18.

Poduval, V.R. 1936-37. *Archaeological Records of Travancore and Cochin*, pp. 7-10. Trivandrum: Government of Travancore.

Poduval, V.R. 1938-39. *Archaeological Records of Travancore and Cochin*, pp. 3-15. Trivandrum: Government of Travancore.

Poduval, V.R. 1939. *Travancore in Revealing India's Past* (Sir. John Cumming Ed.), pp. 297-304. London: The Indian Society.

Poduval, V.R. 1939-40. *Archaeological Records of Travancore and Cochin*, pp. 14-17. Trivandrum: Government of Travancore.

Poduval, V.R. 1946-47. *Archaeological Records of Travancore and Cochin*, pp. 3. Trivandrum: Government of Travancore.

Rajendran, P. 1989. *The Prehistoric Cultures and Environment – A Case Study of Kerala*. New Delhi: Classical Publishing Company.

Rajendran, P. and C.S.P. Iyer 1997. A Preliminary Report on the Characterization of Coper and Gold Ornaments of the Arippa Megalithic Culture in Kollam District, Kerala, South India, *Man and Environment* 22(2): 61-65.

Rao, G.T.A. 1908. *Travancore Archaeological Series*, Vol. 2, pp. 115-92. Thiruvanthapuram: Department of Cultural Relation.

Rao, Gururaja B.K. 1972. *Megalithic Culture in South India*. Mysore, University of Mysore.

Sankalia, H. D. 1974. *The Prehistory And Protohistory of India And Pakistan*. Poona: Deccan College.

Sarkar, H. 1978. *An Architectural Survey of Temples of Kerala*, pp. 2-185. New Delhi: Archaeological Survey of India.

Sathyamurthy, T. 1992. The Iron Age in Kerala, in *A Report on Mangadu Excavations*. Trivandrum: Government of Kerala.

Saunders, A.J. 1928. Dolmens in the Paini Hills, South India, *The Madras Mail Annual*.

Sircar, D.C. 1958-59. Inscription on Stone and Other Materials, *Annual Report on Indian epigraphy*, pp. 71. Delhi: Archaeological Survey of India.

Tampi, S.P. 1976. Maraiyur – a Key to the Prehistoric Archaeology of south India, *Bulletin of the Deccan College Research Institute* 35(3-4): 137-44.

Tampi, S.P. 1983. *Prehistoric Archaeology of south-central Kerala with special reference to the valley of Anjunad*. Unpublished Ph.D. Thesis. Pune: Deccan College.

Thapar, B.K. 1952. Porkalam 1948: Excavation of a Megalithic Urn Burial, *Ancient India* 8: 3-16.

Todd, K.R.U. 1950. Microlithic Industries of Bombay, *Ancient India* 6: 4-17. Trivandrum: Government of Kerala.

Early Historic Trade Mechanism in Central and Western Orissa: A Holistic Perspective

Balaram Tripathy

Abstract

The Early Historic cultures of Central and Western Orissa, despite accomplishments from archaeologists, have not yet been tapped in a holistic approach. An effort is made in this paper to unravel certain important aspects pertaining to urbanization and trade mechanism and the exploitation of natural resources for which the hinterland was known even during the Early Historic period. Classification of major centres in terms of function and production has been discussed to have a clear understanding of hitherto unknown features in Early Indian history in general and of Orissa in particular. Direct and indirect contacts of states/centres with each other have been analysed and discussed in detail. Archaeological objects such as pottery and supplementary antiquities as also the ecological aspects have been taken into consideration to infer the function of urban centres. Stress has been laid on explored and excavated major Early Historic sites in Central and Western Orissa. Most of these sites are fortified and surrounded with moats. Their locational importance and connectivity to each other have been interpreted by drawing inferences from archaeology, literature, numismatic, ethno-history and ethnographic paradigms. The Early Historic cultures in Central and Western Orissa and its relations to the sites located in the coastal part of Orissa are examined. To ascertain trade connection, X-Ray Diffraction Analysis has been conducted on some representative types of pottery found at the sites in hinterland Orissa.

Historical Geography of Central and Western Orissa

The region of Central and Western Orissa (Fig. 1), roughly comprises the present day districts of Boudh, Sonepur, Bolangir, Kalahandi and Sambalpur. This cultural, ethnic and linguistic unit was historically known as South Kosala or Dakshina Kosala. The region, during the ancient times formed a geographic unit and has been corroborated by several literary and inscriptional evidences. Reference of this region is found either directly or indirectly in the Padma Purana (Apte 1893, Vol. 8: 130), the Ramayana of Valmiki (Dutt 1895, Vol. 7, Ch. 108: 4-5) which relates the region with the epic Hero Rama, Laba and Kusha, the Vayu Purana (Mitra 1880), the Mahabharata (Roy 1926, Vol. 2, 13: 591-592) and the Kamasutra of Vatsayana (Upadhyaya 1961, Ch. II, V, Verse 27). The Allahabad Pillar Inscription of Samudragupta (Sahu 1964) refers to the conquest of Kosala under Mahendra and Mahakantara under Vyaghraraja by the Gupta Emperor. Later inscriptions/Copper Plate Grants also referred this area as Kosala which fell under the sway of several dynasties and rulers and the most powerful among them were the Somavamsis. The Somavamsis ruled over this region during the 9th-10th centuries A.D. Even this region is mentioned in travel records of Wuang Chwang, who during his visit/pilgrimage to India, narrates about the potential of the region in terms of its people, religion, and other establishments. The Chinese pilgrim scholar mentions that from Kalinga he had to travel about 1800 *li* (approximately 360 miles) through dense forests to reach the kingdom of Kia-sa-lo or Kosala which was littered with Buddhist establishments (Watters 1988: 200).

Physiographic Features

Topographically, the region of Central and Western Orissa covers the central plains, the middle mountainous country, the rolling uplands and the river valleys (Sinha 1971) (Fig. 2). The arable tract is a stretch of plains with endless stretch of rice fields and enriched by river deposited alluvium. The valleys are fertile and thickly populated. The rolling mountainous, which vary from 153 to 305 m are in elevation than the plateaus and regarded as the product of continuous river action. The vegetation of the region ranges from tropical to sub-tropical with evergreen species and dry mixed deciduous forest tracts. At higher elevations of the hill tracts, open valleys are found which are fertile and abundantly watered by a cross section of perennial streams. The hill slopes are most commonly used for shifting cultivation by a number of indigenous people inhabiting the region.

46

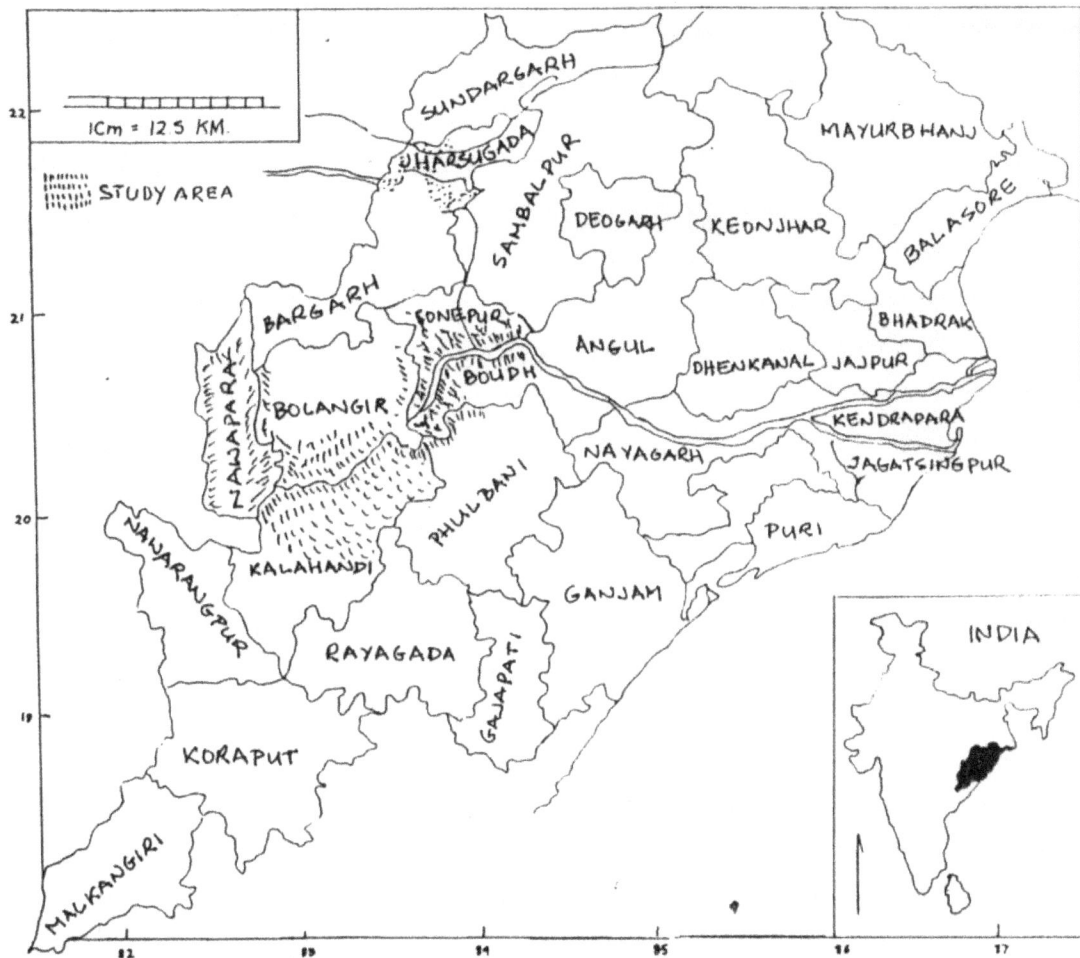

Figure 1: Map of Orissa showing the study region

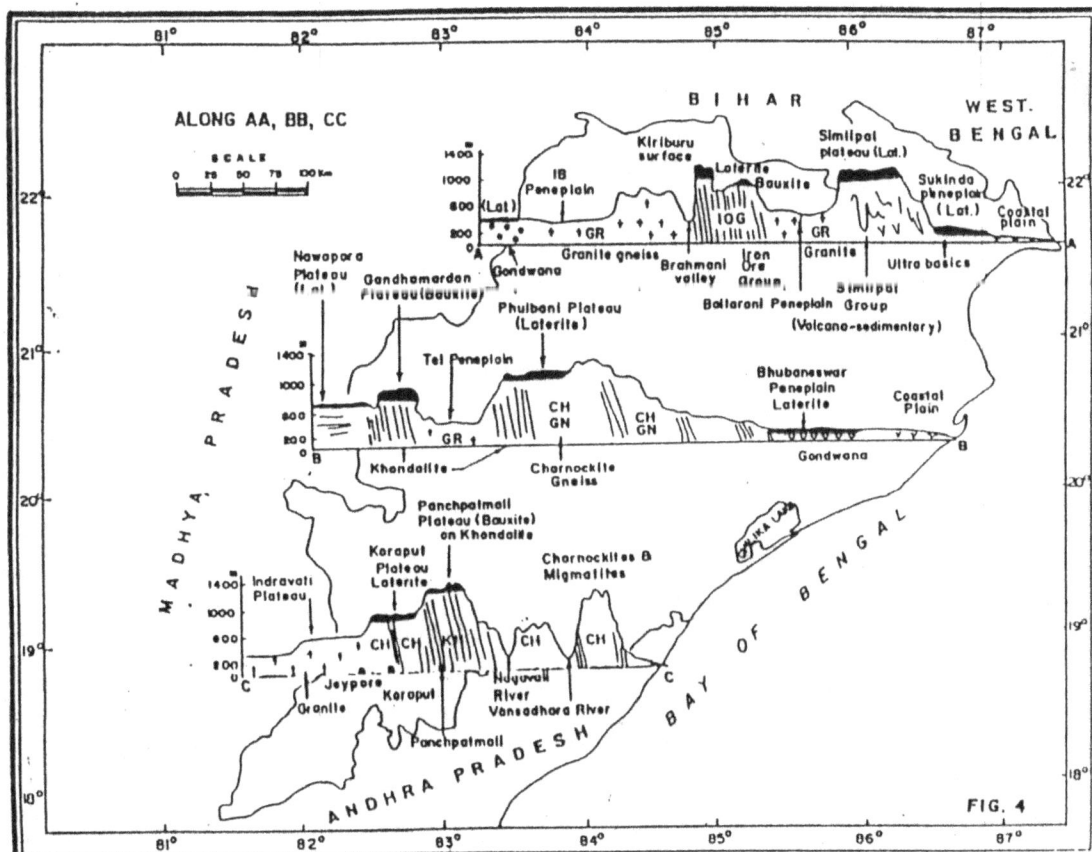

Figure 2: Topographic profile of Orissa

The middle country, covering about three-fourth of the area of Orissa, has deep and broad valleys, cut by the Mahanadi, the Tel and several tributaries and seasonal streams in the central Orissa and rivers like the Tel, Indravati, Jonk and numerous tributaries in the western part. The availability of perennial rivers paved the way for navigation. The navigation pattern and water transport has been vividly described in literatures ranging from the Puranas to the British Colonial ethnographers. Forest resources including timber and khondalite stones, terracotta items and medicinal herbs were transported and the pattern exists even today as a 'living tradition'. Besides, there are also evidences from the Jatakas that the rivers like Telavaha were used for ferry purpose.

Lithostratigraphically, the major portion of Orissa is covered by meta-sediments and granites of the Archean age followed by Cuddapah series, the latter being followed by the Gondwanas. The Eastern Ghats mountain range covers some areas which are characterized by the presence of rocks of khondalite series (Wadia 1961). The vegetation is of tropical deciduous type and the climate is characterized by hot summers, high humidity and well-distributed rainfall. The average annual precipitation is about 1600 mm, which nowadays reduced to a considerable volume due to several natural and man-made factors. The Mahanadi including some tributaries like the Tel is perennial and navigable throughout the year. In fact the entire Orissa has been characterized by the presence of numerous small rivers, rivulets and streams. Up to the British period all the major rivers were navigable throughout the year and most of the transportation system was based on water routes (Deloche 1990) but in recent years almost all rivers have been silted and the riverbeds have become shallow and literally defunct in terms of trade activity.

Early Historic Cultures

In the recent years a number of Early Historic sites datable from 4th-5th centuries B.C. to the early part of the Christian era have been explored in the Central and Western part of Orissa, especially in the districts of Boudh (Tripathy 2002a; 2002b; 2005: 169-179) (Fig. 3) and undivided Kalahandi (Mohanty and Mishra 2005: 97-124) (Fig. 4). The dates assigned are on the basis of ceramic types and hoards of punch-marked coins from both

accidental discovery and systematic excavations at Manamunda-Asurgarh. This proves that the hinterland part of Orissa was heavily colonized by the Early Historic people. This is substantiated by the discovery of more then hundred settlements along the banks of river Mahanadi and the Tel. The sites explored in this part of Orissa have been categorized as major/urban settlements and small hamlets (on the basis of both features and size), located on the periphery of the major centres and acted as satellite settlements. Most of the satellite sites are on the banks of perennial rivers like Mahanadi and the Tel, where as the major settlements are located on the banks of small rivers, except Manamunda-Asurgarh which is located at the confluence of the Mahanadi and the Tel. This exception may be interpreted in terms of trade and commerce, as evident from the rich archaeological material from the site. Besides, several settlements were also noticed on islands which again portray trade activity. The best example comes from Marjkud, an island in the river Mahanadi, this site yielded various types of ceramics and other material having resemblance with the material found in the coastal part of Orissa. It has also been established from the explorations and limited excavations that colonization process during the Early Historic period diffused as a result of the exploitation of natural resources like gemstones, forest produces as also perennial rivers for communication (Tripathy 2002b). Out of the several explored Early Historic sites in the region, the sites of Narla-Asurgarh, Budhigarh, Kharligarh and Manamunda-Asurgarh have been categorized as urban or major centres; all of these have large fortifications and hydraulic management system. Out of the total number of eight Early Historic forts, six are located in the hinterland indicating that these sites also had significant contributions to the early state formation in ancient Orissa. This was centred in all probability around Radhanagar. In this context, the region may be identified with the 'Atavika Territory' mentioned in Ashokan Edicts and the capital of the Atavikas was most probably located at Narla-Asurgarh (Sahu 1982: 1-18). The small centres or satellite settlements, located within a close proximity to the major centres, most probably acted as centres for craft specialization as also gemstone exploitation. Even, in terracotta items, the people had proficiency as revealed through ethnographic observations on the potters and its comparison with the excavated material from the archaeological sites. Almost all the Early Historic sites are located on the banks of rivers, with profuse chance of riverine trade activity and surprisingly the sites are dotted with less than half a kilometre interval.

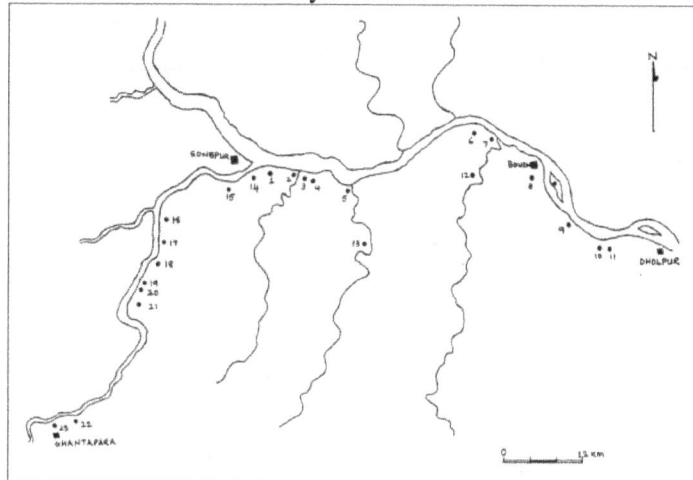

Figure 3: Early historic sites in central and western Orissa

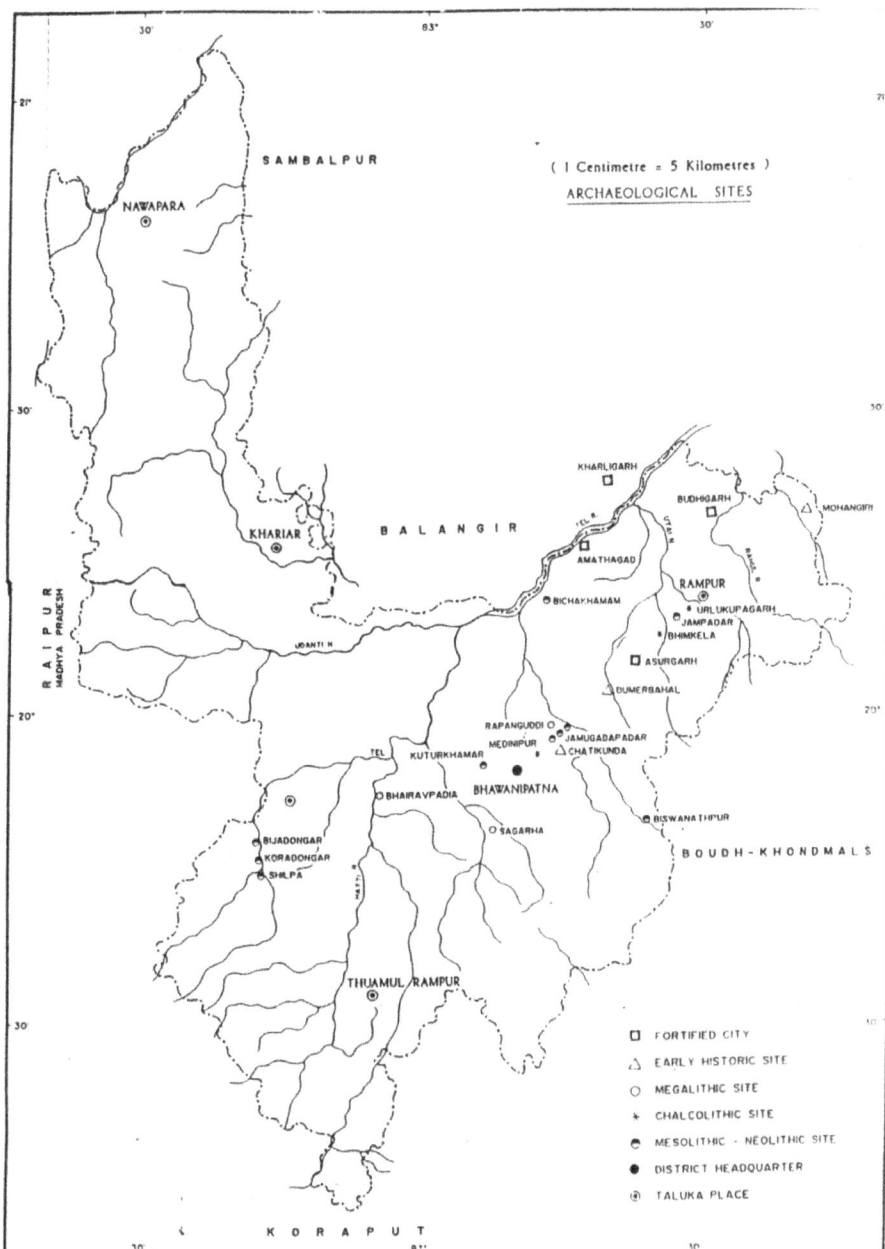

Figure 4: Early Historic sites in western Orissa

49

Manamunda-Asurgarh

Manamunda-Asurgarh is about 49 km to the northwest of the Boudh district headquarters located in the central part of Orissa. The Early Historic fort (Fig. 5) is located on the right bank of the river Mahanadi, a little away from the confluence of the river with the Tel. It is represented by at least six habitational mounds that have formed in a linear fashion. The site was surveyed and interpreted in early twentieth century (Benerjee 1920: 64-86). The site spreads over an area of 1.5 km north south and 0.5 km east west. A defense wall made of burnt bricks, and partly disturbed by the river Mahanadi, is visible along the right bank. In fact, the present day settlement of Manamunda is located just on the ancient settlement and hence its extent could not be traced. The site was subjected for a limited excavation by the Sambalpur University in 1982 (Behera 1982: 16-22) and again in 1990 (*IAR* 1990: 80-85).

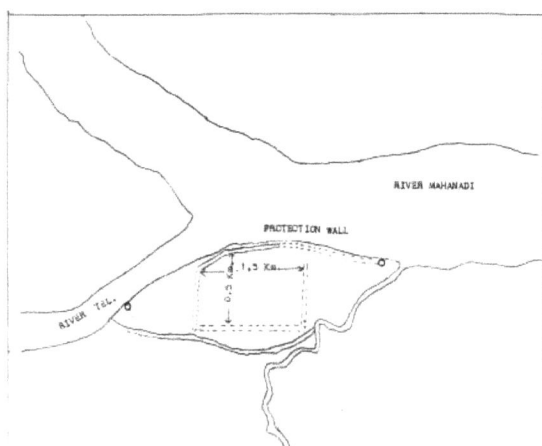

Figure 5: The fort of Manamunda-Asurgarh

In the initial excavation two small trenches were dug vertically in addition to exposing two brick structures as well as two brick pillars around the periphery of the site. Besides, the excavation also yielded the skeleton of a child, Northern Black Polished Ware, Black Slipped Ware, Red Slipped Ware, Fine Grey Ware and Red Ware with a Grey Core. The antiquities of the site included iron objects of war and peace, domestic objects, beads of semiprecious stone and terracotta and other minor specimens of daily use.

In the second phase of the excavation conducted in 1990, two trenches were dug up to the virgin soil. The excavation revealed cultural material from 3rd/4th centuries B.C. to the 3rd century A.D. From the trenches a variety of pottery specimens were collected which

resemble with the findings of the earlier excavation. A punch-marked coin bearing five symbols, reverse-one central symbol i.e., four taurines with a central dot assign the coin to 2nd century B.C. (Pradhan 1995: 26-28).

Further intensive and extensive archaeological work was carried out at and around the site to understand it in a holistic perspective. Several theoretical paradigms were implied to understand the exact function of the site. Interpretations were made after a careful observation of the landscape as also the cultural material found from surface exploration and section scrapping. A detailed study revealed that the site was protected on the north by a massive defense wall running parallel to the banks of the Mahanadi to check the flood activity of the river. The site was bounded by the river Tel and Mehrni (a small stream with reasonable depth and width) on the west and the east, respectively. A moat ran along the southern periphery of the site, joining the Tel and the Mehrni. It is partially visible now in the form of a huge depression and the length of the moat is roughly 3 km and the width is 2.5 m. From the surface as also from, the section scrapping a number of ceramic types were collected and a scientific analysis was conducted on the pottery as also on faunal material. The archaeological material found from the site is very significant as it revealed the existence of coastal Orissa pottery like Knobbed Ware and Black Slipped Ware as also potteries of the Middle Ganga Valley and Chandraketugarh-Tamluk region which was proved by X-Ray Diffraction analysis of ceramic types (Tripathy 2002b). The faunal assemblage of the site has also been dated (Fluorine/Phosphate Analysis) (Fig. 6) and analysed (Tripathy and Joglekar 1997-98: 117-119).

Site	%F	%P	%P$_2$O$_5$	100F/P^{2}O$_5$
Manamunda	0.074	15.00	32.91	0.215
Marjakud	0.072	14.37	34.35	0.218

Figure 6: Fluorine Phosphate dating results

Narla-Asurgarh

Asurgarh, as the name suggests, appears to be the most important Early Historic settlement in the hinterland Orissa, located near Rupra Railway Station, about 2 km from the Narla village. The fort (Fig. 7), square in plan, each side measuring 1200 m, had four wide gates in four cardinal directions, and at each gate was installed one guardian deity. The river Sandul flows by the western side of the fort encircled by a moat on three sides which is fed by a huge tank; this tank exists till today. It has been interpreted that water was being brought through two sluice gates to fill up the moats (c. 4th-5th century B.C. onwards). The entire ancient tank or lake area, which in all probability is contemporary to the site, covers an area of 200 acres. It was designed in such a way that when the fort was surrounded by enemies, a secret sluice could be opened so that the whole area both inside and outside of the fort would be flooded with water and consequently the enemy would washed away. The central part of the fort would remain as an island if such a flood were created because this part of the fort was on an elevated land. Presumably, the palace was constructed at the centre of the fort.

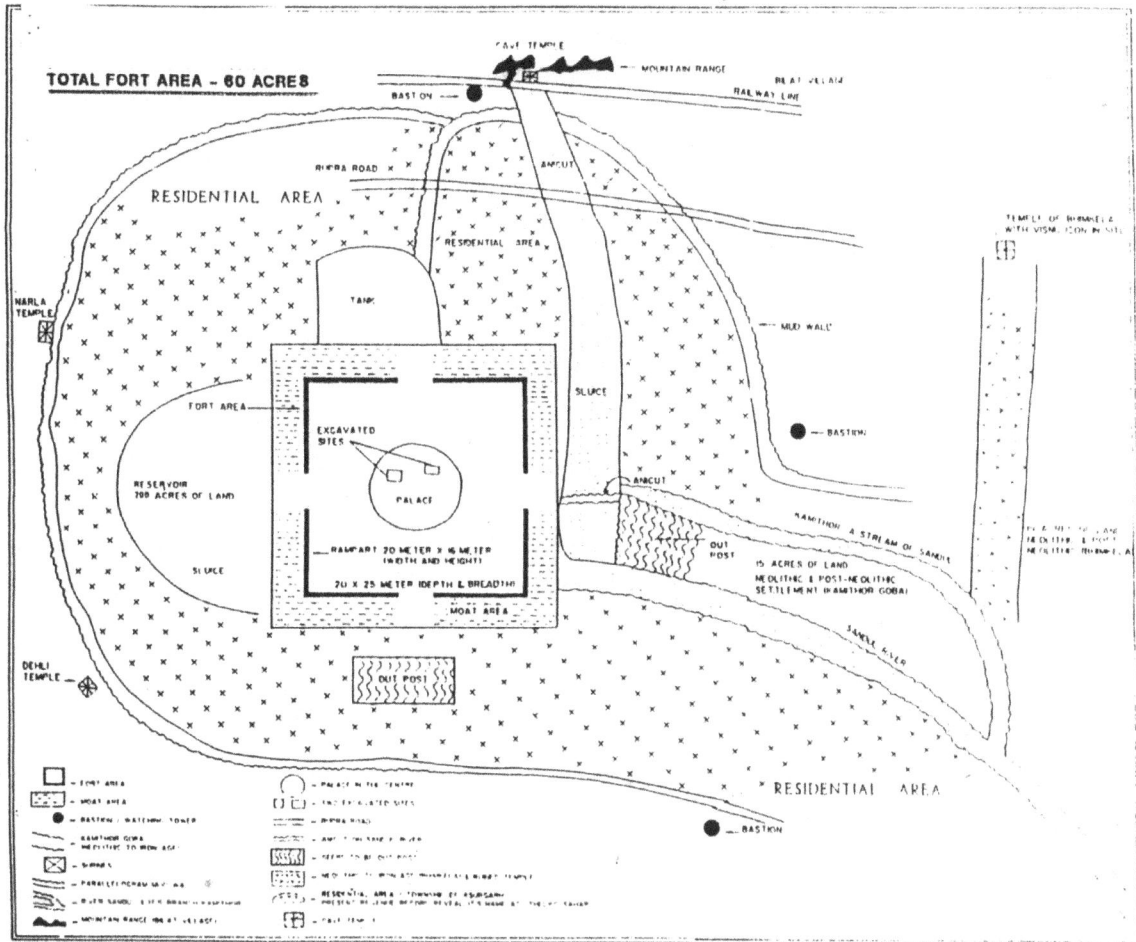

Figure 7: The fort of Narla-Asurgarh

The site was subjected for a limited excavation by the Department of History, Sambalpur University (Sahu 1982: 1-8), which revealed fascinating results. Although it was published in a regional journal, the importance of the site in terms of hinterland urbanization cannot be ignored, as per the archaeological material.

The excavation at the site consisting of two small trenches, have revealed paved house floors, an array of ceramic types such as Black and Red Ware, Black Slipped Ware, Fine Grey Ware, Red Slipped Ware, Northern Black Polished Ware, and most probably Rouletted Ware, iron implements of war and peace, beads made of semiprecious stones, punch-marked silver and copper coins, terracotta figurines, glass bangles, amulets and ornaments. A hoard of 539 silver coins, belonging to the 3rd century B.C. to the 5th century A.D. and collected by the King of Kalahandi furnished considerable cultural data. The first group of coins (69) is assignable to the pre-Mauryan period, the second group (272) to the Mauryan epoch and to the Guptas. The coins found at the site indicate that there was probably a mint at the site for fabrication of punch-marked coins. The similarity of some coins of the punch-marked coins of Asurgarh with those found at Bijnor and Paila near Koushambi, and the similarity in

51

texture of fabric of some pottery types of Asurgarh with those at Ahichchhatra further indicate that there was a brisk trade during the Mauryan period between Asurgarh and prosperous towns like Koushambi and Ahichchhatra in North India as also with Sripura, Vidisha and Ujjain.

While narrating the historicity of the fort, Sahu (1982: 1-8) opines that Asurgarh bears a special importance as far as the Atavika people are concerned. These people find mention in the Ashokan Edicts and are considered to be constituted the fighting forces of Kalinga against Ashoka in his famous Kalinga war of 261 B.C. The Atavika land comprised roughly the present districts of Kalahandi, Bolangir and Boudh-Sonepur regions of Central and Western Orissa and Bastar in Madhya Pradesh. It was an important recruiting ground for the veteran army of Kalinga even as early as the time of the Mahabharata war. Archaeological work at Asurgarh makes us believe that it was the capital city and the most important centre of Atavika territory and the excavation amply indicates that the area was not underdeveloped during the days of Ashoka and the people had a high standard of civilization characterized by well-polished potteries of the Northern Black Polished fabric. No doubt, Asurgarh was an important political and commercial centre situated on the highway joining South Kosala and Mahakantara with Kalinga. In the 4th century A.D., the fort of Asurgarh appears to have belonged to king Vyaghraraja of Mahakantara whom Samudragupta claims to have defeated in course of his south Indian campaign. The excavation indicates that the fort area was deserted after 5th/6th century A.D. and as such, it may be said that Tusti was probably the last known ruler of Asurgarh.

The ceramic industry at the site comprises of dish, bowl and vessels. The dishes are in burnished Black Slipped Ware with inverted simple rim, thin wall; the vessels are in burnished Black Slipped Ware with complex externally projecting short beaked rim; in Red Slipped Ware with narrow mouth, concentric corrugation at the interior body and grey core. All types are of fine core.

Kharligarh

The Early Historic site of Kharligarh is situated in Tentulikhunti block in Bolangir on the border of Kalahandi district, at the confluence of the Rahul and the Tel rivers in a densely forested environment. Two more streams, the Khadang and the Singda, flow on both the sides of the river Rahul at about a distance of 5 km to meet the river Tel off Kharligarh. This area is occupied by a number of primitive communities such as the Gonds, Bhuyas, Khonds and Saoras. The ruin of this fortified city lies in loose lateritic soil, in an extensive area stretching from the Tel to the river Rahul. The fort is almost square on plan, circumscribed in the north, east and south by the rivers acting as natural defense and the west by an excavated moat connecting both the rivers. The rampart consists of burnt bricks of size 40 X 25 X 12 cm^3. The central part of the fort contains a shrine in ruined form, probably the presiding goddess of the fort. Although the northern rampart is greatly denuded by the river exposing the terrace and the basement, the river-worn stone gravels topped by brick wall of about 15 ft. wide, the major part of the fort lies intact. The site has revealed brick structures, a large variety of pottery, iron objects of war and peace, beads of various stones, axes, querns, choppers, microlithic artifacts, smoking pipes, metal bangles, earrings, copper Kushana coins, etc. However, the site needs to be thoroughly plotted and excavated in a horizontal manner. The ceramic assemblage of the site includes a dish in Burnished Black Slipped Ware with slight concave wall, inverted simple rim, flat base, well-fired and of fine fabric; a basin in Black Slipped Ware with internally projecting triangular rim, salt glazed and of medium fabric; the bowls in Black and Red Ware with inverted simple rim, thin wall, well-fired and fine in fabric; and finally Red Ware with disc base (Mohanty and Mishra 2005: 97-124).

Budhigarh

The site of Budhigarh lies 500 m to the east of Madanpur Upper Primary School. It is an extensive mound with a height of 3 m and covers an area of 1000 X 500 m in north south direction. It is situated on the banks of the Puruna Nala, meaning old channel, which could be an artificially dug out moat and the river Rahul which ultimately joins the river Tel. Most part of the mound has remained intact, except the middle portion where the villagers have made a path. The artefactual evidence from the site indicates that the site was occupied from the Early Historic to the late medieval period. The site has revealed a wide spectrum of ceramics, beads, coins, bricks, terracotta objects, iron implements, idol of Durga and Ganesh and a large quantity of faunal remains and human skeletons. The bricks from the site measure 45 X 30 X 8 cm³.

The ceramic assemblage of the site consists of dishes, bowls, miniature bowls, vessels, basins, dish-on-stands and lids. The dishes are of Burnished Black Slipped Ware with slightly inverted, simple rim, convex body and of fine fabric; the type with slightly inverted beaked rim of medium fabric appears to be slightly salt glazed. The bowls are in Dull Ware with external projecting simple, thin wall, traces of slip found on the outer surface and of fine fabric, in Red Ware with externally projecting short-beaked rim and medium fabric. Besides, a miniature bowl in Black Slipped Ware with externally projecting, triangular rim and of medium fabric has been found. Globular vessel (*handi*) in Burnished Black Slipped Ware with externally projecting short-beaked rim, narrow mouth, and thin wall and of fine fabric and vessels in Black Slipped Ware glazing at the surface are the prominent vessel types at the site. The other ceramic types are large basins in Red Ware with inverted simple rim and appliqué design on the neck, dish-on-stand in Black and Red Ware, lid in Grey Ware, bowls of Northern Black Polished Ware and Knobbed Ware (Mohanty and Mishra 2005: 97-124).

The concept of Urbanization

The emergence of state and urbanization in Indian context may be regarded as an extension of the processes of the earlier period like Chalcolithic-Harappan. Research and interpretation have been given by various scholars who term it as "Second Urbanization" or "Early Historic Urbanization" (Ghosh 1973; Sharma 1991, Makhan Lal 1984; Ray 1986; Erdosy 1988; Allchin 1989: 1-16; 1990: 163-173; 1995; Chakrabarti 1995; Champakalaxmi 1996). In a broad sense, in South Asia, the term Early Historic refers approximately to the period from 600 B.C. to 500 A.D. This period saw the emergence of cities and complex politics with the growth of Buddhism among the many other religious philosophies, throughout the subcontinent (Heiztman 1984: 121-138; Erdosy 1988: 430; Kosambi 1989; Sarao 1990; Ray 1989: 42-54, 1994 Chakrabarti 1995a; 1995b: 185-201; Morrison 1995: 203-221). However, the process of urbanization and

city formation depend upon the geographical and ecological setting of a particular region.

By the middle of the 1st millennium B.C., the second urbanization in the region of the Gangetic valley grew up as a result of interaction of multiple factors that were prompted by the conditions of natural situations and previous cultural developments. The process strengthened and enriched the growing divisions within society that came to be institutionalised as economic strata within a hierarchical society (Basa 2005: 69-83). As the divisions within the social organizations increased, existing institutional regions and other social entities came into function to alleviate the attendant stresses, which led to the growth of several small independent kingdoms within the regions of the Gangetic plain.

The process of urban growth or the 'second urbanization' covered in its early phase during the 5th-3rd centuries B.C., in the Ganga valley, Indo-Gangetic Divide, Northwest India, Bihar and Central India. Some of the important early Indian cities included Taxila (Ghosh 1948), Hasthinapura (Lal 1955), Mathura (*IAR* 1973-74: 31-2; 1974-75: 48-50; 1975-76: 53-5), Ahichchhatra (Gosh and Panigraphi 1946; *IAR* 1963-64), Kosambi (Sarao 1968), Sringaverapura (Lal 1993), Rajghat (Narain and Roy 1976), Vidisha (*IAR* 1963-64: 60-70; 1964-65:23-4; 1975-76: 30-31; 1976-77: 33-4) and Ujjain (*IAR* 1956-57: 20-8). Most of the early settlements, besides being enormous in size, are characterized by massive ramparts of brick and mud with elaborately laid out bastions, gateways and moats, evidence of craft specialization, coinage, and incipient polity known from ancient literature, features which elevate them to urban status. The phenomenon of early historic urban growth accelerated during the Mauryan period. This period witnessed the introduction of new political concepts in the form of Mauryan imperialism, in which Buddhism took a leading role. A decentralized administration based on Kautilyan principles of polity (Rangarajan 1994), provinces flourished with immense prosperity in which both inland and overseas trade played a vital role. The expansion of trade network, both domestic and overseas, during this period had far reaching socio-economic impact (Sharma 1983; Begley 1986: 297-321; Lahiri 1992). This development gained further momentum in the post-Mauryan era (*c*. 200 B.C. to 300 A.D.), which is marked by changes in the social and economic fabric of the sub-continent. The same also happened to regions like the Mahanadi and the Brahmani deltas in Orissa as also in the Middle Mahanadi and Tel Valleys of Central/Western Orissa, where urban structure grew with all the essential features. The extension and spread of Buddhism, trade network, development of social fabric had far-reaching implications and were accompanied by a definite system of coinage to promote an organized commercial set up. Besides, the concept of fort building also started due to the extensive trade patterns in precious and costly materials. The social strata also got changed and a very powerful class of businessman rose into power due to their resources and wealth. The Roman trade was an important contributing factor during this period. Recent evidences from the harbour complex of Manikapatana and Palur and Radhanagara have proved that ancient Orissa was well connected with the Roman world which is evident from the finding of several Roman amphorae sherds, medallions, bullae and even Roman glass. The Roman trade particularly influenced the settlement of Tamil Nadu and other parts of South India, as also Orissa.

Urbanization in Hinterland Orissa

Certain traits of Childean urban revolution in particular evidence of brick structures trade and craft specialization, characterize the centres of coastal Orissa. In the absence of written record and evidence for political hegemony, the background of urbanization process in the hinterland Orissa remains unclear. However, the sites of Viratagarh and Kichakgarh in Mauyurbhanj (Mishra 1997), Asurgarh in Kalahandi district (Sahu 1982: 1-8), and Manamunda-Asurgarh in Boudh district (*IAR* 1990: 80-85; Tripathy 2002b) may be regarded as urban centres, in a broad sense of the term. In this context, the application of the World System Approach or 'Centre-Periphery' model propounded by Wallerstein (1974) which focuses a single centre in relationship to its hinterland has been critically examined by Basa (1995: 357-375; 1996: 109-139). The approach to counteract the model is mainly based on the role of ideology and cosmology in exchange network, specific context of the framework and the periphery is not regarded as a passive recipient, but an active agent and is appropriate to imply in a region like hinterland Orissa where independent centres were flourishing during the Early Historic period. The sites of

Narla-Asurgarh and Manamunda-Asurgarh, later with at least six habitational mounds are the standing examples. There are extensive Early Historic settlements in northern Orissa, for example, the site of Viratgarh, yielded evidence of punch-marked and Puri-Kushana coins. If the Mahavamsa, the great Singhalese chronicle is to be believed, there existed many urban centres in the valley of the Mahanadi in the early centuries of the Christian era.

A question that comes to mind in this context is what is the role and status of the urban centres of hinterland Orissa which appear to have not been under the direct control of any imperial administration. This region has not been referred to in any Edict or literary texts as a Mauryan administrative unit except the evidence of Knobbed Ware (Fig. 8), which is often related to Buddhist cosmology. There is a reference in the Allahabad Pillar Inscription to Vyaghraraja of Mahakantara. A folk story refers to this region as the land of Gosimha Daitya, a demon. Interestingly, two important urban centres Manamunda-Asurgarh and Narla-Asurgarh are attached with the suffix Asur and Garh, meaning "Fort of Demons". A probable connotation of this word would be 'the city of the uncivilized' or 'the city of the savages' which can be comparable with the Atavika people mentioned in the Ashokan Edicts. By implication, it would appear that these centres were under the hegemony of tribal chieftains, and hence the name.

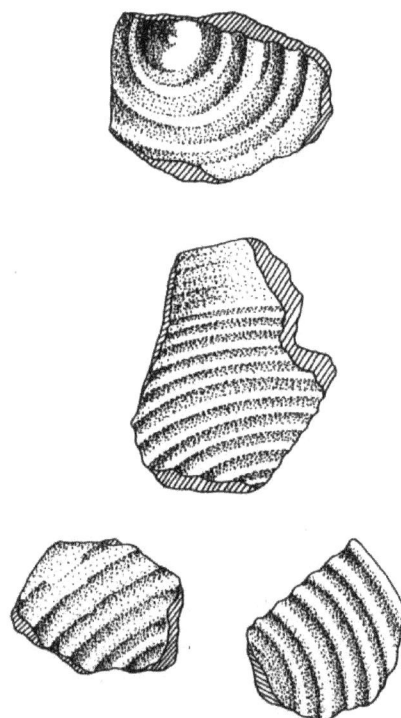

Figure 8: Knobbed ware

54

The archaeological evidences suggest that central and western Orissa was looked upon as a 'resource zone' by the coastal centres. There were both river and land routes that connected these two regions. The process of urbanization in this part seems to have received stimulus from the trade relations of the region with coastal Orissa (Tripathy 2002b).

Central and Western Orissa as Resource Zone

The region of hinterland Orissa covers wide tracts of dense deciduous forest ranges (northern most fringes of the Eastern Ghats) which supports a wide range of flora and fauna (Basu *et al.* 1995: 367-369; Gauerson *et al.* 1995). The region is also quite rich in mineral deposits, especially gemstones which were exploited by the Early Historic urban population with support from local gem exploiters in a very traditional method which

even continues today (Tripathy 2000: 60-67; 2002b). Central and Western part of Orissa, mainly Bolangir, Boudh, Kalahandi and Sambalpur districts have been identified as a gem belt containing emerald, ruby, sapphire, aquamarine, heliodor, cryshoberyle, including Alexandrite, tourmaline, zircon, topaz, moonstone, amethyst, smoky quartz and garnet of different varieties which are associated with the iron ore deposits of the Eastern Ghats (Fig. 9). It is interesting to note that many of the tribal/ethnic deities (especially goddesses) of Central and Western Orissa have been named after the gemstones. For example, Panneswari (Goddess of Emerald), Manikeswari (Goddess of Ruby), Khambeswari (Goddess of Cryshoberyle), and Sambaleswari (Goddess of Resources). These deity names suggest some kind of symbolism pertaining to the gemstone resources of Central and Western Orissa.

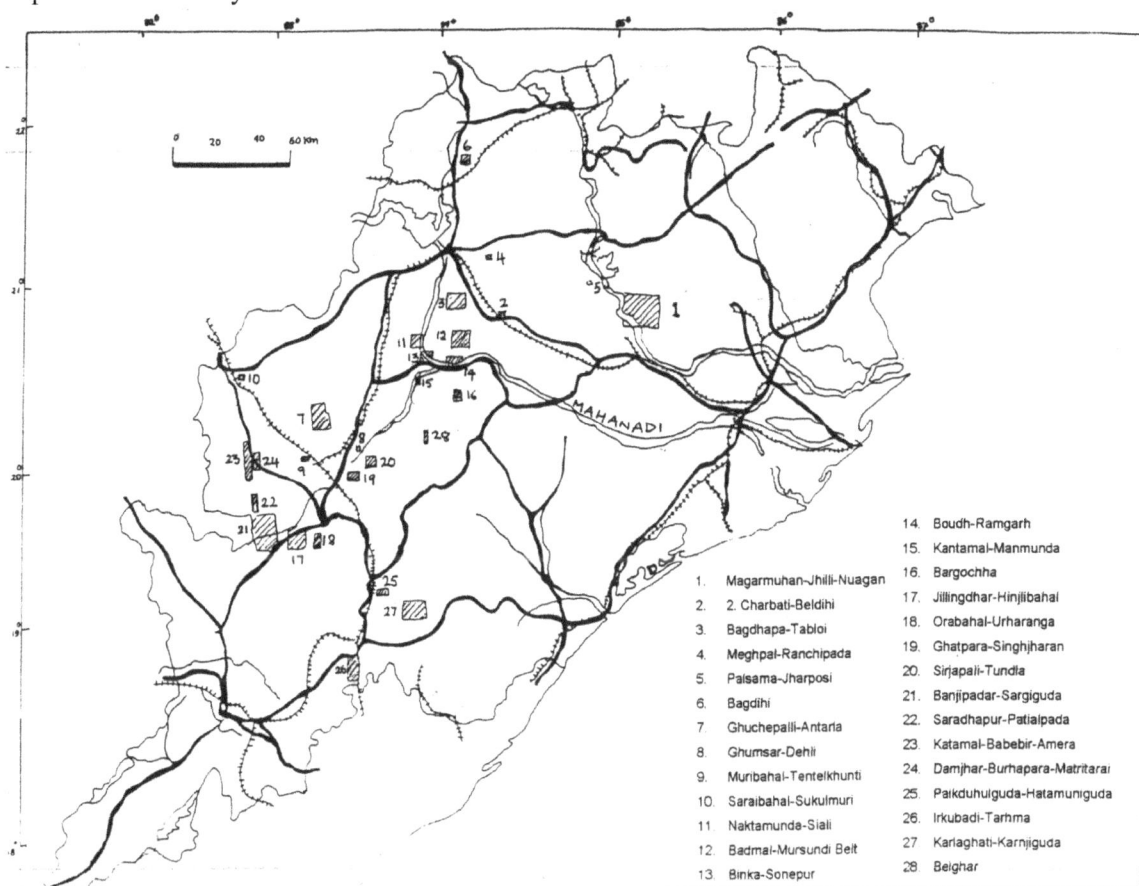

Figure 9: Distribution of gemstones

1. Magarmuhan-Jhilli-Nuagan
2. 2. Charbati-Beldihi
3. Bagdhapa-Tabloi
4. Meghpal-Ranchipada
5. Paisama-Jharposi
6. Bagdihi
7. Ghuchepalli-Antarla
8. Ghumsar-Dehli
9. Muribahal-Tentelkhunti
10. Saraibahal-Sukulmuri
11. Naktamunda-Siali
12. Badmai-Mursundi Belt
13. Binka-Sonepur
14. Boudh-Ramgarh
15. Kantamal-Manmunda
16. Bargochha
17. Jillingdhar-Hinjlibahal
18. Orabahal-Urharanga
19. Ghatpara-Singhjharan
20. Sirjapali-Tundla
21. Banjipadar-Sargiguda
22. Saradhapur-Patialpada
23. Katamal-Babebir-Amera
24. Damjhar-Burhapara-Matritarai
25. Paikduhulguda-Hatamuniguda
26. Irkubadi-Tarhma
27. Karlaghati-Karnjiguda
28. Beighar

More recently, the work of the Orissa Mining Corporation and Geology, Orissa has resulted in the discovery of at least 28 gem belts. The region of Central and Western Orissa yielded kimberlitic pipes containing indicator of mineral grain of pyrope garnet and chromites

which are positive diamond indicators (Das 1997: 18). Moreover, the region is rich in iron ore deposits which were exploited in plenty and transported to the coastal Orissan urban/trading centres. The Manikapatana-Palur Harbour Complex yielded iron ores, slags as also finished implements, suggests local manufacturing activity. But the important forts and trading centres of coastal Orissa such as Radhanagara, Sisupalgarh etc. are devoid of iron smelting activity. Almost all the Early Historic sites of Central and Western Orissa have yielded iron smelting activity which signifies that iron along with gemstones, was a principal commodity to be transported to the coastal/delta part of Orissa. Both land and river routes were preferred to carry the materials and had linkages with each other in terms of trade and its mechanism which has been substantiated with the current ethnographic parallels (Triapthy 2000: 60-67; 2002). Besides gem and iron, forest produces such as medicinal herbs, bamboo, and timber were also transported from this part of Orissa to the coastal Orissan centres.

The trade relations of coastal Orissa with its hinterland have also been corroborated by archaeological evidences (Tripathy 1996-97: 41-54; 2000a: 60-67; 2000b: 397-416; 2002a: 397-416; 2002b; 2005: 169-179; Tripathy and Joglekar 1997-98: 117-119; Tripathy and Mohanty 1998: 69-98). The ceramic evidence is significant in studying trade or exchange and routes by which goods were distributed which serves as an indicator of the interregional and intra-regional trade relations (Anderson 1984: 20-21). The small-scale excavations conducted at the site of Narla-Asurgarh and Manamunda-Asurgarh and the trial trench at Marjakud have revealed several types of pottery which have striking similarity with the pottery found at sites like Sisupalgarh, Radhanagar, Manikapatana, Palur, etc., indicating the fact that such material were transported to the Central and Western Orissan centres as a result of trade and communication. Potteries like Knobbed Ware (Fig. 10), Black Slipped Ware, Red Slipped Ware, Red Ware with a Grey Core (Fig. 11), Fine Grey Ware (Fig. 12), Black and Red Ware, as the X-Ray Diffraction Analysis (Fig. 13) of ceramic types show, were transported from coastal part of Orissa to the hinterland (Tripathy 2002b).

Figure 10: Knobbed Ware

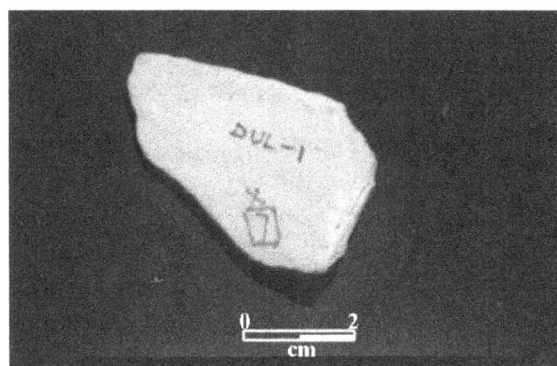
Figure 11: Red ware with grey core

Figure 12: Fine grey ware

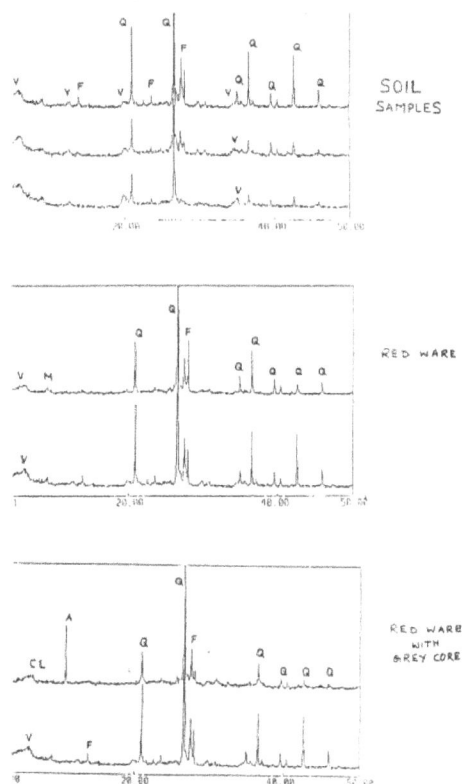

56

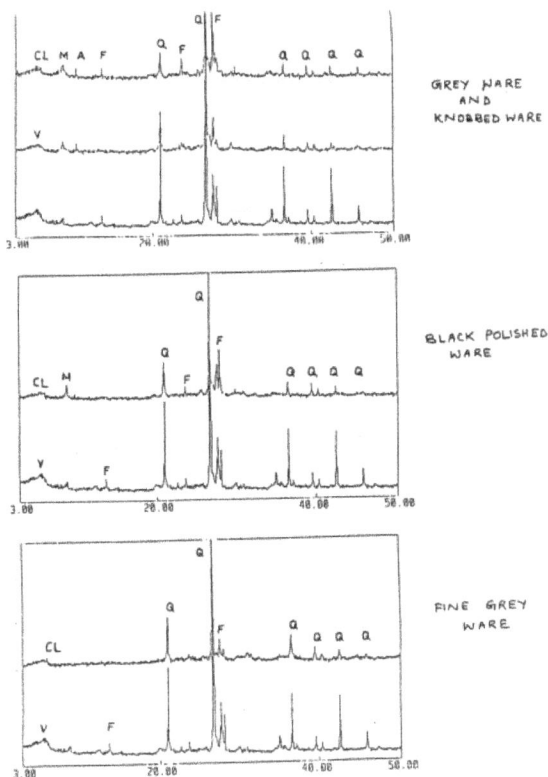

Figure 13: X-Ray Diffraction Analysis: Results

Literary and Traveler's Accounts

Various literary references referring to the region and trade activity, directly or indirectly, give a clear picture of the Early Historic trade and trade routes, and above all, a glimpse of the regional landscape. Even there are references of the existing of large and urban centres in the interior part of Orissa. Some of the ancient sources talk at length about the river systems and their navigable capacity as also auspiciousness. The rivers referred directly in the texts have been identified, either geographically or topographically, with the existing river systems, owing to which, it is now possible to understand the role that these rivers played in the diffusion of cultures that blossomed on their banks.

Several inscriptions and copper plate charters issued by the rulers of different dynasties, ranging from the Gupta to the medieval kingdoms, speak about the contemporary trade activity and the routes, and furnish rich geographical information. Some of the important rivers have also been mentioned in these records, which has helped in identifying the places and the geographical boundary of the regions under different rulers.

The Astadhyayi of Panini (Agrawalla 1955, 1963: 61, 440), ascribed to c. 5th century B.C.

describes the place *Taitilakadru* (identified with present day Titlagarh, a sub-division of the Bolangir district of Western Orissa) as a trade centre. The Sanskrit term *Kadru* meaning a tawny coloured material which may be identified with cryshoberyle (a type of semi-precious gemstone) and is abundant in the region. The text states that Taitila was a famous for the trade of *Kadru*. The description of a remote landmark in the Astadhyayi of Panini is significant and speaks about the importance of the hinterland in terms of resources.

The Serivannijja Jataka (Cowel 1955), a part of the Jataka stories, mentions that Bodhisattva as a merchant in pots and pans crossed river Telavaha for business. This speaks that river Tel was navigated and several big and urban centres were located in the Tel-Mahanadi river valleys in Central and Western Orissa. The river is mentioned as Telavaha (Rangarajan 1994), a name that betokens the profuse trade of oil and oil seeds through it. The Central and Western part of Orissa is rich in plant species like *neem* whose seeds are used to extract oil. These floral materials were traded to different parts of the State in the ancient period also. The mention of a small river like Telavaha or Tel in such an important text elaborates the important role played by this river in terms of trade and transportation.

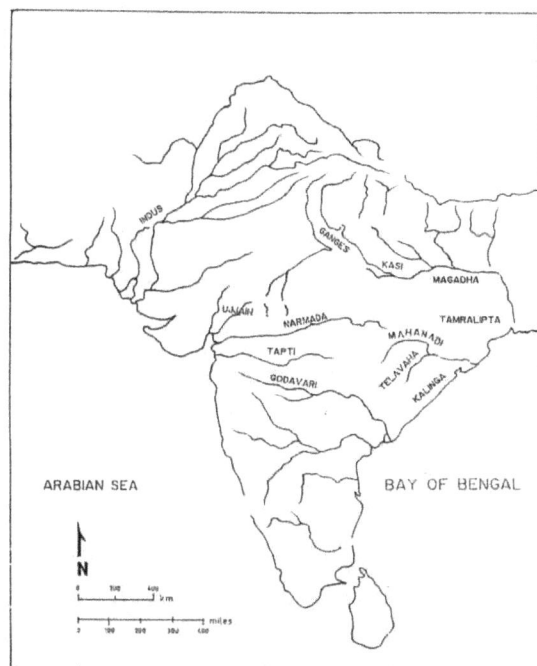

Figure 14: River Telavaha (Tel)

The Arthasashtra Kautilya (c. 4th century B.C.) describes river Tel as Telavaha (Rangarajan 1994) (Fig. 14), and the description of this small river along with several other major perennial rivers of India is significant and implies its role in trade mechanism as also navigation. It mentions a place called Indravana, which may be identified with the area between the rivers Tel and Indravati (Kangle 1965). It also alludes to the rich gem deposit of the region.

The gem deposits and the quality, which fascinated the ancient Roman world, have been referred to in the famous Geograsphia of Ptolemy of the 1st century A.D. (Majumdar 1927), which mentions about the diamond mines at Sambalaka (identified with modern Sambalpur in Western Orissa), the river Manada (identified with river Mahanadi) as rich in gem resources and also the river Tyndis (identified with the river Brahmani). References to these remote locations of Orissa in the geographic map of Ptolemy, is indeed significant. Ptolemy considered Paloura (modern Palur in Ganjam district of Orissa) as a reference point while preparing his map (Fig. 15). One may infer from these references that there was a flourishing trade in diamond and other precious stones in Orissa.

Figure 15: Map of Ptolemy

There are several references by the British ethnographers and officers regarding the navigability and market system of Western Orissa. They briefly discuss about the commodities and the procedure of trade in the region. Even sometimes there are references on trade routes followed by the traders from far off places like Nagpur and Madras. This reference clearly speaks about the possible movement of goods from hinterland Orissa to different urban centres located in the neighbouring states like Chhattisgarh and Madhya Pradesh as also Bengal and to cities like Vidisha, Ujjain and other Early Historic urban centres. This reference has been taken to give a follow up to the Early Historic trade mechanism and surprisingly there is not much change in the trading patterns of these areas with different areas but of course there is a change in the

58

commodities. Surprisingly, still, water transport forms the major thrust for all trading activities.

The travel accounts of British officers travelling in India during the later part of the 19th century and the early part of the 20th century provide valuable data on the use of boats in the Mahanadi; trade transactions through the river; and the navigable distances of different rivers and their tributaries in Orissa. Hunter (1872: 73-74) refers to Mahanadi as navigable up to Sambalpur by flat-bottomed boats of about twenty-five tons borden (a measuring unit), and that a considerable trade were then being carried on. He further adds that, "the river affords valuable facilities for navigation. The boatmen carry rakes and hoes, with which they clear a narrow passage just sufficient to let their craft pass. Where rocks impede the navigation, there is plenty of depth on either side". He also mentions that the Mahanadi is "fed by numerous tributaries like the Salinki, the Bagh, the Mehrni and the Tel. The river Tel divides the Orissa Tributary States from those in the Central Provinces, and forms the boundary between Bod (Boudh) and Sonepur". He observes the presence of a variety of precious and semiprecious gemstones in the riverbeds. A detail account of the trade commodities and materials then in exchange has been given by him. Three towns on the left bank of Mahanadi, he observes, subsist by river traffic, namely Baideswar, Padmavati and Kantilo. The fisherman communities carry salt, spices, coconuts, and brass utensils up to Sambalpur, in the Central Provinces, brining thence, in exchange, cotton, wheat, oil-seeds, clarified butter, oil, molasses, iron, turmeric, *tasar*, cloth, rice etc. There are also several smaller towns on both sides of the Mahanadi, which carry on an extensive trade in timber, bamboos, oil-seeds and other local forest produces.

Motte (1765), a British diamond merchant, followed the trade route ran along the bank of Mahanadi from Cuttack to Sambalpur. In his account he provides picture of the trade, ecological potentiality of the region and above all the traditional settlements located in the area in the 18th century. Settlements fortified with perishable material like timber find mention in his notes. As regards to trade, he refers to the use of boats, both big and small, for trade purpose, and details of the trade contacts of the region with coastal Orissa. He attests the occasional use of land route, which traversed through dense forest tracts, highlighting the role of Mahanadi, which provided an easy path to the coastal locales of Orissa. The commodities generally comprised forest resources, and were exchanged for marine products. He mentions the gem deposit of the region and the quality of diamonds available at Sambalpur and also its fortified settlements (Acharya 1955: 44-50).

James Rennel (1763) in his famous *Memoirs of a Map of Hindoostan* refers to the diamond centres of Western Orissa and the "Jaggannaut Pagoda" of coastal Orissa. He writes, "On the west of Baod (Boudh) and near the Muhannuddy river, Mr. Thams passed a town of the name Bairgarh".

Numismatic Sources

The distribution of punch-marked coins in Orissa of both imperial and Kosala types suggests that Orissa was in a sway of Early Historic trade connections and communication patterns. These coins are found either in hoards or as stray findings (Tripathy 1986). The excavations at Manamunda-Asurgarh yielded in layer 3 a silver punch-marked coin with four symbols datable to the 3rd century B.C. (Pradhan 1995:26-28). Similar discoveries have been found from the excavations at Sisupalgarh (Lal 1949: 62-105) and Jaugada (*IAR* 1956-57: 30-31). The find place and distribution of these coins have been considered as representing trade centres and routes respectively. From the findings it is clear that besides circulating imperial variety or Mauryan types of coins, the sites located in Orissa, especially in the western part, were also circulating coins with local symbols known as Kosala type. It indicates that most probably some sort of autonomy was provided to the sites located in hinterland Orissa due to their importance in terms of either resources or dissimilarities with other localities.

Distribution of Imperial as well as Kosala or Janapada type of punch-marked coins in Orissa

Find Place	District	No. of Coins	Typology	Nature of Find
Narla-Asurgarh	Kalahandi	539	Imperial Type	Hoard
Bahalda	Mayurbhanj	192	Imperial Type	Hoard

Jaugada	Ganjam	01	Imperial Type	Excavation-1956-57
Jharapada	Puri	10	Imperial Type	Hoard
Jagamara	Puri	49	Imperial Type	Hoard
Pandia (Near Jaugada)	Ganjam	334	Imperial Type	Hoard
Manamunda-Asurgarh	Boudh	01	Imperial Type	Excavation-1990
Sisupalgarh	Khurdha	01	Imperial Type	Excavation 1948
Samantarapur	Khurdha	360	Imperial Type	Hoard
Salipur	Cuttack	379	Imperial Type	Hoard
Sonepur	Suvarnapur	162	Kosala or Janapada Type	Hoard
Middle Mahanadi Valley	Bolangir	19	Imperial Type	Stray Finds
Kharligarh	Kalahandi	01	Unidentified	Surface Survey
Budhigarh	Kalahandi	04	Unidentified	Surface Survey

From the distribution of punch-marked coins shown above it is clear that during the pre-Mauryan and post-Mauryan periods, Orissa was a part and parcel to the early city/state formation and trade mechanism. The evidence of large number of imperial variety coins directs towards trans-regional trade activity. The finding of Kosala or Janapada type of coins from Sonepur (one and half km from Manamunda-Asurgarh) is really important in terms of the activity and role of the centre. It may also be presumed that some sort of local autonomy was granted to the centre in terms of circulation of its own coinage. Unfortunately, several hoards of punch-marked coins have been smelted and smuggled by the treasure hunters (Personal observation at Jaugada, Suvarnapur, Kharligarh, etc.).

Archaeological Evidences

The trade activity in any region or culture has a share in the overall development of a society or community, particularly in the domain of economic prosperity. For the interpretation of trade and mechanism operated during the Early Historic period, it was imperative to correlate the ceramic assemblage (Figs. 16 and 17) both by scientific (XRD) as also comparative analyses, numismatic, literary (both religious and secular), traveller's accounts and above all the ecological potential of the landscape, including perennial rivers and navigation systems. It was also felt necessary to conduct an intensive ethnographic study on aspects of current trading patterns as also the boat making tradition, mode of exchange, commodities, season of operation, symbolic aspects and behavioural pattern.

Some of the representative potsherds found from the Early Historic sites of Manamunda-Asurgarh, Deuli and Marjakud were subjected for X-Ray Diffraction Analysis to understand the distribution pattern and possible migration of the pottery, trade contact and the trade mechanism. In this process, samples of local clay used by the potters and representative types of potsherds from Red Ware with Grey Core and Grey Ware, Red Slipped Ware, Knobbed Ware and Grey Ware, Black Slipped Ware were used. It was found that the mineral patterns present in the pottery sample as also in the soil sample do not match with each other. Most of the potsherds like the Black Slipped Ware, Red Slipped Ware and Knobbed ware as also Grey Ware have a striking similarity in the mineral pattern and composition with that of the sites located in the coastal part of Orissa like Radhanagara and Sisupalgarh, Chandraketugarh-Tamluk region of West Bengal and sites in the Chhotanagpur plateau like Kaundinyapura (Tripathy 2002b). It is also observed that the presence of Knobbed Ware, found sporadically in entire Western and Central Orissa, is due to extensive and far-flung trade network operated between the Coastal Orissa with the hinterland, comprising the entire western and a portion of central Orissa. Besides, Red Slipped Ware, Grey Ware and Black Slipped Ware were transported from coastal Orissan centres to the hinterland and were adopted by the local population for both domestic and ritualistic practices. As Knobbed Ware was basically a symbolic landscape pertaining to Buddhist cosmology and its importance, the finding of such variety is meagre in number.

Besides the above scientific analysis of pottery through clay pattern analysis, a wide array of archaeological evidences of early trade and exchange network in Orissa are available. The data for understanding the trade relationships of western and Central Orissa with the coastal regions as also with the Middle Ganga valley and the Vidarbha region comes mainly from the archaeological sites located on the riverbanks of the Mahanadi, the Tel and their tributaries. It has been observed from the evidences that the trade route, which was earlier known as the Dakshinapatha mentioned in various literary and epigraphic sources, passed through Central and Western Orissa touching important places like Nehena, Narla-Asurgarh, Kharligarh, Budhigarh, Manamunda-Asurgarh and Kardi, where hoards of punch marked coins of both Kosala and Imperial varieties have been recorded. The following is a brief sketch of the archaeological evidences that reflect the trade connections of the Early Historic Orissa.

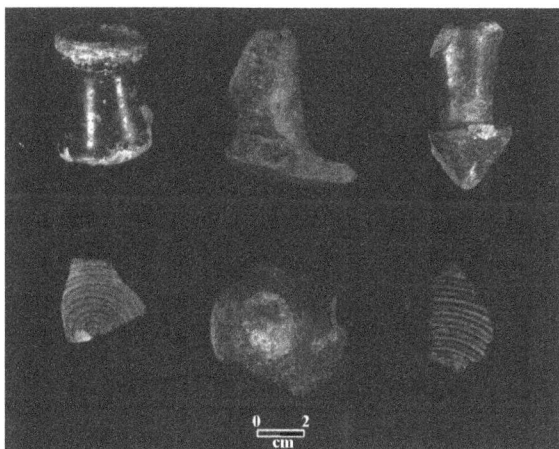

Figure 16: Ceramic assemblage

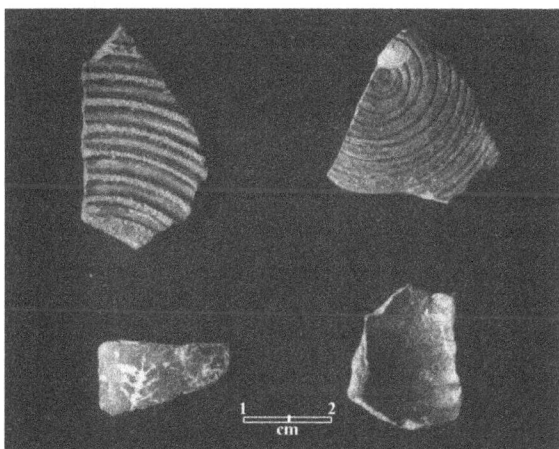

Figure 16: Ceramic assemblage

Knobbed Ware is very crucial in terms of trade, cultural and religious relations/influences in determining trade contacts of Western/Central Orissa with the coastal urban centres. This ware has been reported from the Early Historic sites like Radhanagar (Mishra 2000: 507-549), Sisupalgarh (Lal 1949: 65-102), Jaugada (*IAR* 1956-57: 30-31) in the coastal belt and from Manamunda-Asurgarh (Tripathy 2002),

Marjakud (2000a: 60-67), Deuli (Tripathy and Joglekar 1997-98), Budhigarh (Mohanty and Mishra 2005), Narla-Asurgarh (Behera 1982: 1-8), Nehena (Brandtner 1994: 101-114) from the hinterland Orissa. As most of the knobbed ware-yielding sites in coastal Orissa are associated with early Buddhism, the finding of this ware in the hinterland Orissa indirectly signifies the influence of Buddhism in the area. From the recent explorations and excavations conducted at and around Radhanagar clearly delineates that Knobbed ware was manufactured at the site and then circulated to different parts with whom the people of Radhanagar had trade and ideological connections. The collection of this pottery excels the total collection of Knobbed ware from the Indian sub-continent (personal observation 2006). In fact, this is the only evidence to suggest on the theory of distribution of this pottery in upland/hinterland Orissa. The site of Nehena has shown Knobbed Ware sherds with a thick black slip on both interior and exterior surfaces. The site of Marjakud has yielded the same type but with a graffiti motif, resembling a trident, on the exterior surface (base portion). The Knobbed Ware found at the site of Manamunda-Asurgarh is characterized by a thick black slip on both the surfaces. Hence, it is difficult to understand whether all the sherds of Knobbed Ware were transported from the coastal region to the hinterland or it was also locally manufactured after obtaining sufficient knowledge of its manufacture techniques. It is also difficult to determine whether the settlements were under the firmament of early Buddhism, which was the state religion as evident from a number of Hinayana Buddhist settlements and sites in the coastal part of Orissa. It is plausible that Knobbed Ware was transported and utilized by a section of people engaged in trade activity and who were Buddhists. Interestingly, a large section of Buddhist population inhabit nowadays on the banks of Mahanadi along the trade route in Central Orissa at places like Kantilo, Baideswar, Khandpara. Even Boudh region of Central Orissa has yielded several Buddhist images, of course belonging to the Early Medieval period, which are being worshipped by the Hindus on several occasions. Hence, it is quite possible that Knobbed Ware, especially made out of Black Slipped Ware were being transported to different parts of Orissa too and the Buddhist community formed the community of traders in ancient Orissa which is again testified by the literary descriptions of Tapusa and Bhallika, two merchant brothers of Ukkala (ancient Orissa) attached with Lord Buddha in the 6th century B.C. It is certain from the limited occurrence of sherds that this ware was not used by the common mass of the society. However, the evidence of Knobbed Ware is a direct indication of trade and relations operating between Coastal Orissa, and Central and Western Orissa during the Early Historic period (Tripathy 2000: 60-67; 2002b).

Another most common Early Historic ceramic type is the Red Slipped Ware found at the sites in hinterland western and central Orissa. The scientific analysis of the pottery shows that it was probably manufactured locally, but similar pottery has been retrieved from the coastal Orissan sites such as Radhanagar, Palur, Manikapatana, Sisupalgarh etc., and hence, it is difficult to ascertain whether this technique was borrowed by these sites from the hinterland region or vice versa. So also, this pottery figures commonly in the sites of Middle Ganga valley and Chandraketugarh-Tamluk complex. It is most likely that this technique originated in this region and later on migrated to the eastern part of India and this hypothesis has been drawn from the quantity and percentage of this pottery found in Western and Central Orissa.

So far as the trade contacts of the hinterland with other regions especially coastal Orissa is concerned, the Black Slipped Ware found in profuse amount from almost all the Early Historic sites gives clues for trade activity of the region. This ware is characterized by a glazed black slip on both interior and exterior surfaces, and the basic shapes include dishes and bowls (both shallow and narrow variety). There is an opinion (Brandtner 1994: 101-114; Makhan Lal 1984; Lahiri 1992) that this ceramic originated in the middle Ganga valley and gradually spread towards the east and further towards Orissa. It has also been found at different sites like Ujjain, Vidisha, Chandraketugarh, Radhanagar, Sisupalgarh and at other important Early Historic urban centres. Interestingly, this type of ceramics has been unearthed in profuse amount at the site of Radhanagar which speaks that a sort of inferior NBPW were manufactured in Orissa and this ware was sufficing the need of original NBPWs as it is also deeply associated with Buddhist principles, especially begging bowls (Black Slipped Ware differs from the Northern Black Polished Ware in its fabric, and can be taken as a degenerated form of the latter). Hence, the term Black Slipped Ware is more appropriate for its distinct characteristic. This ware, as the mineral patterns of the clay shows, is an important indicator of the trade contacts of this region with the Middle Ganga Valley as also coastal Orissa.

The presence of Red Ware with grey core in the hinterland has tremendous impact as it is found associated with a number of important sites like Chandraketugarh (West Bengal) and Mahasthan (Bangladesh), Manikapatana-Palur harbour complex (coastal Orissa) and Radhanagar. The occurrence of this ware in a relatively low frequency signifies the trade connection of hinterland with far off places and trading centres. Besides, a few sherds of Fine Grey Ware have been recovered from the Early Historic sites of Manamunda Asurgarh, Sahupara, Marjakud, Budhigarh and Kardi pointing to contacts of this area with regions of the Middle Ganga Valley and Chandraketugarh-Tamluk complex, Radhanagar and Manaikapatana-Palur harbour complex. This evidence suggests a land route and movement of goods from the Middle Ganga Valley to the far south through Orissa via centres like Manamunda-Asurgarh (Tripathy 2002b), Radhanagar (Mishra 2000), Arikamedu (Begley 1986: 297-321), etc. and then traded through sea route to the port site of Manthai in Sri Lanka.

Besides, ceramic coming from distant sources, there are other archaeological evidences supporting a regional trade network, in which iron in both unfinished and finished forms play a vital role. Iron served as a principal commodity to be supplied to the settlements of coastal Orissa. Hinterland part of the State is rich in iron ore deposits and almost all the sites in western and Central Orissa are found to be associated with smelting activity as evident from the findings of numerous pieces of iron ore (Fig. 17), slag (Fig. 18) as also blanks, including finished equipments (Fig. 19) on the surface as also in stratified context at Marjakud (Tripathy and Joglekar 1997-98: 117-119), Deuli and Manamunda-Asurgarh (Tripathy 2002a: 81-97), Budhigarh and Kharligarh (Mohanty and Mishra 2005: 97-124), Narla-Asurgarh (Behera 1982: 1-8) and Nehena (Brandtner 1994: 101-114). None of the sites located in the coastal part of Orissa barring the harbour complex of Manikapatana and Palur from where large amount of iron ores, slags as also iron implements were found (Pradhan *et al.* 2000: 473-494). Even the most important urban centre of Orissa, Radhanagar is devoid of such evidences. From this it is quite clear that smelting was perhaps practiced by the hinterland population specialized in this industry. The hinterland Orissa comprising districts of Bolangir, Kalahandi, Mayurbhanj, Keonjhar and Deogarh where rocks of pyrite, haematite and magnetite deposits are in plenty were exploited by the Early Historic people as a consequence of the 'Second Urbanization' or 'Early Historic Urbanization'. Despite the non-discovery of furnaces at the sites either from the surface or from the trial pits, it is presumed that the sites were engaged in smelting iron, and a systematic horizontal excavation at some of the potential sites from where examples of ore, slag and iron implements are found would definitely reveal this factor.

The region of Central and Western Orissa is rich in precious and semiprecious gem deposits. Gemstones formed one of the major trading commodities of the western Orissan settlements during the Early Historic period as the coastal part of Orissa is devoid of such deposits. Semiprecious gemstone beads have been recovered from the sites like Radhanagar, Sisupalgarh, Manikapatana and other sites located in the plains of Orissa, and it is possible that either raw material or finished beads were transported to these sites from Western/Central Orissa. The sites of hinterland Orissa such as Marjakud (retrieved from stratified context), Manamunda-Asurgarh, Budhigarh and Narla-Asurgarh have revealed semiprecious gemstone beads. Numerous references have been corroborated by literary as also traveller's accounts which delineate that right from the very ancient period hinterland Orissa (especially western and central Orissa) was exploited by the traders which even included the Romans.

Figure 17: Iron ore nodules

Figure 18: Iron Slag

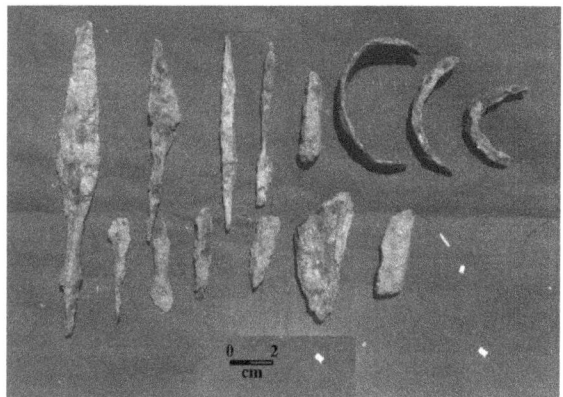
Figure 19: Iron Implements

Ethnoarchaeological Observations

For the interpretation of archaeological materials by which socio-cultural and economic aspects can be observed, the ethnoarchaeological approach has emerged as an analytical tool in recent years (Kramer 1979). Archaeological remains unearthed and located from excavations and surface explorations can be best interpreted with the help of ethnographic parallels of living pattern, material culture and trading patterns which serves as a link between the archaeological record and the ethnographic data and is otherwise known as 'action archaeology' (Kleindeinst and Watson 1956). To quote Longacre (1991: 10), "if we and our students do not undertake ethnoarchaeological research soon, future archaeologists would wonder how we could have been so short sighted. In that spirit let me make a second call to action archaeology-a call with some urgency because if we wait much longer, it will be too late". However, ethnographic studies to correlate the archaeological data is only possible in the areas where socio-cultural and economic changes are scant and in this context, Orissa proves to be one of the best states in India to practice such models.

63

Extensive ethnographic studies were conducted to understand the overall aspects of Early Historic trade mechanism operated by the ancient traders of Orissa (Tripathy 2002b). To establish trade and trade routes, the data on ethno-history, ethnography and archaeological material proves to be imperative. Such data on related topics that has been given equal emphasis in this study is the inland trade network. Ethnographic studies on boat making traditions, forest produces and medicinal herbs (Fig. 20), ceramic and terracotta manufacture (Fig. 21), gemstone exploitation (Fig. 22) and current riverine trade patterns (Fig. 23) were carried out for a better understanding of the functional aspects of the Early Historic sites and of the nature of inland trade connection and trade routes.

It is suggested from these observations and from the archaeological and literary evidences that the availability of a variety of natural resources such as iron deposits (Fig. 24), gemstones and forest produces in the region of hinterland Orissa played a key role in the inland trade network. Most of these sources are absent or partially absent in the coastal part of Orissa, especially in the deltaic portion where the coastal urban centres flourished, which necessitated the development of a trade connection between Central/Western Orissa and Coastal/deltaic Orissa. It seems likely that the establishment of trade relationship stimulated, to some extent, the process of urbanization in Central/Western and Coastal Orissa. This approach was basically undertaken to locate the trade route, resource exploitation, commodities exchanged as also the behavioural pattern of the communities associated with this mechanism.

Figure 20: Medicinal herbs

Figure 21: Terracotta and pottery manufacturing

Figure 22: Gemstone exploitation

Figure 23: Trading boats in Mahanadi

The Routes

The emergence of empires and Mahajanapadas in 6th century B.C. paved the way for a widespread trade network with routes crisscrossing the entire Indian subcontinent and thereby allowing the flow of commodities as well as ideological thoughts. Parallel to this trend was the evolution of trade centres, which became known for their political character as well. In this context, mention may be made of cities like Ujjain, Vidisha, Taxila, Chandraketugarh, Mahasthangarh, Paithan, Sopara, Bharoach, Arikamedu etc. which

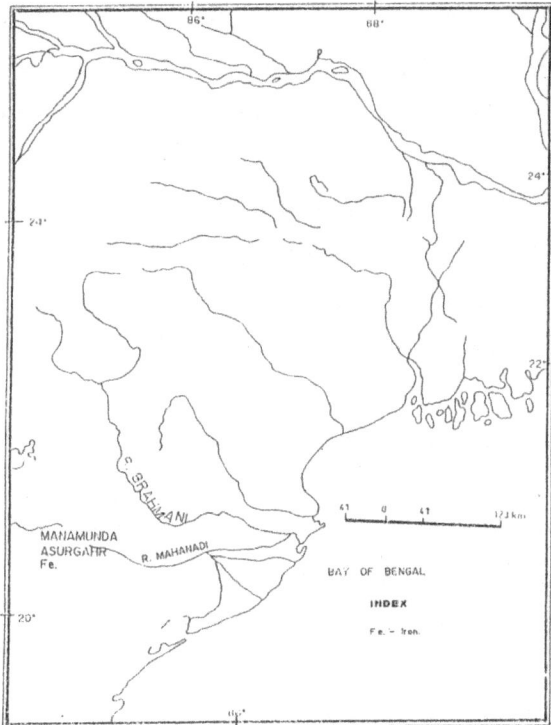
Figure 24: Iron deposits

controlled the trade mechanism during the Early Historic period. Later on due to the establishment of the Mauryan Empire in Central India wielded a great influence on the entire country as it encompassed almost all the parts of Indian subcontinent, including the southern part. To manage such a vast empire, the Mauryan polity required having important strategic places that would function as its provincial headquarters. Besides, there was also a necessity of well-connected trading systems. Hence, there appeared a number of communication routes that linked the northern parts of India with the southern portion. Besides, there were also overseas connections, especially with the South East Asian countries/islands in which the people of Kalinga or ancient Orissa took a leading role. As it is evident from several sources, archaeological, literary and numismatic, long before the advent of the Mauryans, Orissa was well-connected with different lines of trade and communication. Hathigumpha inscription of Kharavela, mentions that the great emperor Kharavela invaded the Magadhan empire and brought back the image of Kalinga Jina and for this purpose he must have needed a route for the mobility of his vast army. Also, the Allahabad Pillar inscription of Samudragupta speaks about the existence of the Dakhsinapatha which he followed during his south Indian campaign (Sahu 1989).

The geographical circulation of punch-marked coins in Orissa (Panda 2000: 551-565) as shown in the table, seem to suggest the existence of at least three trade routes (Fig. 25). This connected Orissa with different centres of India, particularly with the Central and South India. The first route ran from Tosali to Chandraketugarh and then to Mahasthangarh via places like Kichakgarh, Viratgarh and other important urban centres, along the rivers Vaitarani and Burhabalang. This route had a great significance as it passed through one of the important iron ore belts of India. The other route joined Tosali with Ujjain via centres of Madhya Pradesh (Sripura and Vidisha). Within Orissa, this route traversed along the rivers Mahanadi and Tel touching on important settlements such as Manamunda-Asurgarh, Narla-Asurgarh, Kharligarh, Budhigarh, Nehena etc. and joined Ujjain through sites in Vidarbha like Kaundinyapura. The discovery of punch-marked coins from these areas corroborates the fact that this route was widely followed for trade and transportation during the Early Historic period. The third route, which is yet to be ascertained, might have ran from Toshali Nagara (most possibly present day Radhanagar) within the passage between the Mahanadi and the Brahmani. Unfortunately, very less exploration has been conducted in this passage and hence the route followed by emperor Ashoka in his famous Kalinga war remains unexplored and enigmatic. It is quite clear that the two routes mentioned above were not followed by the Mauryan army as none of the sites have yielded sufficient archaeological material like Northern Black Polished Ware, Mauryan weapons, or any other pottery or antiquities. It is neither supported by epigraphic records of Ashoka. Hence, it would be imperative to explore the areas between the valleys of Mahanadi and the Brahmani to determine the exact route followed by the Mauryan army. The region between Mahanadi and the Brahmani is approachable and nearer to the Mauryan capital city of Pataliputra, then the other two routes. There was absolutely no necessity for emperor Ashoka to follow a distant route viz. Toshali-Ujjain via Central and Western Orissa and Toshali-Chandraketugarh via Kichakgarh and Viratgarh in northeast Orissa. However, this requires more extensive and systematic research to interpret and conclude.

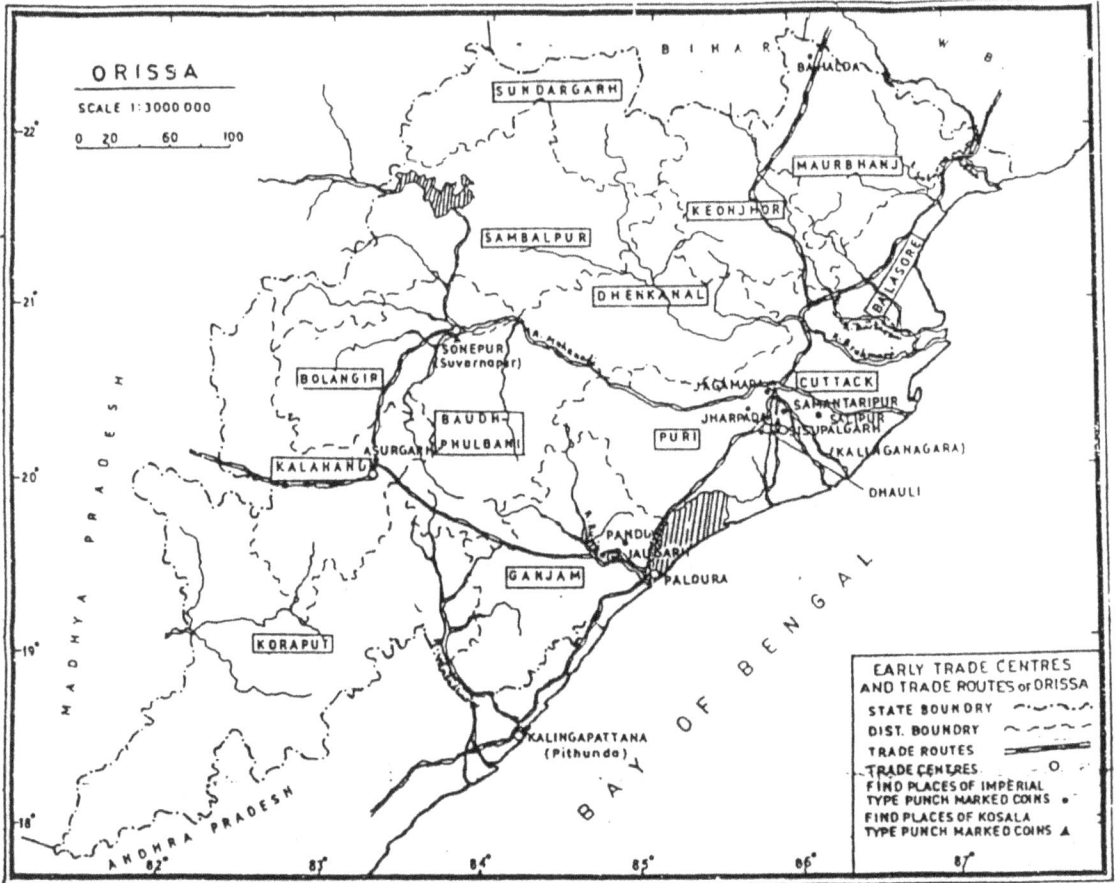
Figure 25: Trade routes in Orissa

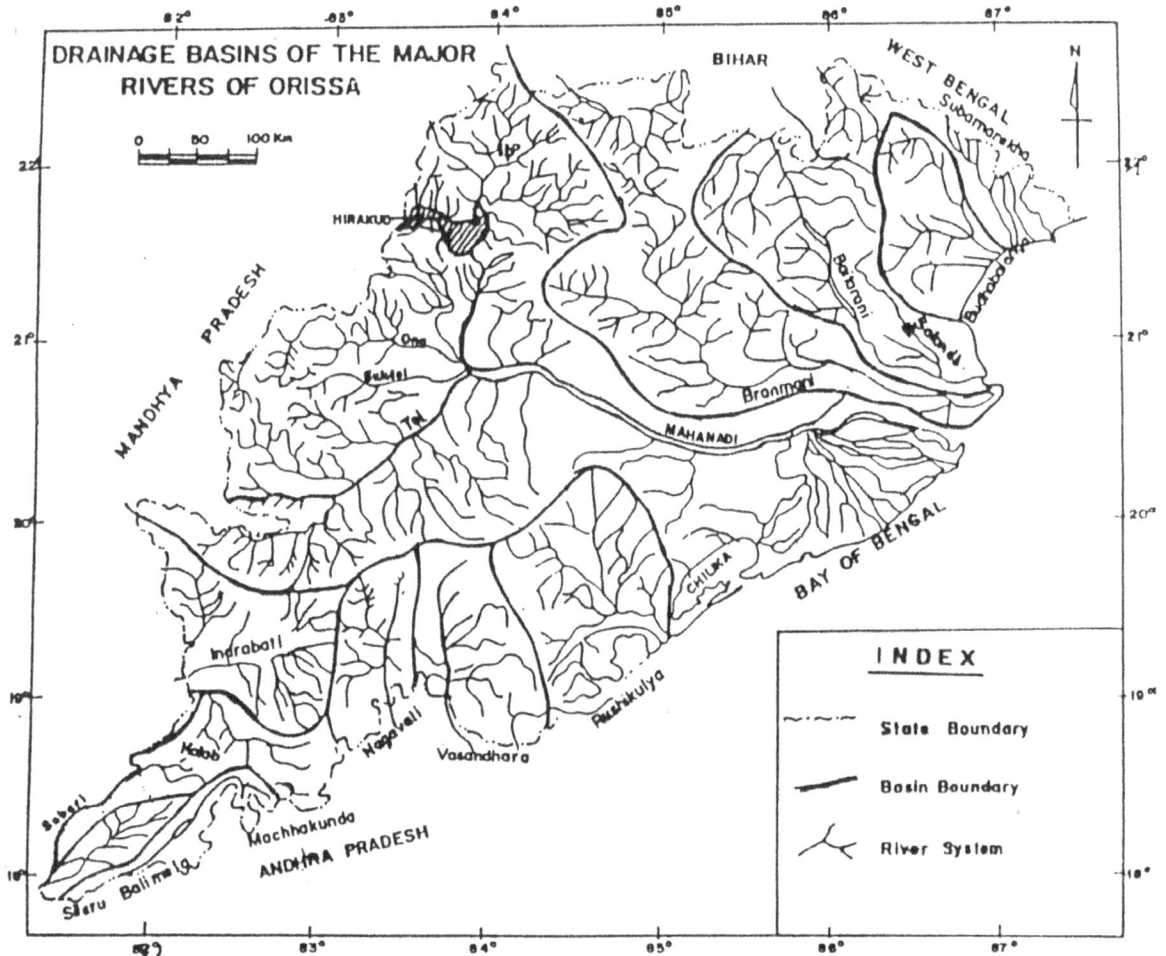
Figure 26: Drainage map of Orissa

It is also evident from the available sources that the rivers, including some small ones contributed a lot for the flourishing of the routes and trade patterns. The major rivers of Orissa (Fig. 26) viz. the Mahanadi, Brahmani and Tel served as routes in impenetrable forest tracts of Central and Western Orissa. This is evident from the discovery of a number of Early Historic sites with borrowed material located on either their banks or on islands (Fig. 27) and dunes.

Figure 27: Early historic site of Marjakud

In the present discussion, it is important to discuss the pattern of communication in Central and Western Orissa. It has been observed from both the colonial accounts and ethnographic parallels that the Mahanadi served as the main route of trade and transportation. The route through the Mahanadi connected the coastal parts of Orissa (Cuttack) with the Central and a portion of Western Orissa (up to Manamunda-Asurgarh in the Middle Mahanadi Valley). At Manamunda-Asurgarh the route took a turn and followed the river Tel. Simultaneously, there was also a parallel land route along the river Tel, as the river is not navigable in its upstream beyond Budhigarh. The discovery of a number of Early Historic sites along the Mahanadi and the Tel indicates that this route was widely followed. Along the banks there were many market centres like Kantilo, Baidyapur,

Marjakud, Kardi, Boudh, Baunsuni and Manamunda-Asurgarh. This route with some deviations at certain points is still being followed. This riverine route had a parallel land route running along it, which is now known as the Old Jagannath Road and followed by the pilgrims from Chhattisgarh and entire Western Orissa even today. There is no sufficient archaeological or any other evidence for the use of water route upstream of Manamunda-Asurgarh. Most likely, the route took a turn at the confluence of the Mahanadi and the Tel, from where a parallel land route was followed up to the Vidarbha region. This is substantiated by the discovery of a large number of urban and small sites on the banks of the Tel and its tributaries. The material culture represented at these sites clearly highlights the role of the Mahanadi and the Tel in the diffusion of trade in ancient Orissa.

To connect southern part of the subcontinent, Orissa was having several land and river routes and in some cases sea-route was also adopted. It is also evident from the archaeological material from Manikapatna and Radhanagar that there was a direct link of Orissa with sites like Arikamedu and Korkai in Tamil Nadu and Manthai in Sri Lanka. The ceramic findings from the site of Palur-Manikapatna harbour complex and from Radhanagar has a striking similarity with the pottery found from Arikamedu, Korkai and Manthai. However, this needs more comparative as well as scientific analysis of the material. It is also evident from the literary and epigraphic records that ancient Orissa spreaded up to the Krishna-Godavari delta in the Tamil Nadu-Andhra border.

The Arthasashtra recommends the use of river routes (*nadipatha* or *baripatha*) over the land route (*Sthalapatha*), as in those times large forest tracts covered most parts of the Indian peninsula impending access and communication (Kangle 1965). Major navigable rivers therefore assumed importance and functioned as the routes of trade and commerce.

Problems and Prospect

Major Early Historic sites of Orissa like Narla-Asurgarh and Manamaunda-Asurgarh were excavated in a limited scale and hundreds of Early Historic sites have been brought to light, but unfortunately none of them have been excavated horizontally which is essential for interpreting the data (Tripathy 2002b). However, the archaeological material from these limited excavations has yielded very significant results. Narla-Asurgarh excavation limited to three trenches, that also not up to virgin soil has yielded a hoard of 539 silver punch-marked coins as also a number of Northern Black Polished Ware sherds and Rouletted Ware (later ware is author's personal observation at the Museum of Khariar, Kalahandi). This possesses utmost importance in terms of urbanization and trade as it reveals Mauryan material in hinterland Orissa. The archaeological material yielded from Manamunda-Asurgarh excavation provoked several thoughts among young archaeologists to study the site in a holistic perspective. A thorough analysis of pottery and other antiquities including the landscape of the site was conducted by the present author (Tripathy 2002b). The archaeological material yielded from the site indicates towards a close relationship with almost all important urban centres like Radhanagara, Sisupalgarh and Jaugada in coastal Orissa and the port site of Manikapatana and Palur. There is absolutely no doubt that the site played an important role in the diffusion of urbanization and state formation. The site yielded several types of ceramic wares such as Red Slipped Ware, Black Slipped ware and Black and Red Ware. Besides, the Red Ware with a Grey Core is also transported from outside. The pottery assemblage of Manamunda-Asurgarh has been subjected to X-Ray Diffraction Analysis (Tripathy 2002b) which speaks that Knobbed Ware, Black Slipped Ware, Black and Red Ware as also Red Slipped Ware were brought from Coastal part of Orissa to the central/western Orissa through extensive trade network. Ethnographic parallels were also drawn from the existing trade activity between western/central and coastal Orissa (Tripathy 2000: 60-67; 2002b; 2007).

It is imperative to note that all urban centres in Orissa are located on the banks of small rivers than bigger ones as also in a little distance from the seacoast and to the major rivers. Probables reasons could be it is not possible to carry large fleets for attack on the small rivers, less flood dangers and for protection. For example, Radhanagara is located on the banks of Kelua, a tributary of the Bhahmani, Sisupalgarh on the banks of the Gangua a small rivulet of the river Daya, Jaugada on the banks of river Rishikulya, Narla-Asurgarh on the banks of the Sandul, a tributary of the Tel, Kharligarh and Budhiagarh on the banks of Rahul, a tributary of the Tel. The Early Historic site of Manamunda-Asurgarh is the only urban centre, which is located at the confluence of the Mahanadi and the Tel, indicating the centre's flourishing and briskly trade and merchandize. With a meeting place of at least three trade routes 1. Sisupalgarh-Ujjain via Tel and the land route along the Tel, 2. Radhanagara-Manamunda Asurgarh-Vidisha-Ujjain, and 3. Manamunda-Asurgarh-Sripura-Vidisha-Ujjain, the site has the maximum trade potential like Sisupalgarh and Radhanagar.

From the archaeological, literary and other evidences it is quite clear that Orissa like the Gangetic valley also came into the firmament of the Second Urbanization. The evidence of a number of Early Historic forts with elaborate planning for protection and hydraulic system and a number of peripheral settlements clearly indicates the character of urbanization in Early Historic Orissa. Out of the eight forts, only one i.e., Radhanagara is honeycomb shaped. The archaeological material from the site dates back to pre-Mauryan era on the basis of the comparative analysis of the ceramic assemblage and other antiquities. This clearly suggests that Radhanagara served as the capital of ancient Orissa and is the earliest fort in entire Orissa. On the other hand the site of Narla- Asurgarh most likely served as the capital of the Atavika territory mentioned in Ashokan Edicts. Manamunda–Asurgarh being located in between these two great centres served as a principal trading centre with having brisk trade network with several parts of the Indian Sub-continent, especially with the Coastal Orissa, West Bengal, Chhotanagpur plateau and sites in Middle Ganga Plains.

From the above discussion it is quite clear that trade in various forms was mainly responsible for urban growth in Orissa. The thriving trade network of ancient Orissa with several Southeast Asian urban centres as also sometimes with the Roman world was the principal factor for the formation of complex society in Orissa. Even the hinterland parts of Orissa, which were connected to each other by several water and land routes, acted as resource bearing zones as the entire region is replete with gemstone deposits and forest resources. The flourishing nature of the coastal urban centres was possible due to the rich resources which were exploited in a systematic manner for trading. More archaeological work in this respect will unravel the hidden aspects pertaining to urbanization and state formation in early Orissa. The concept of urbanization in hinterland Orissa has to be studied in detail by keeping in view the landscape and resources and the early state formation in Orissa as a whole.

Acknowledgement

I am indebted to my Guruji, Prof. V.N. Misra who encouraged me in several ways and gave me opportunities to work on different aspects of archaeology. His contribution to my archaeological career is immense and in personal level also he inspired me as a guide, friend, philosopher, and above all shaped my research aptitude in a systematic way. However, I shoulder the responsibility of mistakes, if any.

References

Acharya, P. 1955. *Sambalpur Yatra* (in Oriya): Translations of the Account of British Diamond Merchant T. Motte (1765). Cuttack: Utkal University.

Agrawalla, V.S. 1963. *India as known to Panini.* Poona: Deccan College.

Allchin, F.R. 1989. City and State Formation in the Early Historic South Asia, South Asian Studies 5: 1-16.

Allchin, F.R. 1990. Patterns of City Formation in Early Historic South Asia, South Asian Studies 6: 163-173.

Allchin, F.R. 1995. *The Archaeology of Early Historic South Asia-The Emergence of Cities and States.* Cambridge: Cambridge University Press.

Anderson, A. 1984. *Interpreting Pottery.* Oxford: Oxford University Press, pp. 20-21.

Archaeological Report. Pp. 430.

Apte, M.C. 1893. *The Padma Purana.* Poona: Anandsharma Sanskrit Series.

Basa, K.K. 1995. Early Westerly Trade of Southeast Asia: A World System Perspective, *Bulletin of the Deccan College Post-Graduate and Research Institute* 53-54: 357-375.

Basa, K.K. 1996. Archaeological Approach and Ethnographic Models for Trade and Exchange: A Critical Study, *The Eastern Anthropologist* 49(2): 109-139.

Basa, K.K. 2005. *River Systems and the Emergence of Complex Society in Orissa,* in *River Valley Cultures of India* (K.K. Chakravarty and G.L. Badam Eds.), pp. 69-83. Bhopal: Indira Gandhi Rashtriya Manav Sangrahalaya.

Basu, S., H.P. Dani and D.P. Pati 1995. *Eastern Ghats,* in *Advance in Ecology and Environment* (P.C. Mishra, N. Behera, B.K. Senapati and B.C. Guru Eds.), pp. 367-369. New Delhi: Ashish Publishing House.

Begley, V. 1986. *From Iron Age to Early Historic in South Indian Archaeology,* in *Studies in Archaeology of India and Pakistan* (J. Jacobson Ed.), pp. 297-321. New Delhi: American Institute of Indian Studies.

Brandtner, M. 1994. Archaeology of Western Orissa: Finds from Nehena, in South Asian Archaeology 1993, Vol. 1 (A. Parpola and P. Koskikalio), pp. 101-114. Helsinki: Suomalainen Tiedeakatemia.

Chakrabarti, D.K. 1995a. *Archaeology of Ancient Indian Cities.* New Delhi: Oxford University Press.

Chakrabarti, D.K. 1995b. Buddhist Sites Across South Asia as Influenced by Political and Economic Forces, *World Archaeology* 27(2): 185-201.

Champakalaxmi, T. 1996. *Trade, Ideology and Urbanization.* Delhi: Oxford University Press.

Cowell, E.C. 1955. *The Jataka (Serivannijja Jataka),* Vol. 1. London: Luzac and Co.

Das, J.N. 1997. Mineral, Ores, Output Growth Doubles, *Odisha Today* 11: 18.

Deloche, J. 1990. *Transport and Communication in India: Water Transport* (Vol. 2). Oxford: Oxford University Press.

Dutt, M.N. 1895. *The Ramayana.* Calcutta: Chaukhamba Publication.

Erdosy, G. 1988. *Urbanization and Early Historic India.* London: BAR International Series.

Gauerson, H., P. Legris, V.M. Meher-Homji, J. Fontanel, J.P. Pascal, K. Chandrahassan and A. Delacourt 1995. *International Map of Vegetation and of Environment Conditions, Notes on Sheet of Orissa.* Pondichery: Publication du de'partment d' e'cology.

Ghosh, A. 1973. *City in Early Historical India.* Shimla: Indian Institute of Advanced Study.

Heitzman, J. 1984. *Early Buddhism, Trade and Empire,* in *Studies in the Archaeology and Palaeoanthropology of South Asia* (K.A.R. Kennedy and G.L. Possehl Eds.), Pp. 121-138. New Delhi: Oxford University Press.

Hunter, W.W. 1872. *Orissa,* Vol. 1. London: Smith Elder and Co.

IAR-Indian Archaeology: A Review. Journal of the Archaeological Survey of India. New Delhi.

Kangle, R.P. 1965. *Arthasashtra of Kautilya* (Translated from the Original Text), Vol. 2, Section 29, Para 37, P. 115. Bombay: Bombay University Press.

Khuntia, S. (n.d.) *Geology of Gemstone Resources of Orissa.* Orissa: Orissa Mining Corporation.

Kleindeinst, M. and P.J. Watson 1956. Action Archaeology: The Archaeological Inventory of a Living Community, *Anthropology Tomorrow* 5: 75-78.

Kosambi, D.D. 1989. *The Culture and Civilization of Ancient India in Historical Outline.* New Delhi: Vikash Arya Publishers.

Kramer, C. 1979. *Ethnoarchaeology: Implications of Ethnography for Archaeology.* New York: Columbia University Press.

Lahiri, N. 1992. *The Archaeology of Indian Trade Routes Up To c. 200 B.C.* New Delhi: Oxford University Press.

Lal, B.B. 1949. Sisupalgarh: An Early Historic Fort in the Eastern Coast, *Ancient India* 5: 62-105.

Lal, Makhan 1984. *Early Human Colonization in the Ganga-Yamuna Doab with Special Reference to Kanpur District.* New Delhi: B.R. Publishers.

Longacre, W. A. 1991. *Ceramic Ethnoarchaeology: An Introduction,* pp. 1-10. Tuscon: The University of Arizona Press.

Majumdar, S.N. 1927. *Ancient India as Described by Ptolemy.* Calcutta: Baptist Mission Press.

Mishra, J. 2000. *Radhanagara: Early Buddhism, Urban Structure and Trade,* in *Archaeology of Orissa* (K.K. Basa and P. Mohanty Eds.), pp. 507-549. New Delhi: Pratibha Prakashan.

Mohanty, P. and B. Tripathy 1998. The Prehistoric, Protohistoric and the Early Historic Cultures of Orissa, *Pragdhara* (Journal of the U.P. State Department of Archaeology, Lucknow) 8: 69-98.

Mohanty, P.K. and B. Mishra 2005. *From Stone Age to the Early Historic: Recent Archaeological Discoveries in Kalahandi District, Orissa*, in *River Valley Cultures of India* (K.K. Chakravarty and G.L. Badam Eds.), pp. 97-124. Bhopal. Indira Gandhi Rashtriya Manav Sangrahalaya.

Mohanty, R.K. and Monika, L. Smith. 2006. Sisupalgarh Excavations 2005, Man and Environment XXXI (1): 27-32.

Morrison, K.D. 1995. Trade, Urbanism and Agricultural Expansion: Buddhist Monastic Institutions and the State in the Early Historic Western Deccan, *World Archaeology* 27(2): 203-221.

Narain, A.K. and T.N. Roy 1976. *Excavations at Rajghat. Varanasi.* Benaras Hindu University.

Panda, S.K. 2000. *Trade and Trade-Routes in Orissa*, in *Archaeology of Orissa* (K.K. Basa and P. Mohanty Eds.), Pp. 551-565. New Delhi: Pratibha Prakashan.

Pradhan, S. 1995. A Note on a Punch-marked Coin found from Manamunda Excavation, *Journal of the Numismatic Survey of India* IIV (1-2): 26-28.

Prusty, H. and P. Mohanty 1995. Langudi: A Unique Rock-Cut Buddhist Site in Orissa, *Bulletin of the Deccan College Post Graduate and Research Institute* 53: 325-327.

Rangarajan, C. 1994. *Kautilya Arthasashtra*. New Delhi: Penguin Books.

Ray, H.P. 1986. *Monastery and Guild*. Delhi: Oxford University Press.

Ray, H.P. 1989. Early Maritime Contacts between South and Southeast Asia, *Journal of South Asian Studies* XX (1): 42-54.

Ray, H.P. 1994. *The Winds of Change, Buddhism and Maritime Links of Early South Asia*. Delhi: Oxford University Press.

Rennel, J. 1783. *Memoirs of a Map of Hindoostan*. London: M. Brown.

Roy, P.C. 1926. *The Mahabharata*. Calcutta: Bangavasi Edition.

Sahu, B.P. 1996. Situating Early Historical Trade in Orissa, in *Indian Archaeology Since Independence* (K.M. Shrimali Ed.), Pp. 95-109. Delhi: Amit Printing Works.

Sahu, N.K. 1982. Excavations at Asurgarh, District Kalahandi, in *Interim Excavation Report* (S.C. Behera Ed.), Pp. 1-8. Jyoti Vihar: Sambalpur University.

Sahu, N.K. 1964. *History of Orissa*. Bhubaneswar: Utkal University.

Sarao, K.T.S. 1990. *Urban Centres and Urbanization as Reflected in the Pali Vinaya and Sutta Pitakas*. Delhi: Vidya Nidhi Oriental.

Sharma, R.S. 1983. *Material Culture and Social Formations in Ancient India*. Delhi. Munshiram Manoharlal.

Sharma, R.S. 1991. *Urbanization in Early Historic India*, in *The City in Indian History* (Indu Banga Ed.). Delhi.

Sinha, B.N. 1971. *Geography of Orissa*: Delhi: National Book Trust.

Tripathy, B. 1996-97. Archaeological Exploration around Boudh District, Orissa: A Preliminary Report, *Bulletin of the Deccan College Research Institute* 56-57: 41-54.

Tripathy, B. 2000a. Early Historic Trade Network in Central and Western Orissa: An Ethnoarchaeological Perspective, *Man and Environment* XXV(1): 60-67.

Tripathy, B. 2000b. *Archaeology of Boudh: Central Orissa*, in *Archaeology of Orissa* (K.K. Basa and P. Mohanty Eds.), Pp. 397-416. New Delhi: Pratibha Prakashan.

Tripathy, B. 2002a. *Mesolithic and Early Historic Cultures in the Middle Mahanadi Valley, Boudh District, Central Orissa*, in *Nilabdi* (Pdt. Nilamani Mishra Commemoration Volume) (D. Pathy and B. Panda Eds.), Pp. 81-97. New Delhi: Herman Publishing House.

Tripathy, B. 2002b. *Archaeology of Boudh District, Orissa With Special Reference to the Early Historic Settlement Pattern.* Unpublished Ph. D. Dissertation, Deccan College Deemed University, Pune, Maharashtra.

Tripathy, B. 2005. *Mesolithic and Early Historic Cultures in the Middle Mahanadi and Salunki River Valleys of Boudh District, Central Orissa: An Ecological and Ethnoarchaeological Perspective*, in *River Valley Cultures of India* (K.K. Chakravarty and G.L. Badam Eds.), Pp. 169-179. Bhopal: Indira Gandhi Rashtriya Manav Sangrahalaya.

Tripathy, B. 2007 (in press). Early Historic Cultures of Orissa: A Broad Perspective, *Journal of the Asiatic Society of Bangladesh*.

Tripathy, B. and P.P. Joglekar 1997-98. Archaeological Investigations in Central Orissa, *Puratattva* 28: 117-119.

Tripathy, S. 1986. *Early and Medieval Coins and Currency System of Orissa, c. 300 B.C. to 1568 A.D.* Calcutta: Punthi Pustak.

Upadhyaya, S.C. 1961. *The Kamasutra of Vatsyana* (New Edition). Bombay: D.B. Taraporewalla and Sons.

Wadia, D.N. 1961. *Geology of India*. London: McMillan and Co. Ltd.

Wallerstein, T. 1974. *The Modern World System: Capitalist Agriculture and the Originsof the European Economy in the Sixteenth Century*. New York: Academic Press.

Watters, T. 1988. *On Yuan Chwang's Travels in India (629-645 A.D.)*, Edited by T.H. Rhys Davis and S.W. Bushell. New Delhi: Asian Educational Service.

A Study of the Nepalese Bronzes from Ancient to Medieval Periods

Mala Malla

Geographical Background

Nepal is a small, broadly rectangular country situated almost in the lap of the Himalayas. It is a buffer state between Tibetan Autonomous Region of China in the north and India in the east, west and south. Its border on the east ends at the Mechi River and the Mahakali River in the west. The elevations too vary, ranging from 40 metres in the south and 8848 metres in the north (the peak of Mt. Everest, also called Sagarmatha - "the summit touching the sky"). Glacier Rivers and high mountains make some regions difficult for access (Joshi 1986: 51-56).

The two neighbouring countries have played their own roles in influencing Nepal's culture, religion, and language, but Nepal too has had its own role in influencing their cultures. This country is inhabited by various ethnic groups having their own traditions, customs, culture and dialects. Kathmandu Valley has a unique character, which combines traits of both, Hinduism and Buddhism. Of all the Himalayan regions, Kathmandu Valley is the most developed one in the terms of civilization - the records of different periods in history amply indicate this.

Political History

Due to lack of proper exploration and excavation, the early history of Nepal is still covered in mist. The *Puranas*, like *Skanda Purana*, mention that the Valley of Kathmandu was a lake surrounded by the Siwalik Hills (Yogi *et al.* 1956: 334). According to Hindu chronicles, Lord Krishna, one of the incarnations of Vishnu, visited Nepal to rescue his grandson from the demon Shankashura also known as Mahendradamana (Yogi *et al.* 1956: 334). He was accompanied by the cowherds ('*gwalas*'). He cut the rock of Chovar, nearly eleven kilometers south of Kathmandu, with his disc and helped drain out the water of the valley. The Buddhist chronicles of Nepal ascribe the same credit to Manjusri, who came from Greater China (Wright 1877, 1972 reprint: 78). Nepal's ancient name *Nayagrad* was replaced by *Manjupattana*, named after him (Gautam 1966: 120-121).

According to the fourteenth century Gopal Raj Vamsavali, once the water was drained out of the valley, the *gwalas* established their settlement there, which were characterized by Neolithic traits (Vajracharya and Malla 1985: V). However, these accounts do not help as far as the date of these events is concerned. Scientific research has now proved that the Kathmandu Valley was actually a lake around two hundred thousand years ago (Hagen 1971: 69). A volcanic eruption might have split the rock of Chovar and the water found its way to southwards. Slowly, the water was drained out and the dampness produced different kinds of flora and fauna to grow here and setting the ground for the development toward civilization. Archaeologists and geologists have found large number of prehistoric fossils of aquatic plants and animals here (Hagen 1971: 69). Some stone tools were also discovered at Dhobi Khola, which lies between Baniyapakha and Panditgaon, near Buddhanilakantha (north-east of Kathmandu) (Sharma 1982: 250). These tools cannot be properly dated as they come from surface collection. The tools were examined by some Russian archaeologists who dated them to about 30,000 BP (Setencko 1978-1979: 1). From the above account it seems that the civilization in the Kathmandu Valley started around the beginning of the first millennium BC. Although the origin of the early inhabitants is not identified, but it has been assumed that both Mongoloid and Caucasoid races composed the population of Nepal, at least from the first millennium BC (Regmi 1969: 16).

The first authentic mention of Nepal is found in the *Arthasastra* of Kautilya, written around 4th century B.C. The writer of this treatise, in the chapter of *Kosapravesa*, recommends that the rainproof woollen blankets, made of eight pieces joined together and of black colour known as *Bhingisi*, as well as blankets known as *Apasaraka* made in Nepal were highly appreciated in Pataliputra, the kingdom of Magadha (Aryal 1967: 131; Shamsastry 1956: 81-82). In modern Nepal, the blanket weavers belong to a community by name Kirata, who are of Mongoloid type. The Gopal Raj Vamsavali mentions that the first inhabitants of the Valley were the Gopalas (cowherds), followed by the Mahishapalas (buffaloherds). During the rule of the Mahishapalas, the Kiratas from eastern Nepal invaded this Valley and began their rule (Vajracharya and Malla 1985 Folio 17: 25). The Kiratas' rule lasted for thirty-two generations. If we allow twenty-five years for one generation, then it appears that the Kiratas ruled Nepal for about eight hundred years (Regmi 1969: 56). The Gopal Raj Vamsavali enlists eleven rulers before the beginning of the Kirata rule (Vajracharya and Malla 1985: 25); so using the same counting method, the rulers before Kiratas can be estimated to have ruled for 275 years. Thus, the first dynastic rule, according to the chronicles, started a little before 1000 B.C. The inscription executed by king Vasantadeva (506-532 AD) of Lichhavi dynasty carries some words of so-called Kirata dialects, which bears out the earlier rule of Kiratas (Vajracharya 1973: 122-23, Inscription no. 25). According to the inscriptions, Sanskrit was the court language during the Lichhavi period. But a few non-Sanskrit words are also found along with the Sanskrit words, for example *Kuthera*, *Lingwal*, *Mapchok*, *Solla* also called *Sulli*, *Brahmamuga*, etc (Vajracharya 1973: 122, Inscription no. 25).

The Hanumandhoka inscription of Amsuvarma (early 7th century AD) contains a description of a palace, built by the Kiratas; that was damaged by birds, but was renovated by king Amsuvarma (Vajracharya 1973: 374, Inscription no. 91). From this description also, one can assume that the Kiratas ruled here before the Lichhavis. But all the early dynasties like Gopala, Mahishapala and Kirata, before the Lichhavis, are known only from the Vamsavalis like Gopal Raj Vamsavali, Kirkpatrik and Wright Vamsavali, but no other authentic documents are so far available to support their existence. The real history of Nepal begins with the Lichhavi rulers (Regmi 1969: 54).

It is said that Kiratas were succeeded by the Lichhavis who came from the south (Regmi 1969: 59). We do not know for sure that the Lichhavis of Nepal were the same as the Lichhavis of Vaisali in India. There are no authentic documents to prove the connection between the Lichhavi dynasties of Nepal and Northern India though there are some references in the Puranas like Himavatkhanda (Yogi *et al.* 1956: 306). According to Nepalmahatmya of Skandapurana, Vaisaladhipati Dharmadatta attacked the Kiratas and the defeated king Shankhu fled to

the forest. Some historians also claim a link between the two dynasties (Levi 1925: 53). From the available sources, scholars assume that the Lichhavi rule might have started in Nepal sometime around the beginning of the Christian era (Levi 1925: 53; Regmi 1969: 64). Recently archaeological excavations in Kathmandu have unearthed a stone statue of a king dating back to Samvat 107. One of the historians, Dr. D.C. Regmi (1992: 1) on the ground of the Pashupati inscription of Jayadeva II dated to 733 AD, has related this statue to the Lichhavi king Jayadeva I, who ruled before Manadeva I in and around first/second century AD. But the question of authenticity is still there.

The first authentic written records of the Kathmandu Valley are found only from the middle of the fifth century AD, that is of Manadeva I of the Lichhavi dynasty who ruled from c. 460-505 AD (Vajracharya 1973: 9-13, Inscription no. 2). An assessment of the position with regard to his predecessors can be made on the basis of facts provided in the chronicles. The Lichhavi rulers were contemporaries of the Gupta rulers of Northern India as it is mentioned in the Allahabad pillar inscription of Samudra Gupta (Chattopadhyaya 1958: 158). In this inscription, Samudra Gupta mentioned Nepal as border state who paid tribute to him. The Gupta overlordship continued till the rule of Skanda Gupta. After his death in 647 AD, Nepal was perhaps successful in freeing herself from this influence, as later Gupta rulers were weak (Jha 1970: 107). According to Dr. Hit Narayana Jha (1970: 108) the Changunarayan pillar inscription of Manadeva I indirectly echoes the feeling of the rebellion and he reads the date of this inscription as 467 AD, which coincides with the year of the death of Skanda Gupta.

The Lichhavi period is the beginning of Nepalese dynastic history. Nepal's independent political relation as a sovereign state with Tibet and China in the north began for the first time in this period (i.e. in the early half of the seventh century AD). The Lichhavi rule ended around ninth century AD. There are more than two hundred stone inscriptions and hundreds of Hindu and Buddhist icons belonging to Lichhavi period. The Lichhavi kings constructed huge palaces, which were praised by the Chinese travellers. They promoted the contemporary Indian script, culture and religions in Nepal.

The history of Nepal from ninth to twelfth centuries is not clear. It is said that the Lichhavis were succeeded by a new dynasty of the Thakuris (Sharma 1968: 74). At the end of this new dynasty, new states like Tirhut, Palpa and Sinja emerged on the southern border of Nepal. Drawn by the prosperity and higher culture of the Valley, these border states were inspired to invade it again and again, rendering the Valley very weak and politically disunited.

The twelfth century (Nepal's medieval period) saw the rise of the Malla dynasty in Nepal. The Malla dynasty was founded by king Ari Malla in the year 1200 AD who ruled till 1216 AD. The Malla rule is divided into two periods - Early and Later Medieval (Malla) periods. The Early Medieval falls within the time bracket of 1200-1482 AD till the death of king Jaya Yakshya Malla and the Later Medieval period started from the death of Jaya Yakshya Malla to 1769 AD. After the death of Jaya Yakshya Malla, the Malla kingdom was divided among his three sons which led to the establishment of three individual petty kingdoms, at first centred in Bhaktapur (Bhadgaon), Kantipur (Kathmandu) and Bhonta (Banepa). After sixteenth century, Banepa was annexed by Bhaktapur while Lalitpur (Patan) was separated from Kantipur. These three independent kingdoms were ruled by three petty kings. The political domination of the Malla rulers of these three kingdoms lasted almost for six centuries, from 1200 to 1769 AD, and in that year, Nepal was annexed by the Gorkha king Prithvinarayana Shah who founded the Shah dynasty, which continues to date.

Importance of the Study

The early inhabitants, of Nepal, the Newars are the indigenous people of Nepal Valley, known for their skills in arts and crafts. The *Arthasastra* of Kautilya (1967) highly praises the woollen blankets of Nepal. Huen-Tsang, a Chinese traveller, who visited India and certain parts of Nepal in seventh century of the Christian era, spoke very highly of the artistic skill of the people of Kathmandu Valley.

Historical research in Nepal started about 100 to 120 years ago only, and whatever work has been done so far by foreign as well as native scholars has provided us with only a skeleton of the political history of the country. What we know now is only the dynastic history and the contribution of famous rulers of Nepal.. One has also to study the socio-economic, religious and art history to get a holistic perception. The socio-economico-religious and art histories add flesh, blood, vein and skin to the skeleton and would make it complete. For last few decades the academic attention has been drawn to these aspects of Nepalese history.

The history of Nepalese art is yet to be properly studied and evaluated. All the books, so far published, deal with all aspects of the Nepalese arts. So it is the need of the time to study specific art forms in detail. Realizing this fact and being impressed by the wealth and techniques of bronze art, it has been attempted here to examine the bronze art of Nepal. The Nepalese bronzes so far have been considered only as the objects of display for their exquisite beauty, but not of discussion. They are deprived of serious academic concern from art historians. The Nepalese bronze sculptures exhibited in different museums of the world have been highly praised by the art critics, but no proper and complete history has been written. U.V. Schroeder in his Indo-Tibetan Bronzes (1981) has written about the stylistic differences of the Nepalese bronzes from historical time to the present day. His pioneering contribution remains to highly important, though it is not complete. He being a foreigner was not allowed to visit and study the vast collections of Nepalese bronzes in temples and Viharas. This made the researcher to select this topic and to attempt to fill the lacuna. The study was carried out by actually working out in the field with people, artists and the priests so as to enable me to present a near complete history of Nepalese bronze arts. This practical approach to the study has made it possible to provide a detailed background on the Nepalese bronzes starting from the very beginning till the middle of the eighteenth century. The knowledge derived from the practitioners in the field in an important aspect of this study.

So far all the scholars, who have published books and articles on Nepalese art in various academic journals, have written the importance of Nepalese art studies, but among them none has described the technology in detail. Schroeder has provided a brief account of oriental bronze casting in general, but not with specific reference to indigenous Nepalese technology. He quotes the classical Indian literature and scriptures regarding the technique and technology of Cire-Perdue, but has written very little about the present technology of Newar artists of Nepal. So I have attempted to provide a detailed account of the technology and the stylistic changes with respect to temporal changes with specific references to Nepalese bronze art.

Thus this study deals with the history of bronze casting in Nepal, and also describes in detail its origin and development of the stylistic changes through the ages mainly between Lichhavi and Medieval bronze arts. Various technological aspects like Cire-Perdue, embossing, engraving, chiselling work and finishing by painting and applying gold on the bronze objects has been elaborated in this work.

This work based on detailed interviews with the artists and observations at various stages of the bronze work from the wax model to the final touch provides a list of various tools (in vernacular as well as in English) and the unique but complete technology still practised by the Newar artists.

Most of the pictures and art objects described in this research work had never been photographed and published before. They are being published for the first time.

Furthermore, this work has also focused on the socio-religious background of the Nepalese bronzes. The Nepalese bronzes were exported to Tibet on large scale and so were executed according to the need of the Tibetan market. This aspect of Nepalese bronze was just hinted by A. K. Coomaraswamy and Pratapaditya Pal but the present work provided an extensive insight on the subject.

Objectives

The research work, related with Nepalese bronze art, is specifically guided by the major objectives listed below:

1. to trace the origin and development of the various techniques of the Nepalese bronze art, viz., the Cire-Perdue, embossing, engraving, chiselling and so on;
2. to determine the extent of Indian and Tibetan influence on Nepalese bronzes and to discuss the opinions of the earlier scholars in this context;
3. to search the antiquity and the continuation of the tradition of bronze casting of Nepal;
4. to provide a guideline for the dating of bronze figures of Nepal;

5. to prepare a detailed index of Nepalese bronze art;
6. to trace the stylistic changes of Nepalese bronze art of different eras;
7. to trace whether the techniques of applying gold and inlaying semi-precious stones on the bronze figure of Nepal is of indigenous origin;
8. to suggest probable solutions for the development of bronze art in Nepal, in order to ensure the continuation of the ancient tradition.

In the context of this research work on "A Study of the Nepalese Bronzes from Ancient to Medieval Periods," the researcher, under Review of Literature, had studied quite a good number of publications; but a great limiting factor arose out of the fact that most of them did not mention the bronze arts. Gopal Raj Vamsavali - though having the widest coverage (from nearly 1000 BC to 14th century AD) - also does not have any description on the subject in reference. The few publications, which do touch the subject, are not very elaborate. They too do not describe the techniques and technology of bronze arts.

The study has tried to trace the development of bronze art history during fifth to eighteenth centuries - this period of 1300 years is very extensive. Sometimes (especially during ninth to twelfth centuries) the historical development seems to have lost in mist. When we say that there is no traceable history for many centuries (from ninth to twelfth centuries), this amounts to saying that the same holds good for bronze art development. Lack of historical sources for these centuries, therefore is a major limiting factor faced during the course of this work.

The situation would look paradoxical that while the research in the present context, focuses on the ancient and medieval periods – that is from Lichhavi to Malla periods (from 5th century AD to third quarter of the 18th century, i.e. up to 1769 AD), the scholar has also studied the extant techniques and technology used by the Nepalese artists. But this is neither paradoxical nor machronic because Nepal's art tradition is deeply rooted in its ancient wisdom and ritualism endowing the art an unbroken continuity. The craftsmen - as they informed the researcher - can't / don't deviate even slightly from the age-long established practices of idol making. Despite this, the age-old wisdom associated with idol-making was not preserved in a written form, but this gap seems to have been compensated because of its cryptic formulations manifested in ritual-based process of making bronzes.

Methodology

The study is based on primary as well as secondary sources of classical India as well as Nepalese literature. It may be looked upon as a micro-based scrutiny of bronze objects in the museums of India and Nepal and of private collections. This has been carried out with the help of field observation of various procedures like casting, chiselling and gold gilding of bronze objects. Almost all the extant specimens in Nepal, especially in the Kathmandu Valley were subjected to examination. The scholar also had an opportunity to see some exhibits in India's Prince of Wales Museum (Bombay) and National Museum (Delhi). Thus, observing the actual operations of manufacturing, examination of several specimens and referring to previous publications are three major stages of the approach adopted in this work.

The bronze art of Nepal can be divided into two main periods, viz., Ancient (Lichhavi) and Medieval (Malla). After the Lichhavi period, the technique and style of bronze art seem to have undergone a great change - the former was highly influenced by the Gupta art, while the latter was influenced by the Pala art of eastern India. The art style and the forms of the icons also changed as numerous Buddhist deities were introduced to Nepal from the early medieval period. This age also witnessed the development of repouse art. These all aspects were studied by interviewing the artists of Kathmandu Valley, especially of Patan city and by observing them at work.

An approach of personal interviews and observation was adopted, though it was not free of hurdles. In some cases, some of the icons were covered with cloth and kept inside the temple where no outsiders can get any access. In most of the cases, only the priests of the temples and monasteries are allowed to enter the main shrine. However, fortunately, enough the contemporary artists themselves have been very co-operative and they imparted useful information. Many places of importance in Nepal and India were also visited. Some of the artists of Patan, who have kept the tradition of making bronzes alive, were also interviewed. From one of them the artist Moti Kaji Shakya of Bhinche Bahal (Patan) gave me

the information of two types of wax available only seasonally (like summer and winter) and also about the technique of making models in wax. Badri Kaji Shakya of Uku Bahal (Patan) allowed me to observe the process of casting images in bronze. Mana Kaji Shakya of Patan Bhinche Bahal showed how gold is cut to small pieces for making slurry to apply on the face of an image. Singha Raj Shakya of Patan showed me how facial features of an image are painted and the making of colours used in painting the eyes, face, hair, ear and eyebrows.

The researcher has reviewed the literary work of earlier scholars like A. K. Coomaraswamy, S. Kramrisch, P. Pal, D. Barrett, N. R. Ray, A. Ray, K. Khandalavala, M. V. Krishnan, D. R. Regmi, S. M. Joshi, R. N. Pandey, L. S. Bangdel, R. Reeves and many others for developing an academic perspective regarding the historical development and technology of making bronzes.

Thus, the research is based on a multi-disciplinary and holistic approach of the bronze art. It is based on the records (including *Vamsavalis* and inscriptions) and bronze art objects of Nepal specimens of which are found in the Kathmandu Valley as well as abroad. Different Newar communities have contributed in the enrichment of this art.

History of Bronze art in Nepal

The beginning of the art form of stone sculptures in Nepal can be dated to the middle of the fifth century AD. Its history prior to this period is represented by a few specimens, such as the stone sculptures of Virupakshya of Pashupati Aryaghata, Rajpurusha of Mrigasthali of Pashupatinath, the latter now is exhibited in the National Museum, and Chakrapurusha (also called Rajamata) of Pashupati Aryaghata. All these sculptures are influenced by the style of Mathura School of the second/third century BC and are the products of Kirata period (Sharma 1968: 75).

The art of Nepal from fifth to ninth centuries can be termed as the real Lichhavi or the classical Nepali School. It is represented by numerous stone sculptures. Vishnu Vikranta sculptures of Kathmandu's Tilganga and Lazimpat dated 467 AD (the latter now preserved in the National Museum) are the first available images with dated inscriptions on the pedestal. Besides, Garudasana Vishnu of Changunarayana, Visvarupa Vishnu of Changu, Chaturmurti

Vishnu of Sankhu, Laksmi exhibited in the National Museum, Jalasayana Vishnu of Buddhanilakantha, Varaha of Kathmandu Dhumvarahi, Ravananugraha of Mrighasthali, Pashupatinath, Uma-Maheshvara panel of Patan's Kumbhesvara, Buddha of Chabahil, Bangemuda, Pashupati Aryaghata, Avalokitesvara of Dhvaka Bahal chaitya, Avalokitesvara of Ganabahal, Kathmandu, are the prime examples of the Lichhavi sculptures and they exhibit considerable influence of Gupta school in modelling and refinement (Sharma 1968: 77).

The Malla rule of medieval period can be considered as the golden period of development of Nepalese art and architecture. Thousands of specimens found in Nepal, belong to this period. Some of which are Vishnu Vikranta of Changu, Surya of Patan's Thapahity and Bhaktapur's Panauti, Indra of Panauti (Bhaktapur), Mahishasuramardini of Bhaktapur Darbar Square, Uma-Mahesvara of Kumbhesvara (Patan), Narasimha of Hanumanadhoka, Padmapani Lokesvara of Kva Bahal (Patan), Tara of Banepa (Bhaktapur), Bhagavati images of Bhaktapur's Palanchowk, Kathmandu's Sobha Bhagavati and of Naxal are the prime examples of the medieval period. Along with the sculptural art in stone, making of the bronze images also made a beginning at about the same time.

Bronze art occupies an important place in the art of Nepal. Nepalese bronzes are exhibited in various museums and also form part of a number of private collections all over the world. Although Nepalese bronzes are well known throughout the world, their history is still obscure. Attempts have been made to throw light on various aspects by a number of foreign scholars, but a comprehensive study is not yet available. Writing on the art history of Nepal, the seventeenth century Tibetan historian, Taranatha, mentions the names of two famous artists, Dhiman and his son Bitopalo, who lived in Varendra region (northern Bengal) during the reign of Pala kings, Dharmapala and his son Devapala ruling Magadha, around ninth century AD. These two artists founded two distinct schools of art. Bitapola, the son appears to have been expert in bronze casting. The images cast by his followers began to be called as Eastern style. The followers of his father, Dhiman, were the creators of the School of Eastern paintings (Chattopadhyaya 1970: 348 Folio 138A).

These two artists flourished under the rich patronage of Nalanda. In this context, it may be noted that a brick structure, discovered at the temple site No. 13 at Nalanda, has been identified as smelting furnace, with metal pieces and slag in it (Sahai 1981: 6).

Scholars like Lain Sing Bangdel, Stella Kramrisch, Douglas Barrett and Karl Khandalavala assign the origin of Nepalese bronzes to the Pala Bronzes of eastern India. According to Bangdel (1970: 12-13) the Eastern School underwent many changes in Bihar and Bengal, whereas the school of bronze art in Nepal followed the tradition of Pala art till the twelfth/thirteenth centuries. According to Barrett (1957: 95), the bronze art tradition started in Nepal only during the Pala dynasty of eastern India in the early Medieval period and Nepalese artists learnt the techniques of bronze casting from the Pala artists. According to Kramrisch (1964: 39-40), during the rule of Pala dynasty (750-1150 AD) in Eastern India, bronze images were made in large numbers in Nalanda and Kurkihar in Bihar and being easily portable found their way to Nepal where their form at once became re-cast in the Nepali tradition. But there is a strong possibility that bronze casting in Nepal existed prior to this time and it closely followed the styles of Gupta art. Taranatha mentions the presence of the influence of Western art (Chattopadhyaya 1970: 348 Folio 138A). A.K. Coomaraswamy, the first scholar, who introduced Nepalese bronze sculpture to the world, placed the history of making sculpture in bronze in Nepal in the ninth century (Sharma 1967: 10). According to him, Nepalese art is best known by the metal images, usually copper or brass, and of fine workmanship and in the Nepalese bronzes are found the influence of late Gupta art (Coomaraswamy 1927: 145). However, the Padmapani exhibited in the Boston Museum dated to ninth century AD by Coomaraswamy has been dated to as late as the thirteenth or fourteenth century by Khandalavala (1950: 24).

However, Pratapaditya Pal does not see Pala influence on Nepalese bronzes. He says that, it has become axiomatic with modern scholars to assert that post-ninth century, Nepali art was strongly influenced by the Pala art of India. Yet it is curious that the Nepali temples and monasteries have not yielded a single Pala bronze. On the contrary, several Nepali bronzes have been discovered in India, in and around Nalanda. A comparison between Nepali and Pala bronzes of about tenth and eleventh centuries completely belies such an assumption (Pal 1975: 14).

From this statement it appears that Nepalese bronzes did not indicate any Pala influence even up to tenth/eleventh century. In other words, it can be said that Nepalese bronze art developed independently while retaining few characteristics closer to the Gupta model. Pal (1975: 14) further says that, the bronzes that are here attributed to the Lichhavi period of Nepali history (ca. 400-800 AD) unquestionably demonstrate the predominant influence of the aesthetic tradition of Gupta art of India (ca. 300-600 A.D.).

The bronze images of post-Lichhavi and of pre-Medieval periods, shows a pronounced Nepalese character though there is some foreign influence as well. As Amita Ray says that Nepal's dependence on Indian forms, styles and technique is equally obvious. It is equally obvious that eventually Nepal made a successful venture towards the formation of a Nepali style (Ray 1973: 38).

According to Dr. R.N. Pandey (1968: 26), the influence of Pala style on Nepalese bronze art is beyond doubt, but it is seen in the art that developed only in the medieval period. There are ample evidences to show that the art developed from the Lichhavi period itself. There are several metal figures, assigned to pre-Pala period (Pandey 1968: 25-26).

**However, according to the inscriptional evidence, the authentic history of bronze art in Nepal can be traced to fifth century AD, along with the development of Mahayana Buddhism. Among the earliest bronze images is the image of a standing Buddha with a dedicatory inscription dated to 591 AD which is now exhibited in the Cleveland Museum. It resembles the bronze Buddha of Northern India of Gupta period (Czuma 1970 Fig. 8; Slusser 1975-76 Fig. 5; Pal 1978 Fig. 76; Schroeder 1981 Fig. 74E; Ray *et al.* 1986 Fig. 26). This bronze Buddha was initially believed to be of Gupta period (Ray *et al.* 1986: 97). But scholars like Gautamvajra Vajracharya and Marry Slusser, studied the pedestal inscription and consider it to be the work of an artist from Patan (Slusser 1975-76: 81-84). The pedestal inscription reads as follows:
"This image is the pious gift of the Sakya nun Purisuddhamati at Yamgval monastery in

Laditagrama in the year 591 AD. May the merit from this deed result in the attainment of supreme wisdom for all sentient being. From the proceeds of pindaka a feast should be provided at the locality east of Chaityakuta Jinabandhu monastery" (Schroeder 1981: 299).

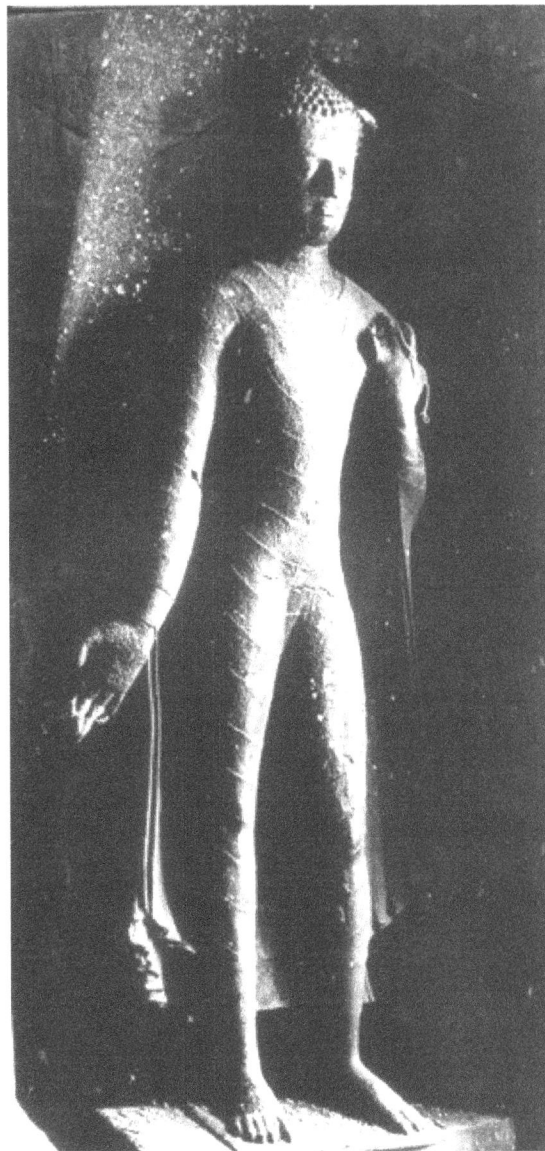

Figure 1: Buddha, Sankhu, 7th century AD

Besides, we have bronze images, which are still worshipped in the temples and monasteries of the Valley itself and some are displayed in the National Museums Among them are the Vishnu image preserved in the storehouse of Changunarayana temple of Changu, dated to fourth century AD (Khanal 1983: 65, no. 7), the Garudasana Vishnu of Changunarayana temple, of which the golden *kavaca* and Garuda were renovated by king Amsuvarma (605-621 AD) (Vajracharya 1973: 317, Inscription no. 76) and the early seventh century Buddha of Sankhu Vajrayogini (Fig. 1) (Srivastava 1967-68: 85 pl. IX). This Buddha of Sankhu is known as the

Queen of blacksmith (Sharma 1970: 1). Padmapani Avalokitesvara of Patan Kva Bahal, dated to eighth century AD (Fig. 2), Sankhu Buddha, also called Ratnasambhava, of ninth century (Fig. 3) (Thapa 1970: 29, Fig. 27), Vishnu of National Museum, dated to tenth century AD (Fig. 4) and sculptures unearth from Tukan Bahal Stupa, Kathmandu (Shrestha 2002: 20-38) confirm that bronze art in Nepal existed prior to the Pala period of eastern India and it was closely followed the Gupta styles (Pal 1974: 14).

Figure 2: Padmapani Lokesvara, Kwa Bahal, Patan, 8th century AD

Of all the art, Nepal achieved great fame for metal work from the Lichhavi period onwards. From the fifth century onwards, we have dated inscriptions, copper coins, dated as well as undated images in bronze, found in storehouses of temples and in private collections in Nepal and abroad.

Copper coins like *Mananka* of Manadeva I, *Vaishravana, Kamadohi* type of coin, and *Pasupati* coins related to king Amsuvarma (Regmi 1968: 150-214), stand testimony to the developed form of art, that flourished in Nepal (Walsh 1973: 10-13). The Chinese traveller

Wang-Huien-Tshe, who visited Nepal during the reign of king Narendradeva (643-657 AD), mentions that, Nepalese have coins of copper which bear on one side a figure of a man and on the reverse a horse and a bull, and has no hole in the middle (Jayaswal 1936: 238).

Figure 3: Buddha, Sankhu, 9th century AD

In the beginning of early seventh century AD, Nepal made significant achievements in metal sculpture. During the time of Amsuvarma, Nepal exported iron and copper utensils (along with woollen goods) to India (Vajracharya 1973: 209-11, Inscription nos. 73 and 74). Changunarayana golden *kavaca* inscription of Amsuvarma dated to 607 AD, states that the Garudasana Vishnu Kavaca was renovated by king Amsuvarma (Vajracharya 1973: 317, Inscription no. 76). This shows that the bronze image was already dedicated there at the beginning of early seventh century AD. The chronicle states that king Haridatta Varma (who ruled nine generations before Manadeva I) had built four Narayana temples in four directions of the Kathmandu Valley and one of them was of Changunarayana (Vajracharya and Malla 1985: 28, Folio 20). The image of Garudasana Vishnu also might have been established then. Since no one is allowed to check and touch the image, we cannot say definitely whether it is made of pure gold or is only gold-gilded.

The *kailashakuta Bhavana*, a palace, which was praised by the Chinese travellers, was built by king Amsuvarma in the beginning of early seventh century AD (Vajracharya 1973: 290-91, Inscription no. 71). The history of T'ang Dynasty includes the observations about the palace as:

"In the middle of the palace, there is a tower of seven storeys roofed with copper tiles. Its balustrade, grills, columns, beams and everything therein are set with fine and even precious stones. At each of the four corners of the tower there projects a water pipe of copper. At the base, there are golden dragons, which spout forth water. From the summit of the tower, water is poured through funnels which find its way down below, streaming like a fountain from the mouth of the golden makara" (Jayaswal 1936: 238-239).

Another description of the same palace is found in the account of Wang-Hiuen-Tshe, who visited Nepal in the seventh century that has been translated by Levi (1925: 62) as follows:

"In the capital of Nepal there is a construction in storeys which have more than 200 cheu of height and 80 peu of circumference. Ten thousand men can find place in its upper part. It is divided in three terraces and each terrace is divided in seven storeys. In the four pavilions, there are sculptures to make you marvel. Stone and pearls decorated them."

According to the Chinese accounts, mentioned in T'ang Annals, the king of Tibet, Srong-brtan-Gampo, married the Nepalese princess Bhrikuti, who is said to be the daughter of Amsuvarma (Jayaswal 1936: 162). She took the images of Maitreya Boddhisattva, Aksobhya Buddha and Arya Tara with her to Tibet (Joshi 1978: 4). Temples were constructed for those images in the heart of Lhasa (Jha 1970: 159). Scholars assume that those images most probably were of bronze, as bronze images are easier to transport than

stone images (Joshi 1976: 42; Joshi 1978: 4). In the joint inscription of Sivadeva I and Amsuvarma of Lele at Patan, dated to 604 AD, there is a mention of *archa gosthi,* one of the organizations dealing with images (Vajracharya 1973: 282-83, Inscription no. 70).

Beside these, the Minanatha Lokeshvara of Tangal Tole of Patan can be cited as one of the best examples of developed forms of Nepalese bronze art. Along with Red Machhindranath Yatra, the Lokesvara's Yatra is performed every year. Devamala Vamsavali has related this Lokeshvara with king Amsuvarma (Joshi 1978: 3).

Several accounts compiled by contemporary Chinese visitors to Nepal during the Lichhavi period are available. Yuan Chwang, the famous Chinese Buddhist pilgrim, who travelled in India during 629-645 AD, wrote that the "*Nepalese people had no learning but were skillful metal workers*" (Watters 1904, 1988 reprint: 83). His comment is of interest since it is the earliest available literary reference concerning the skills of Nepalese artists working in metal.

During the reign of king Narendradeva (c. 643-657 AD), a Chinese delegation, led by Wang-Hiuen-tshe, visited Nepal twice. His accounts, included in the history of the T'ang Dynasty, remarks about the people of Nepal as having all their utensils made of copper. They adore five celestial spirits and sculptured their images in stone (Jayaswal 1936: 238). The Chinese traveller further mentions about king Narendradeva as, "*their king Na-ling-ti-po adorns himself with true pearls, rock crystal, mother of pearl, corral and amber; he has in his ears rings of gold and pendants of jade and trinkets in his belt adorned with the golden figure of the Buddha*" (Levi 1925: 59).

According to the chronicles, the Red Machhindranath, whose *ratha yatra* (chariot festival) is still performed annually at Patan city, has been related with this king Narendradeva (Wright 1877, 1972 reprint: 142-148).

The above accounts of the chronicles and inscriptions are adequate evidence of the artistic achievements of the Nepalese during the Lichhavi period.

For the intervening period between the ends of the Lichhavi supremacy up to the beginning of twelfth century, the history of Nepal is almost unknown. It is marked by a dearth of inscriptions and coins though such material is not totally absent. Sivadeva III, who ruled in the twelfth century AD, is credited with issuing two types of coins, named *sivaka* and *damma* (Vajracharya and Malla 1985: 58 Folio 48) of gold and silver, respectively (Petech 1958: 177-78). These coins were in circulation till the end of the Malla period. Beside these, the pedestal inscriptions, sculptures from Nepal and abroad, the colophons of the religious scriptures and the Gopal Raj Vamsavali of the fourteenth century refer to a few important events of this period. The image of Sankhu Buddha of the ninth century (Fig. 3), the tenth century image of Vishnu in the National Museum (Fig. 4), Kva Bahal Padmapani images of ninth and twelfth centuries (5), Chandesvara in Indian Museum, Calcutta dated to tenth/eleventh century (Bangdel 1976: 89, Fig. 3), Muchhalinda Buddha in Virginia Museum (Gairola 1978, Fig. 1a) and Devi in Newark Museum (Pal 1974, Fig. 226) are among the best specimens of this dark period. Beside these images, pedestal inscriptions of these periods (9th to 12th centuries) are found in private collections, in the museums, viz., Cleveland Museum, British Museum, Boston Museum, Virginia Museum, Stanford Museum, Prince of Wales Museum, National Museum of Delhi, Indian Museum of Calcutta, National Museum of Kathmandu and in the temple courtyards in the Kathmandu Valley.

Pratapaditya Pal has published the bronze image of Vishnu, having the dedicatory inscription dated to 'Samvat 172' (Pal 1971-72, Figs. 5&6; Pal 1974, Fig. 31). The pedestal inscription of this image states that the bronze image of Vishnu was installed by some Hetujeeva, Vastramitra, Devaswami, Dharamitra, and others to obtain the blessings (Alsop 1984: 33-34). Pal took this date under the Nepal Samvat, which he converted to Christian era 1052 AD (Pal 1971-72: 60-61). However, Gautamvajra Vajracharya has opines the view on the basis of the palaeography, that the date of the inscription should have been referred to the Manadeva era rather than to the Nepal Samvat meaning that the date of the inscription is 748 AD (Pal 1971-72: 66). He has also stated that, *"the script is unquestionably in the Gupta character"* (a personal letter from Vajracharya to P. Pal dated Feb. 23, 1982, as mentioned by Alsop 1984: 45). Another scholar Dhanavajra Vajracharya (1973: 590-91, Inscription no.

171) published his readings on the same inscription confirming Gautamvajra Vajracharya's version.

Figure 4: Vishnu, National Museum, Kathmandu, 10th century AD

In the medieval period, the bronze art developed in various ways. Though the Lichhavi rule came to an end in the early ninth century AD, the art movement, which had started during this period, continued up to the medieval period. This period is considered as the *golden period* of the development of Nepalese art and architecture. Most of the art works found in Nepal are stated to be of this period (Regmi 1966a: 862). The Malla rulers of this period, not only patronized sculptural art, but they actively participated in activities like building of temples, setting up of images and encouraging manuscript painters to draw on leaves and large canvases called *Thanka* (*paubha*), depicting deities and religious events (Regmi 1966a: 862). During this period the dominant religion in Nepal was Vajrayana Buddhism. Although it was practised from the time of the Lichhavis (Vajracharya 1973: 370-371 and 523-524, Inscription Nos. 89 and 141), it was formally adopted only after the visit of Atisa Dipankara Srijnana from India in the eleventh century AD (Rajendra Ram 1978: 117) and its fullest development took place during the medieval period (Regmi 1965: 547). Between ninth and thirteenth centuries, Nepal maintained an intimate cultural link with India through scholars from Nepal visiting the university centres in Bihar and Bengal (Regmi 1965: 543). Nepal, being a centre of Buddhist learning, scholars from India also visited Nepal (Ray 1973: 38).

In the early thirteenth century, Muslim Sultan Bakhtiyar Khilji conquered the whole of eastern India (Majumdar 1957: 39). In the centuries prior to the Muslim invasion, Bihar and Bengal had played a vital role in the development of Vajrayana Buddhism. But this invasion caused panic among the Buddhists who were ruthlessly persecuted. This invasion was accompanied by the wholesale destruction of Buddhist monasteries like Vikramasila, Nalanda and Odantapuri. As a result, Buddhism collapsed in India and a large number of Buddhist monks, scholars, painters and sculptors from these Buddhist universities migrated to Nepal, Tibet and south India (Majumdar 1957: 425).

The arrival of Buddhist refugees was beneficial to Nepal in many ways. Among them, there were many eminent Buddhist scholars who brought collections of the Buddhist manuscripts with them and also many artists came with them to Nepal. These artists carried their art designs and skills with them (Agrawala 1950: 203). As a result of contact with these Indian Buddhist monks, scholars and artists, Nepalese Buddhists also accepted the Vajrayana philosophy and Tantrism, a cult of profound mysticism and magic in temples and monasteries. A large number of bronze images of Tantric deities were produced during the medieval period. This was the beginning of a new era in the world of metal art in Nepal.

From the beginning of the early medieval period, the Nepalese artists were actively engaged in the work of decorating temples and monasteries in Nepal as well as in Tibet. The artist A-ni-ko (also called Arniko or Balabahu by the Nepalese) (1245-1306 AD), a descendant of the royal family of Nepal, achieved everlasting fame in the court of Mongol emperor Kublai Khan of China (Levi 1925: 63-64). This shows the important role of Nepalese artists in regard to the stylistic development of Tibetan as well as Chinese art during thirteenth-fifteenth centuries.

Father Desideri, who visited Nepal in 1722, remarked on Newars, who were the inhabitants of the Kathmandu Valley that they are *"clever at engraving and melting metal"* (Regmi 1966a: 1009).

Because of the contact with Indian refugees and as a result of the new cultic practices making inroads into the various rituals of the country, religious and social life of Nepal changed to a great deal. Vajrayana pantheon of eastern India got established throughout the Kathmandu Valley (Regmi 1965: 541).

A large number of Tantric and ritualistic Sanskrit treatises, both of Shaivite and Buddhist origin, were copied and preserved in the monasteries of the Valley during the medieval period (Majumdar 1957: 426; Rajendra Ram 1978: 164-65). During this period, the casteless character of Buddhist monkhood underwent a change and gave way to the formation of rigid caste structure at the top. Under the Mahayanism, Vajrayana pantheon developed. Some of the monks turned into priests and most of them entered a householder's life. This gave an impetus to the introduction of complex caste structure among the Buddhists also. This development in its own turn supported the development of Tantrism (Regmi 1965: 543). This added new deities and new cults to already existing tradition (Regmi 1966a: 557). The Buddhist text *Sadhanamala* mentions invocations to numerous female and male deities, viz., Prajnaparamita, Kurukula, Vasudhara (also known as Vasundhara in Nepal), Nairatma and male deities like Hevajra, Heruka and Samvara, deriving their origin from Vajrayana Trantrism (Regmi 1966a: 576-98). Many deities of the Vajrayana pantheon continued to enjoy popularity till the end of the seventeenth century. By then Vajrayana pantheon had become part of both the faiths of Shaivism and Buddhism (Macdonald and Stahl 1979: 54). Under the influence of this pantheon, Shiva, the principal deity of Shaivism, known as Pashupatinath, also came to be worshipped by the Buddhists. On the eighth day of the bright fortnight of the month of Kartik (October-November), the Pashupati *linga* is crowned and is worshipped as Avalokitesvara (Macdonald and Stahl 1979: 54). The Buddhists believe that Guhyesvari is the root of the lotus on which the Adi-Buddha became manifest as a flame at Svayambhunath (north of Kathmandu), while the Hindus, she is the vagina of Satidevi (Macdonald and Stahl 1979: 48). Likewise, Vajrayogini is one of the mother goddesses of the Vajrayana pantheon, but for the Saivites she is worshipped as Ugratara (Regmi 1966a: 596). Such newly introduced commonalities tended to bind the Buddhist and Shaivite groups closer. As a result, they developed the same rituals, language and script.

The fifteenth century was propitious in Nepalese history. During the reign of king Yakshya Malla who ruled from 1428 to 1482 AD, trade link with Tibet was established which proved to be beneficial for artistic community, especially Buddhists (Pal 1974: 134).

After the sixteenth century, Tantric influence is more pronounced in bronze images. The rulers of the three near independent Malla kingdoms of Kathmandu Valley (Kantipur, Bhaktapur and Lalitpur) were very rich. Nepal Valley had become the centre of trans-Himalayan trade, so they could control all the entry points to Tibet and levied duties on all trade (Regmi 1966a: 537; Dhungel 1986: 49). Being of the same families and jealous of each other, these Malla kings were constantly competing with each other. So they built temples, Darbar squares and patronized artists. They minted coins and cast images for the Tibetan market and earned gold and silver in exchange (Regmi 1966a: 533-34; Dhungel 1986: 49). Nepalese bronzes can be seen in the monasteries of Tibet even today (Schroeder 1981: 410).

Over many years in the past following the Chinese occupation of Tibet and subsequent destruction of its monastic orders, thousands of images were removed and dispersed all over the world. Among these images were many of Nepalese origin - they were either taken to Tibet in earlier times or cast there by the itinerant Nepalese Newar artists. Often the relatively unaffected or unworn appearance of such images results in the ascription of a later date. In addition, these images are frequently regarded as indigenous works of Tibet or as later copies of earlier Nepalese prototypes. N.R. Ray (quoted by Regmi 1965: 617) says that the Tibetan art owes its inspiration to Nepalese art tradition and the latter was definitely superior to the former in quality and standard. Since the eleventh century, Tibet received a number of skilled artists along with learned monks from Nepal (Regmi 1965: 617). Nepalese went to Lhasa and other areas in central Tibet. The legacy of art they carried with them to these places was the classical Nepalese style and its distinct features were indelibly printed on their art creations (Pal 1975: 21; Regmi 1965: 632-33).

During the medieval period, most of the images were cast in bronze and the influence of Tantrism is evident in their making (Figs. 6-10). The Nepalese images in bronze are worth studying as excellent specimens of art works of the medieval period. Occasionally, they were studded with semi-precious stones, coral, amber, pearls, rubies and turquoise. As early as in the seventh century AD tradition of embellishing the images with jewels had been testified by Chinese travellers and the continuation of the same craftsmanship and taste is borne by the specimens of medieval period too (Figs. 11 & 12). Several bronze works of this period are found. They include the images of the reliefs in tympannums as reflected in the many floral and geometrical designs and illustrations of finials, double drum and similar other objects. Some of them are gilded. But the early medieval bronzes are very few in number and mostly they are exhibited in the museums of India, Europe, America, Britain and form part of private collections all over the world. As stated by Father D'Andrade, the Nepalese artists worked on metal in Tsaparang (Regmi 1966a: 1004). Most of the inscriptions of fourteenth/fifteenth centuries also commemorate the installation of bronze images in temples for worship.

The Tibetan monk Dharmaswamin recorded seeing a golden image of Sakyamuni also known as Lord Abhayadana, inside the Tham Vihara built by Atisa Dipankara Srijnana (Roerich 1959: 55). Dharmaswamin also noted in his memoir how he saw in the Tham Vihara an abbot's seat gilded and adorned with pearls for which eighty ounces of gold was used (Rajendra Ram 1978: 115; Roerich 1959: 55-56).

The image of Dipankara Buddha of Patan Guitatole, which has an inscription of thirteenth century, is the earliest inscriptional evidence found in Kathmandu Valley (Regmi 1965: 615). The Kathmandu Itumbahal inscription of Madansimharam Vardhana (a Bhotia feudatory) commemorates the occasion of setting up of gold image of Arya Tara at Paravarta Mahavihara by Jaitralaksmi, wife of Madansimharama in the year 1382 AD (Rajbansi 1970: 38-39, Inscription no. 53).

The copper plate inscription of I-baha-bahi in Patan dated to 1427 AD mentions gold image of Boddhisattva installed by Mahapatras Rajasimha

Malla Varma and others (Regmi 1966b: 56, Inscription no. LIV).

The most important image of the early medieval period in the Kathmandu Valley itself is the image of Padmapani of Patan Kva Bahal of twelfth century - this is still worshipped (Fig. 6). Besides, Vajrapani of twelfth/thirteenth centuries in the British Museum (Barrett 1957, Fig. 7) and Maitreya of twelfth century in the Prince of Wales Museum are among other notable specimens. Another image is the gilt copper Indra of twelfth century in a private collection that has been referred by Stella Kramrisch (1964 no. 16). Matrika of twelfth century in the Prince of Wales Museum and Chamunda of thirteenth century in the San Francisco (Schroeder 1981: 352, Fig. 92A) are the images of note of female deities of early medieval period. The golden image of Narayana was installed by king Yakshya Malla in 1427 AD in memory of his late son Rajmalla. This gold image enshrined in the temple of Bhaktapur is a form of Narayana known as Hrishikesha (Regmi 1966c: 80-82, Inscription no. LXXII). One of the Yakshya Malla's copper plate inscriptions has a description of the installation of an image of Gauri within the temple of Pashupatinath in honour of the sacred memory of the deceased queen mother, Sansaradevi Thakurani in the year 1441 AD (Regmi 1966b: 58-61, Inscription no. LVI). Vasudhara in the collection of B.S. Cron dated 1467 AD (Barrett 1957, Fig. 2) is another figure of this type, which was installed during the reign of king Yakshya Malla.

The image of Vajrapani of fourteenth/fifteenth century in the British Museum (Barrett 1957, Fig. 5), Samvara images of fourteenth century in the National Museum (Figs. 7 and 8) are among the graceful specimens of this phase. The four handed Shiva in the Indian Museum, Calcutta (Mehta 1971, Fig. 12), Padmapani in the National Museum (Fig. 11), Padmapani of Boston Museum (Coomaraswamy 1927, Fig. 276), Kva Bahal Padmapani and Manjusri also can be cited as the main pieces of art of this period. The image of Agastya of fourteenth/fifteenth century preserved in the Art Institute of Chicago (Bolon 1991, Fig. 4) and Vishnu with Garuda and Lakshmi in the Prince of Wales Museum, bearing dedicatory

Figure 5: Padmapani Lokeswara, Kwa Bahal, Patan, 12th century AD

Figure 6: Heruka with Prajna, Prince of Wales Museum of Bombay, 1544 AD

inscription dated to 1698 AD are other important bronze pieces of this period. On the back of the pedestal of Vishnu, there is a dedicatory inscription, which records the gift of Lakshmi Narayana and Garuda idols by one Narasimha Bhatta in 1698 AD (Gorakshkar 1971: 31). The other images like Bhrikuti in the Prince of Wales Museum, National Museum's Surya images, Amoghasiddhi, Sukhavati Lokesvara, Simhanada Lokesvara, Durga, Bhairava, Varahi. Vasudhara (Fig. 12), Tara, Prince of Wales Museum's Tara and Prajnaparamita which has a dedicatory inscription dated to 1699 AD, Virginia Museum's Prajnaparamita (Gairola 1978, Fig. 4a), Humphrey Prajnaparamita (Barrett 1957, Fig. 6), Virginia Museum Bhadrakali (Gairola 1978, Fig. 10a), Prince of Wales Museum's Heruka holding his Shakti Vajravarahi (Fig. 6), having a dedicatory inscription on the back of the pedestal dated to 1544 AD and Indra, are the prime examples of the late medieval period, showing the influence of Tantrism. Above all, an image of Visvarupa, one of Hanumanadhoka, Kathmandu, set up by king Pratap Malla in 1657 AD (Vajracharya and Panta 1961 III: 19) and another of Kva Bahal are the most elegant figures of this period. Images of Ananda Bhairava (Fig. 9) and Ananda Bhairavi, having an inscription dated to 1702 AD, usually exhibited during the period of *Indra yatra* in the verandah of Bhagavati temple at Kathmandu's Hanumanadhoka (Vajracharya 1976: 173, Inscription no. 50) and Tara of Svayambhunath - they are the prime examples of late medieval period.

Besides, bronze images are found in the Viharas of the Kathmandu Valley itself; they are mostly of Dipankara, Sakyamuni Buddha (Fig. 10). The gilt images of Dipankaras, which are carried in processions during festive occasions, are often called *Samhedyo* who receives *samaye* (offerings of delicious food consisting of beaten rice, soyabean, garlic, ginger, meat, bean, dry fish, etc.). Some of the Shaivite temples also housed bronze images. Images of Indra and Vairocana installed at Indresvara temple at Panauti (one of the ancient places of Bhaktapur) are dated to thirteenth century (Thapa 1970, Figs. 28 and 29).

Figure 7: Samvara, National Museum, Kathmandu, 14th century AD

Figure 8: Samvara, National Museum, Kathmandu, 14th century AD

Figure 9: Ananda Bhairava, Hanumanadhoka, Kathmandu, 1707 AD

Figure 11: Padmapani Lokeswara, National Museum, Kathmandu, 15th century AD

Figure 10: Sakyamuni Buddha, Prince of Wales Museum of Bombay, 17th century AD

Figure 12: Vasudhara, National Museum, Kathmandu, 17th century AD

Other specimens of seventeenth century of gilt bronze used as embellishments on the stoned wall of the water conduit are found in the courtyards of the Bhaktapur Darbar (Fig. 13), Patan Sundari Chowk and Kathmandu. Similarly Devi images of the same period are placed in the three royal palaces of Kathmandu Valley (Regmi 1966a: 914).

Figure 13: Water Conduit of Bhaktapur Royal Palace, 1688 AD

The bronze art also includes some images on the tympannums, also called *torana (tolan)*. One such image is the four-faced Shiva of the southern gateway of Pashupatinath temple. Similarly the image on the tympannum (Fig. 14) of the famous *Golden Gate (lun dhvaka)* of Bhaktapur palace, built by Ranajeet Malla, the last Malla ruler, in 1753 AD, can also be cited here. It consists of an embossed image of Taleju Bhavani flanked by small Devi images. Similar type of *torana* is also to be seen in the main courtyards (*mu chuka*) of Kathmandu and Patan Darbars. The *toranas* of Indrayani and Sobha Bhagavati temples, situated on the banks of Vishnumati river of Kathmandu city, are also beautiful examples of late medieval period. Besides these *toranas*, doors of Kathmandu Taleju temple built by king Pratap Malla in 1671 AD and 1692 AD respectively (Vajracharya 1976: 224-30, Inscription nos. 32, 34 and 35), Pashupatinath temple, set up by Devidas in 1676 AD (Regmi 1966a: 910), Changunarayana temple (which indicates no idea of its date) are the best examples of bronze art of this period. Another excellent example of such doorways is the *Golden Gate* of Bhaktapur's royal palace (Fig. 14), built by Ranajeet Malla in 1753 AD (Regmi 1966a: 911). Percy Brown (1912: 75) in his "Picturesque Nepal" has appreciated the beauty of this doorway and the skill master artist in the following words:

"A doorway of brick and embossed copper gilt, the richest piece of art work in the whole kingdom, and placed like a jewel flashing innumerable facts in the handsome setting of its surroundings and further and the artificer of this wonderful doorway has proved in this great work that he was not only a past master of his craft, but a high priest of his cult. There are many other beautiful and absorbing features on the various buildings in the Darbar Square of Bhatgaon (called Bhaktapur), but this, the door of gold-molten, graven hammered, and rolled-forces these into comparative insignificance by its depth of meaning, richness of design, wealth of material, and the excellence of its workmanship. As a specimen of man's handicraft, it creates a standard whereby may be measured the intellect, artistic and religious, of the old Newars."

After the sixteenth century, images of devotees were also made which are found in and around Kathmandu Valley. Bronze statues of the Malla kings like Bhupatindra Malla (Fig. 15), Yoganarendra Malla (Fig. 16), Pratap Malla, Parthivendra Malla, statue of so-called Bhupatindra Malla, exhibited in the National Museum, a lay devotee's statue exhibited in the same museum and a devotee in Prince of Wales Museum can also be cited here.

Thus the art of image making in bronze began languishing in north India from the thirteenth century, on account of the suppression it faced at the hands of the iconoclast Muslim rulers, but the art not only survived in Nepal, but tradition was preserved without any break till the present day (Regmi 1966a: 908). The countless surviving temples and shrines along with their sculptural embellishments, which are concentrated in the Valley of Kathmandu, are almost exclusively the works of the Newar artists and artisans, whose skills were well acknowledged outside Nepal as well. It is said that in the court of Kublai Khan, a Nepali master, sculptor and builder, A-ni-ko was serving as the head of the Art Department (Levi 1925: 63-65). Taranath, in his autobiography, has mentioned twenty Nepalese sculptors in Tibet working in bronze. They were honoured by paying *dakshina* (gift in coins) implying they were not mere workers hired on daily wages. In their honour the articles they were offered were Chinese clothes, dust silk, turquoises. He further states that a statue of Jambhala and haloes for seven other statues were created by the Nepalese artists in his presence (Regmi 1965: 633). The fifth Dalai Lama in his works has named some Nepalese artists working in Lhasa. Their names were Dsyo bhan, Siddhi, Kar sis (Mangal), Dhar ma de vo, Dsai sin (Jaysing), A ma ra dsa ti (Amarajati), and Dse la K'ran K'ra pa su tsa. Amongst other images made by them one was of the Dalai Lama (Regmi 1965: 633).

Coomaraswamy (1921: 1) saw the Nepalese metal images as characterized by certain features of composition, a very full modelling of the flesh and almost florid features, the bridge of the nose is markedly round and the lips full. On the other hand, those of the later date and up to modern times are no longer so robust and fleshy, but svelte and slender waist and more sharply contoured; the nose becomes aquiline. Sometimes even hooked, the lips clear-cut and thin and the expression almost arch.

He further states that the Nepalese bronze art of the late medieval period had tended to become a goldsmith's art with more ornamentation and less plastic which was an inherent quality of the earlier creation (Coomaraswamy 1921: 1). His observation may be correct but only to a certain degree. It does not certainly apply to the images up to the fifteenth/sixteenth century in general. Even for the later period, it can be stressed that most of the earlier features were retained. The bronze was the only field where an unbroken stream of the art tradition was maintained with its finer qualities, but it must be admitted that to a certain degree of deterioration in the composition seems to have encroached in the images of seventeenth/eighteenth centuries.

The dating of Nepalese images is often made difficult because of the different states of preservation over the centuries. This problem is also related to the different customs of worship practised for different deities. For example, the image of Nepalese origin in a Tibetan monastery, viz. of Jo-Khong, Lhasa (Schroeder 1981: 413), has remained as fresh as original because it remained untouched throughout. It has retained its full coating of gilding and inset semi-precious stones and in perfect condition, whereas an image of the same period in a temple or a monasteries or a private shrines of the Kathmandu Valley used for ritualistic purpose would have lost most of its gilding and inset stones.

**Nepalese bronzes of fourteenth and seventeenth centuries denote a true Nepali style than the earlier pieces and they are easily recognizable. Tantric bronzes, belonging to this period, are inspired works displaying a distinctly Nepalese character (Pal 1975: 15). Nepalese art after sixteenth century follows to a great extent the prototypes of Buddhist and Brahmanical deities that developed earlier in India but it does not naturally presuppose that Newar artists blindly duplicated such models. On the contrary, Nepalese artists had greater freedom in conceiving the mental images of their gods and goddesses before they actually executed it. The predominant use of bronze as a major medium of artistic expression is a unique feature of Nepal, at least up to the early eighteenth century, among Asian cultures. Even after Nepal was taken over by the Gorkha king Prithvi Narayana Shah in the year 1768 AD. Nepalese artists continued casting images in bronze but the craft seems to have moved away from the traditional norms.

ii **Technology**

In the whole of Indian sub-continent metal has been used from the very ancient times as evidenced by the findings of Indus Valley Civilization (Marshall 1931; Vats 1940) and a number of sites throughout northern India mainly in the Gangetic Basin, where hoards of copper objects of certain types were deposited (Lal 1951). Among them, the most notable are two figures of the famous dancing girls from Mohenjo-daro, one exhibited in the National Museum of India, New Delhi and the other is exhibited in the National Museum of Pakistan, Karachi (Schroeder 1981 Figs. 1E & 1F). They are probably the earliest bronze sculptures to have been cast by Cire-Perdue or Lost Wax process; the process that continued till date.

The history of casting in Nepal is not yet adequately known while the excavations show the development of this art from many centuries before Christ. The archaeological excavations carried out by Nepal-German Archaeological Project in 1992 at the caves of Mustang have revealed many copper hoards, viz., arrow heads with a tang strip made of bronze, iron blades (Simon 1992-1993: 1-19 figs. 4:2, 9:1), iron ritual objects, embossed bronze or copper sheets (Simons *et al.* 1994: 51-75 figs. 10, 16) also called anthropomorphic object by Tiwari (1984-85: 1-12), bronze objects like cross shaped, copper bangles (Simons *et al.* 1994: 51-75 fig. 9), likewise iron spatula (blade?), metal

88

jewellery, long tubules made of brass and of copper, brass bell and iron belt buckle (Simons *et al.* 1994: 93-129 figs. 2:1, 3:2-5, 21:1, 2) and anthropomorphic figures of copper also have come to light from Jagatpur village of Kailali District (Darnal 2002: 39-48 fig. V). The findings of Mustang have been called Megalithic and Neolithic by Mr. Tiwari (1984-85: 1-12 Figs. 6 and 9), Dr. Schuh (1992-93: c-m) named them as Neolithic and Megalithic. According to Angela Simons (1992-1993: 8), this was a Prehistoric and Iron Age Culture. T.N. Mishra (1994: 151) is of the opinion that the findings from Mustang are comparable to the Neolithic, Chalcolithic and the Megalithic sites found in the south Asian region. Besides, the successive excavations at Tilaurakot, the ancient Kapilvastu, in the western Tarai region of Nepal during 1962, have yielded nearly three thousand silver and copper coins, dating from fifth to second centuries BC (Mitra 1972: 84-99). Mitra is of the opinion that these coins were issued locally at ancient Kapilvastu when it was a sovereign state. Besides, melting furnace along with it, metal pieces and slag have been excavated at Kapilvastu (Rijal 1979: 37). These evidences suggest the possibility of having the knowledge of casting metal art objects at Kapilvastu during the said period. However, no other place from the Kathmandu Valley, has so far yielded similar contemporary evidence. But the art of casting is still being practised in Nepal. It is, therefore, possible to have a direct access to the technology of image casting which has its roots in the ancient tradition. By the end of second century and beginning of third century AD, the Lichhavis migrated to Nepal from India (Regmi 1969: 64). The ornaments and *mukutas* (coronets), used in the so-called ancient images such as Virupakshya, Chakrapurusha, and Rajapurusha suggest that the technique of image casting in bronze had already been developed in Nepal before the arrival of the Lichhavis (Marie Laure de' Labriffe 1973: 185). According to R. J. Mehta (1971: 22), however, the art of image casting was introduced in Nepal only during the regime of the Imperial Guptas in India (320-600 A.D.). There is no doubt that the artistic vision of the Guptas indeed had a strong influence on Nepal's Lichhavi artists. The influence is apparent in the bronze Buddha dated to 591 A.D. preserved in the Cleveland Museum of Art (Schroeder 1981 Fig. 74E; Ray, N. R. et al. 1986, Fig. 26).

Presently Nepalese artists apply the technique of casting in bronze in various ways. The images are either made of known subjects or according to the new ones chosen by the artist to his own choice. Two types of techniques are applied:

(a) Hammer beating process (*manjya thyojya*)

(b) Lost wax or Cire-Perdue casting (*than jya*)

(a) **Hammer Beating Process**

This process is applied to a sheet of metal by beating it with a hammer. It has two variants:

(i)   Embossing or Repouse (*thakaya*);
(ii)   Engraving (*kohmuya*)

(i) Embossing or Repouse

In this process a bronze sheet is attached by a wooden instrument to a wooden anvil and the artist beats with an iron hammer. The object created in this manner are either custom-made or artist's independent creations. First the desired form is outlined on the bronze sheet. If a large sized image is to be made, then the sheet is cut into several parts according to the desired size and the image is outlined on it. Then it is placed over the anvil and beaten with a flat hammer. In this process, iron rods of various sizes and round hammer are used for beating the sheet. Usually embossed objects are hammered and subsequently gilded. Items such as plaques, *prabha* and masks are normally made from a single metal sheet. Objects having complicated composition are made in parts using several metal sheets, and afterwards are assembled together. Certain parts of an image, such as feet, arms, attributes and other details, which are too complicated to be embossed, are appended after having been carved from wood or cast in metal using lost wax process. After employing matrices of wood, metal sheets are systematically hammered and partially enlarged until they take a proper required shape. Doors of Kathmandu Taleju temple set up by King Pratap Malla in 1671 AD and 1672 AD respectively (Vajracharya 1976: 224-30, Inscription nos. 32, 34 and 35), Pashupatinath temple set up by Devidas in 1676 AD (Regmi 1966a: 910), *Golden Gate* of Bhaktapur royal palace built by king Ranajeet Malla in 1753 AD (Regmi 1966a: 913) are the best examples of this type.

The major centre of embossing tradition is in and around Patan area, one of the ancient townships of the Kathmandu Valley, where the sounds of hammer and chisel can still be heard in the monastery areas and the *toles* (narrow lanes), streets of the city of Patan.

(ii) Engraving

In this process, the artist takes a thick metal sheet according to a model or to the required size. Occasionally, this process is carried out by the hammer beating. He cuts the sheet according to his need. Then he outlines of the figure that to be engraved is tentatively drawn. After that the sheet is placed upon a wooden anvil that matches the outline. Then the outlined figure is engraved by using an iron hammer. The portion of the sheet that was askew while engraving is again put on the anvil and beaten by the wooden hammer to put it in shape. For making the beating easier, the sheet is heated in fire. After removing it from the fire the sheet is again engraved by hammering. In this way, the artist will make a rough figure. The worked metal sheet is then fixed on the wooden anvil layered with lac. With the help of a small fine flat iron-cutting tool and iron hammer, the main figure is separated which is finally extracted by heating the sheet. When the lac melts, the figure is freed. By using this technique frames and tympannums are made (Fig. 14). The square type tympannum and the large figure of Kama Raj Gumba at Svayambhunath are the best-known examples made by this technique.

Figure 14: Artist making Torana, applying embossing technique

(iii) Cleaning and Polishing

After embossing and engraving, objects are cleaned and polished. They are first finished by chisselling and then for about two hours put in liquid with acidic nature made out of sour substance. But such indigenously made liquid substance is not available these days, so the artist uses acid. After soaking sufficiently in the sourly substance, the objects are scrubbed either by a metal brush or polished with a brick powder and hay to produce a shining effect. These days, however, the objects are polished on electric machines.

If the figure is to be coated with gold, it is first painted with a sourly element and then dipped in mercury. Then gold slurry is applied on the figure and heated slowly so that the mercury evaporates and only yellowish, whitish glaze of gold will be seen. For shining and polishing, the figure is rubbed by using agate and ultimately it is washed in an herbal solution. This process of furnishing is known as *lasan thayagu* (brightening the object) in the local dialect. After that the object is immersed in boiled herbal froth of sweet taste (*majitho*). This process is called *jha: kayagu*. The door, Lokesvara attached windows and the three artistically engraved windows attached in one form (*sanjhya*) of Patan Darbar, the statue of the Malla king - Yoga Narendra Malla (Fig. 17), the life size images of Ganga and Jamuna known as Shree Lakshmi of the main courtyard of Patan Darbar, the *Golden Gate* of Bhaktapur Darbar, constructed during the reign of king Ranajeet Malla (Fig. 15), the door of Navadurga temple, statue of king Bhupatindra Malla (Fig. 16) and the images of Shree Lakshmi in the main courtyard (*mu chuka*) of Bhaktapur Darbar and images in the Hanumandhoka Darbar (old palace of Malla kings) at Kathmandu, are all made of using these techniques. The images of Samyak Devata or Dipankar Buddha known as *kwapa:dyo* among the Buddhist Newars are also examples of this technique. These are taken out only occasionally from the storehouses by the Buddhist Acharyas in various monasteries.

(b) **Cire-Perdue Casting or Lost Wax Process (*Madhuchistavidhana*)**

Most of the images made in the Patan area are manufactured by the Cire-Perdue or lost wax process. It is generally believed that this technique in Nepal is probably an extension of the process followed by the Pala artists of Bengal and Bihar (Krishnan 1976: 29). At present, it is mainly carried out by the Newar artists of Patan city known as *bare* (one of the castes of Buddhist Newars). The artists of this caste claim that they use an ancient iconographic text known as *dya dekegu saphu*, which literally means as Text of Making an Image of Deity as a manual that is similar to the Silpa Sastras used

Figure 15: Golden Gate of Bhaktapur Royal Palace, Bhaktapur, 1753 AD

Figure 17: Statue of King Yoganarendra Malla infront of Degu Taleju Temple, Patan Darbar Square, *c*. 1700 AD

Figure 16: Statue of King Bhupatindra Malla on a stone pillar infront of Golden Gate, Bhaktapur, *c*. 1706 AD

by the Sthapatis of south India. However, in practice they carry out their work on the basis on their experimental expertise. But what they follow is a multitude of rules set by traditional norms. Unlike the south Indian Sthapatis, who invariably make solid casts, the Newar artists mainly practise hollow casting. Only in the case of images smaller than 15 cm. in height they make solid castings.

The image casting is a complex process, which is carried out by specialized artists belonging to specific sub-castes. As the manufacturing proceeds in several stages, there are artists who specialize only in particular skills according to what suits the particular individual. There is, however, always a chief artist who supervises and co-ordinates the complete process. His job also includes the responsibility of securing adequate patronage as well as managing the inventory.

The process of image casting by lost wax technique is divided into following stages:

1. Wax modelling: modelling of the envisaged image in wax;

2. Casting mould: covering the wax model with layers of clay (Fig. 18);
3. Casting: melting out of the wax model, filling the empty cavity with molten metal and finally breaking of the mould to reveal the cast image;
4. Finishing: polishing and engraving of the raw cast image;
5. Gilding: fire gilding with mercury, gold leaf or painting with cold gold;
6. Inlaying: inlaying with gold, and setting of semi-precious, imitation stones.

Figure 18: Wax model covered with clay, mixed with husk and cow dung

Technique of Modelling of the Image in Wax

The first step in the process of casting an image is the modelling of the envisaged image in wax. The *Vishnu-Samhita* mentions that "If an image is to be made of metals, it must be first made of wax" (Reeves 1962: 32). The shape and form of the finished image depend upon the wax model, and is, therefore, from the artistic and stylistic viewpoint; this is the most important and vital part of the process. The traditional wax model is prepared in two different types: (i) Solid and (ii) Hollow. For this work materials like wax, rosin, mustard oil, big vessel that contains nearly about five litres of wax, oven, leather sheet, iron cutting tool, iron rod, iron hammer, wooden hammer, traditional spoons of 3ft in size used for cooking purpose called *dhaga* and *panyue* in local dialect, wooden flakes of 3" x 5" x 1" in size, rough cloth, stone slab, towel, coal or wood fuel, small pointed knife, bucket made of clay, bowl made of wood, flat iron rod of about 30 cm, flat and smooth brick of 14" x 20" x 4" in size, wax mould or replica, tools made of buffalo's horn, clean water, and tray are required

After removing honey, beeswax is put on a clean plastic sheet and with the help of iron cutting tool and hammer it is broken into many small pieces and is put in a brass or aluminum pot. Before splitting the beeswax, it is weighed so that rosin can be mixed in the correct ratio to ensure that beeswax would not melt while heating. For example, in 2.2 kg beeswax nearly 600 grams of powdered rosin is added. This admixture depends upon the season of the year, so as to have the necessary consistency to work with. The Newar artists distinguish between the winter and the summer wax. In the dark wax produced during winter months, rosin of about 400 gms is mixed in 2.2 kg beeswax, while rosin of 400 to 500 gms is mixed with same amount of light beeswax that is produced during summer months. The light or summer wax is stiffer and does not melt easily in the summer heat. The light wax generally replaces the winter wax in March, and it is used until October. As confirmed by the Newar artist Moti Kaji Shakya of Patan, the wax of either type is called '*shee*' in Newari parlance.

The wax is boiled in a metal pot and charcoal or wood is used as fuel in the oven. It must be stirred continuously by a long handled spoon, when the wax starts melting, During boiling, the pot is removed several times from the oven to avoid spill - over of the wax. If stirring is not done, the bubbles of wax may catch fire. Half an hour after heating the wax gives out a good aroma. Then a bit of wax is tasted for thickening after cooling in order to check whether it is ready for moulding. After about forty-five minutes of heating, the colour and smell of the wax will change. Then the rosin, made into powder on a stone slab and filtered through muslin cloth, is added to it, according to the prescribed ratio to wax. While rosin is being added, the wax pot is removed from the oven and the mixture is continuously stirred for nearly fifteen minutes by a big spoon. After adding the rosin, the pot is again put on the oven for heating the mixture. Whether the rosin melts or not, is observed by stirring the wax. The flame is also to be watched carefully. As the froth comes out from the wax, it comes out from rosin also. At such moments, the pot is removed from the oven and kept away, so that the danger of the spill - over catching fire should not arise. It is also necessary to watch that even a drop of water should not fall into the boiling wax pot, otherwise there would be a rapid rise in the level of the mixture and hence a spill - over.

When the mixture is cooked properly then, with the help of two persons, the wax is filtered through a muslin cloth in a clay bucket. There must be some water at the bottom of the bucket, so that the wax will not stick to it.

While pouring the wax, for the purpose of filtering it, a square, flat metal rod or strong stick is used to stir the wax continuously. If the wax does not filter properly, or if it becomes thick, it will again be put on the oven for heating. The wax should not be thicker; and while filtering it through the cloth in the bucket, it is not supposed to be poured from height, so that the water should be remixed in the wax and it will not be sticky. The wax is aired with winnowing fan (*hasha*, made of bamboo chips) or a leather sheet so that the wax will spread to take the shape of the bucket and its edge will be plain and smooth. At this stage wax becomes a *prepared wax,* as it is mentioned in the *Manasara* (Reeves 1962: 30).

Artists use different types of tools and equipments for making a wax model. These consist of a long wooden roller, a smooth marble slab, a wooden mallet, a compass, a pair of calipers, modelling tools of various shapes made out of horns and ivory, steel knives, pincers and a small charcoal brazier.

For the actual modelling of the wax image, the artist exposes the wax either to the sun or heats it on fire. Then it is spread on a smooth stone slab, beaten either by a wooden beater or an iron hammer or by hard flat stone (Fig. 19) to discard the water out from the wax that was mixed while filtering the wax in the bucket. Once devoid of water, the wax becomes sticky enough for moulding. The wax is spread on a stone slab and beaten further with millet to make it a homogenous lump. After beating the wax, mustard oil is added so that it can be handled freely while working. The flat sheet is sliced into small pieces, which are used for making the model, and rolled into hollow tubes. In order to prevent the tools from sticking to the wax, they are moistened at regular intervals. To retain the malleability of the wax, a constant temperature is maintained with the help of a small handy lamp or oven.

After bringing out the envisaged image in full form, by conforming to the *laksana,* gestures/postures (*mudras*) by modelling the head, hands, legs, and rest of the parts are also prepared. Facial features like mouth, nose, eyes, etc., are the last to be shaped with the help of a tool made of horn of a female buffalo. Different parts of the image like limbs are modelled separately and subsequently added in the sockets in the torso (Fig. 18). These socket joints are located at such points

where it can be concealed by the ornaments like necklace and bracelets over them. Likewise parts like *kirita mukuta* on the forehead, *prabhamandala, kamarbandha,* and clothes are fixed at a later stage. After finishing the model, the pedestal for the image is to be prepared either in the shape of square, rectangular, cylindrical or of floral shape and socket to the main figure.

Figure 19: Wax model and hard stone used as a tool for beating wax sheet

Next, in order to ascertain the quantity of metal required for casting, the modelled parts are weighed and the amount is calculated in proportion to the wax used. In the case of brass, it is ten times the weight of wax. The modern artists have no clear idea regarding the proportion of silver and gold, as nowadays in these metals are not used for casting. However, they claim that they retain the knowledge of making cast in alloy known as *panchaloha* (alloy of five metals) and *astadhatu* (alloy of eight metals).

ii. Techniques of preparing Die Replica or *Sancha (Thasa)*

For making a replica, the artist prepares the wax sheet using the same process as in modelling. This wax sheet is placed on the original figure of wax. Before placing the wax sheet, compound of oil, water and saliva is put all over the main figure so that the wax sheet will not stick to it. After wrapping the wax sheet around the figure, and then slowly pressed with fingers carefully maintaining uniformity of thickness of the wax sheet. The surplus wax is removed by knife. After firmly pressing the sheet over the whole figure and ensuring that it has assumed the proper shape it is carefully removed by cutting out. The replica then is put in the cold water for cooling, so that the shape should be retained.

iii. Technique of making Solid Images from Replica

In making solid images, the artist puts a compound of oil, water and saliva all over the replica from inside. After that, the wax sheet is wrapped to the replica. While the wax is warm, it is applied to the replica from the inside by pressing gently with fingers to give shape of the figure. The wax is repeatedly heated on a low flame to keep it warm and malleable. The extra portion that jults out of the replica is removed by a knife. The model prepared thus is kept for cooling for sometime and with the help of a spindle (*lattu*) made of wax itself, the wax image within wax replica is slowly and gently removed from all sides, parts by parts. These parts will be rejoined by using molten wax. After that the joints are smoothened out by using horn tools.

iv. Technique of making Hollow Images from Replica

The prepared wax sheet is heated again in such a way that it will not melt by the heat of fire or sun. After heating the wax sheet, it is placed inside the replica, which is then quickly spread and pressed all over the replica by fingers. The uniformity of thickness all over is carefully maintained while taking the shape of the interior mould. While pressing, the artist has to be careful not to change the shape of the replica itself. If the wax cools in the process, the whole object will have to be heated again. After completing the pressing, the prepared model is kept in water for sometime for cooling if the model is still warm. After cooling it is pulled out with the help of a spindle. The pulling process is continued till the whole wax model comes out. Then the shape will be rectified and finished either by hand or by horn tools. The surplus wax sheet will be removed by a knife.

All the parts of the wax models prepared thus are joined together by using molten wax to give the original form. Then the models are observed carefully against sunlight or artificial light to ensure the uniformity of the thickness. If at some points it is translucent then it is possible that the joints are weak and shape may change because of it. To resolve the problem molten wax is put all over the figure and joints with the help of pointed stick that is wrapped with fine muslin cloth. This process is called *ti payegu* meaning putting the liquid. This process will be repeated several times till it is absolutely certain that the edges of the replica are completely smoothened to the required extent. In this way the chances of leaving any flaws while actually making the bronze cast are reduced to minimum possible degree.

For metal casting, a wax pipe or channel is needed. This is prepared according to the shape of the objects to be made. It is meant for the funneling the molten metal and for circulating the displaced air inside the mould. In the case of very complicated wax models, especially multi-armed images, additional channels are attached to the outer parts of the extremities to ensure that the molten metal reaches every nook and corner of the clay mould. The channel also increases the stability of the wax model, which must support its own weight whenever it is laid down.

v. Casting Moulds

Once the wax model is completed, clay mould, which will receive the molten metal, is prepared. The clay is put in three to five layers, depending on the size and nature of the image to be produced. This particular process is crucial, because the mould and wax will ultimately determine the quality of the casting.

After making the wax model and putting the channel, it is covered with clay. This process is known as *mesin payegu* meaning covering by soft clay. In this process, the moulding materials consist of soft clay, which is mined out from a depth of fifteen feet from the field, yellow clay from a depth of five feet (*gicha*), cowdung (*sappa*), rice husk (*hema*) and water. For the first coat, soft clay and cow dung are soaked in two different vessels overnight. After mixing soft clay and cow dung together, thin slurry is prepared for the first coating. Similarly, soaked yellow clay and rice husk are mixed. For the second coat this mixture is kept away. After that the thin slurry, that is prepared for the first coat, is filtered through a muslin cloth and the wax model is dipped in it. Then the mould is kept in shade for drying. The first coat is applied many times and each layer is allowed to dry completely in the shade before the next coat is applied. The first two layers are a light application of very fine-grained gray clay. Care is taken so that the first application of clay reaches every corner of the wax figure so that a tight fit is assured around the wax. The model is then covered with several layers of the second coat of clay to which charred husk, tiny bit of cotton and salt, all finely grinded on a stone, are added. When the model is ready for casting, under successive coatings of clay, its shape can only be dimly discerned in the outlines of the bulky mould (Figs.19). This clay mould is known as *saya*. The mouth of the channel is left free in the shape of a cup throughout during the process of applying various coats.

The process of applying various layers of clay is the most time-consuming process in the entire casting procedure, taking as long as two months. The artist is at the mercy of the weather during this time, since the clay must dry evenly in the sun to ensure that the wax model is not distorted nor the clay cracked by uneven drying. Obviously, for this reason, certain seasons are considered more suitable than others for the manufacture of images. The best season is from March to May, when the sun is moderately strong and the monsoon has yet to arrive.

vi. Image Cast

The foundry establishment of dewaxing, baking and casting consists of dewaxing and baking oven (*sayaga:*), melting furnace, dry earth, sand, a shallow pan or bowl, clay or iron crucibles, clip tongs, lifting tongs (*sanasa*), pointed chisel, hammer, and charcoal.

Once the mould becomes completely dry, smaller clay mould is dewaxed by heating in the charcoal brazier or oven (*agucha*). The larger mould is heated inside a specially made oven named *sayega:* used for dewaxing and baking the mould. It is built on the floor and is similar to wood fired muffle furnace used for baking pottery. It consists of a hearth at the bottom and a chamber with a grilled floor over it. This chamber has an opening on one side for loading the mould inside. After baking the clay mould from every side, the artist makes a hole with a knife in that portion where the channel is kept. The melted wax is poured from the mould in a bucket or pan, containing cold water. This wax is reused. The mouth of the channel is made bigger for the sake of pouring the molten metal. Then the mould is left undisturbed for several days before casting, although the period between the melting of the wax and casting should not exceed one week, as the interior of the mould is then subject to deterioration.

For casting, two ovens are prepared and fired. The baking of the mould and melting of the metal go on simultaneously to get the mould prepared in time when the metal is ready for pouring. After dewaxing, the mould is given a fresh coat of fine clay mixture in order to seal off any cracks that might have developed while dewaxing. Then the empty mould is once again shelved inside the oven, which is fed with wood fuel and covered with charcoal. The opening is closed by two terracotta slabs (*kopu*) and the baking is done.

The oven used for melting the metal (*bhonchaga:* also called *kwa jhya:*) is constructed of bricks and clay, and it is fed by charcoal rather than wood and is constantly attended to by mechanical bellows. The raw metal is pre heated and broken into small pieces and loaded into open crucibles (*bhoncha*). These crucibles are constructed of special fireproof clay, which is of sufficient thickness to hold the molten metal and not to break when removed from the furnace with tongs (*sanasa*) and turned over for pouring during the moment of casting. According to the artist Badri Kaji Shakya of Patan, in earlier days, these crucibles were made in Nepal itself. These were made of a combination of clay and rice husk. But now they are imported from India and are made of clay and cement mixture According to the same artist, while melting the metal, some part of zinc is added for melting quickly and also for cleaning the metal. In 2.2 kg metal 100 gms of zinc is to be added. The alloy is proportioned according to the weight of the figure. After keeping the raw metal in the crucibles, its mouth is covered by a clay plate.

For melting metal, the crucibles are kept inside the furnace (*kwajhya*) and covered with charcoal. The space between the crucibles is packed with charcoal and fire is ignited. According to the artist Moti Kaji Shakya, blasting is done either by leather sheet or by winnowing fan (*hasa*) or mechanical bellows are used. Using thumb rules based on long-standing experience, the artist ascertains the exact time when mould and metal will be ready for casting. In other words, the flame, heat, colour, odour and smoke are also used as indicators of readiness of the metal. As for casting, only the observation of the temperature of the molten metal is not sufficient; the temperature of the receiving mould is also to be checked before pouring the metal in it. For this, a long stick that is tied with wax or cloth (*alancha*) is kept on the opening of the mould. When the metal is completely ready, the artist removes the terracotta lid with the help of tongs, and breaks the temporary wall. The artist opens the furnace chamber and the crucibles are carefully lifted with tongs and the metal is poured into the mould (Fig. 20). After filling the molten metal, the clay mould is left to cool and harden completely for about fifteen to twenty minutes. The cooling is speeded also by pouring cold water over the mould, which emits huge volumes of steam. Finally, the entire mould is placed in a large bucket (*atha*) containing water to complete the cooling process (Fig. 21).

Figure 20: Artist pouring molten metal in clay mould

Figure 21: Clay mould dipped in water to cool down

The melting of the metal inside the sealed crucibles prevents oxidation. The size of the crucible is such that the operations could be carried out by two persons without difficulty. The casting is done in parts as a solution against short supply of metal. So some moulds can be safely stored for later use.

vii. Finishing

When the mould becomes sufficiently cool to touch, the clay is removed carefully with chisel and hammer (Fig. 22) and the cast is released slowly, so that it might not be damaged. After the image is cast, it is handed over to other artist who would proceed to the job of retouching for smoothing and engraving. The cast image, when it emerges from the clay moulds, its surface is rough, due to the impression of the clay particles stuck on the metal. Thus the first step of retouching in engraving is called sanding. If the image is to be ultimately painted with gold, then only sandpaper is used for the purpose. If the image is poorly cast or has some minor flaws, which are not so serious as to justify melting down the metal, then it is repaired by welding other pieces of the same material to the affected areas. Otherwise in case of serious flaws the cast may be discarded completely for remitting the material.

Figure 22: Image emerged from clay mould

When the sanding is finished, the actual process of engraving begins. Using a small chisel and a hammer, the engraver redefines and sharpens the details built into the original work, and, in some cases, he does innovative engraving work, chiselling scroll-like designs into clothing. Similarly the ornaments, *mukuta, kundala, vaju*, paujeb (*pauju*) are engraved on the image. In some cases, artist may do some inlay work by using other metals into the surface of the object. Lastly features like eyes, nose, mouth and ears, will be chiselled in a balanced way to create a perfect face. Polishing, as per the customer's demand, is also done. After this process only, the process of gold or silver plating is started.

viii. Technique of making Slurry of Gold

There are several stages of making a paste of gold. As the gold is a malleable metal, thicker gold sheet is beaten into very thin sheet almost like a paper. In olden days, it was done by manually beating the gold with hammer, but, now, the old method is replaced by the electric pressure machine. According to the artist, in traditional method, the gold was first heated in fire and is beaten with the hammer several times. This process is repeated until the gold sheet becomes as thin as paper. At present, there are iron rolls fitted with electric motor through which the gold is passed several times. Each time after passing through the gold sheet gets thinner and thinner and ultimately to the thinness of a gold ribbon. Then the golden ribbon is cut into small pieces.

Another method as described by the artist Mana Kaju Shakya of Patan is to cut the gold sheet into small pieces, then mix with mercury in the ratio of 1: 4. Then these two combinations of metal are put in on the iron anvil and by adding sand and water, it is slowly ground with the help of a pestle. The grinding is done very slowly to prevent the unstable drops of mercury and fine pieces of gold escaping from the mortar. The necessary amount of salt and citric acid is added periodically to help the gold and mercury completely amalgamate into a paste. This process of grinding is continued till both the materials change into the paste and sand is removed. The grinding process is a very slow and tedious job. A trained person can grind maximum of twenty to twenty five grams of gold in a day's work.

ix. Technique of Pasting Gold

Gold slurry or paste is used specially in the making of silver and copper objects. Since the gold is the noblest metal, it could be gilded only on these two metals. In traditional method, no other base metal shall be considered capable of taking gold plating.

To start with, the object on which the gold is to be gilded must be in proper shape, should be cleaned thoroughly and then rubbed with sandpaper. In olden days, the *ko appa* (over burnt brick) was used for rubbing the surface, but now sandpaper is used. The object should be rubbed in such a way that it should obtain maximum shine and should be absolutely smooth. Then the object is dipped in the mercury without any delay, otherwise, due to the atmospheric reaction; it turns dark within a couple of hours. If it turns dark, it has to be cleaned and rubbed again and the process will be repeated for gilding the gold until it shines and becomes smooth as described above before it is taken up for the gilding process.

Once the object is thus ready for gilding, it is again dipped in mercury, mixed with salt, citric acid, woodash and water and then rubbed vigorously either with cloth or iron brush so that it shines brightly. Once the mercury is fully coated, the object looks as if made of steel. Then once again it is carefully cleaned in fresh water to wash out the salt and citric acid. If this is not done properly then it will leave unwanted patches after gold gilding. This is because the residual portion of salt and citric acid reacts with mercury, gold and copper resulting in unwanted patches.

Then the gold paste is applied to the required portion only. In olden days, it was rubbed either with a finger or with an iron rod covered with muslin cloth or cotton on its top. At present, it is done by a small brush with the help of nitric acid and washed by water so that the dirt will be washed away and it will be easy for pasting. After rubbing pasting is done with a small stick or flat spoon (*panyu*). Then the gold-pasted object is heated for about ten seconds on charcoal fire and then brushed with a brush topped with a cotton swab. The action is repeated eight to ten times depending upon the intensity of the fire. Once the gold paste has been coated on the intended places of the image, the real gold gilding starts. The image is cleaned with cotton. By doing this, the paste gets balanced in every part where it has been applied. While giving heat to the image, the mercury will evaporate, which is very harmful to health. It especially affects the jaws. As a measure against the harmful fumes spiced but uncooked raw piece of meat of buffalo known as *kachila* in the local dialect, is held in the mouth and only after completing the application of the gold paste, the meat is thrown out and the mouth is washed with local alcohol. The act of heating and brushing is done very carefully; otherwise the image gets overheated and gets unevenly spotted and darkened. If the mercury is not evaporated properly the gold image may get patinated with green and white blotches indicating the presence of residual portion of the mercury. To proceed with care and without haste is therefore, absolutely necessary.

Once the mercury evaporates, the gold comes out bright and then the image is washed in herbal froth. This froth is prepared by boiling an herb of sweet taste *magitho* till it becomes thick. After washing in the herbal froth, the colour of gold, though not shiny is seen. To give a shiny look the image is rubbed with agate or hakib stone (*hathan*). This process is called *lasan thayegu* or *lasan tayegu* meaning brightening the image. The particular technique applied to pasting gold in the image described so far is very indigenous in character and has been developed by Newar artists.

x. Technique of Gilding the Face

This is done only after finishing the process of modelling, casting, chiselling and pasting the amalgamated powder of gold and mercury. For preparing the gold paste to paint the face, the gold is cut into small tiny pieces. These pieces are soaked in hot water in small bowl for nearly ten minutes. When the gold melts and remains on the surface of the bowl, water is discarded. The remaining gold, that is wet, is mixed with *saresh* (leather glue). The consistency of the mixture of these two components is observed whether it is thick or thin either by dipping the end of a brush that will be used for painting or by a small stick of wood in the mixture. After this, gold paste is applied to the required face of the image and other parts with the help of a brush. This process is repeated several times. But, at present, before applying the gold, a primer, mixed with white stone coloured leather glue, is applied as a lining (*aster*) on the face and other parts. A mixture of ochre coloured powder (*ramatilak*), leather glue and ready-made wet powdered gold that are readily available in the market, are also applied. After applying the primer or *aster*, the single coat of gold will be enough. After completing the gold coat on required parts, individual features are painted. Thus for eyes, the mixture of white stone coloured leather glue is used; for cheeks the mixture of leather glue with white and red colour giving a reddish tinge is used for painting; for hair, blue stone colour is applied, whereas eyes, nose, ear, the eyebrow, are outlined in the blue stone colour.

Thus finishing is done by adopting the various processes like chiselling, engraving, sanding, cleaning, and fitting the different parts together, over all polishing, gilding and encrusting with precious and semi-precious stones. The inlay pieces are inserted in the gaps left for them and then skillfully riveted. These joints are concealed with jewellery, attached with precious and semi-precious stones. Gilding is done with gold leaf by applying it to an adhesive lacquer. It must be said that the art of engraving has not maintained the same high standard over the years as that of sculpting. This is largely due to the change of the mass market for cast images, all of which must be finished. Though most of the processes are similar to those of Indian artists, there exists, however, a fundamental difference with regards to the technique applied in India and Nepal. In India every object, except the very big one, is modelled, moulded and cast as a whole (Krishnan 1976: 32). In Nepal, except for very small objects, each part of the image is done separately (modelling, moulding and casting) and after casting the parts are assembled together.

Conclusion

Art and literature are the expression of man's experiences, emotions and feelings. As regards history and culture, various activities of the rulers and ruled, scholars and men of literature concerning politics, art, architecture and other creative expressions provide background for the elaboration and illustration of history.

As regards the present study of Nepalese bronzes, a systematic survey of the bronze art has been made in a historical perspective. Bronze art occupies a pre-eminent position in the art history of both India and Nepal.

Indus or Harappan Civilization (3000 to 1800 BC) indicates the beginning of the tradition of bronze art in India. Among the metal objects unearthed from excavations at Mohenjo-daro, Harappa and several other sites, the figure of dancing girls from Mohenjodaro are the earliest sculpture to have been cast by *madhuchistavidhana* (Cire-Perdue or Lost wax process) - the process also adopted in bronze art of later periods.

Due to the lack of sufficient exploration and excavation activities and scientific research in Nepal, the authentic history of bronze art does not go back to the period before the Lichhavis.

The civilization itself began in Nepal with the draining out of the water of Kathmandu Valley and appearance of different kinds of flora and fauna and gradual increase in the habitat of the people. A more visible development of art and architecture, sculptures and stone images can be seen in the Malla period. However, there is no denying the fact that the Lichhavi period introduced the beginning of the bronze art along with the tradition of stone art.

Studies of bronze art of Nepal have been carried out by many renowned scholars of Nepal and abroad viz., A.K. Coomaraswamy, Gautamvajra Vajracharya, U.Von Schroeder, Marry S. Slusser, Pratapaditya Pal, Stella Kramrisch, Duglos Barrett and Karl Khandalawala. Though they assign different periods of the development of bronze art, most of the scholars like Gautamvajra Vajracharya, Schroeder, Slusser and Pal agreed that the history of bronze casting can be traced to as early as the fifth century of the Christian era. One of the earliest images that resembles with the Gupta bronze Buddha of India is the image of a standing bronze Buddha of Samvat 513 Saka era preserved in the Cleveland Museum, USA. Equally important are the undated bronze Vishnu image of Changunarayan of the fourth century and Buddha image of Sankhu of the early seventh century. The discovery of silver and copper coins in the excavations at Tilaurakot in the western Tarai of Nepal suggests the possibility of an older beginning of bronze art in Nepal.

The bronze casting in Nepal has been heavily influenced by the styles of the Gupta and the Pala arts of India. In Nepal, it is only from the fifth century onwards along with the Manadeva I's Changunarayana pillar inscription, we see the development of bronze art through the dated inscriptions, copper coins, and dated images. *Mananka* coins of Manadeva I stand first in the history of coins to trace the development of bronze art. During the reign of Amsuvarma (early 7th century A. D.) also, there was development of bronze art. During his time, Nepal used to export objects like iron and copper goods to India and images of Maitreya, Aksobhya and Arya Tara to Tibet. The most ancient and developed form of bronze art is supposed to be the image of Minanath Lokesvara of Patan Tangal Tole, which has been related to Amsuvarma. Chinese accounts after the visit of Chinese travellers to Nepal during the fifth and seventh

centuries also indicate that Nepalese people were highly skillful in metal work.

The eleventh/twelfth century saw the rise of Malla dynasty in Nepal. The Malla period is the developed age of the bronze art of Nepal. Indian character in style and technology of bronze art was predominant during the Malla period. During this period, Tantrism, Buddhist pantheon, monastic orders, floral and geometrical designs, gilt bronze, images on the Tantra were in vogue. Newari artists in Kathmandu Valley were strongly influenced by the Pala and Sena styles of India, which were also adopted by Tibetans and Chinese artists from the Newar artists. Nepalese bronze art, therefore, has received foreign influence that was adopted and transmuted by indigenous artists. .

From the study of the bronze art from the ancient to the present periods, we come to the conclusion that there are ample accounts, statements of the chronicles and inscriptions providing evidences of the techniques and methods, artistic activities and achievements. Most of the activities were due to the cultural and religious contacts with the artists and people of India, China and Tibet. The tradition of casting of bronze images in Nepal has gone through changes over the centuries. All the images are dedicated to religion and because of them aesthetic value, artistic vigour and taste, they constituted a unique style. Further study is required to find out the authentic historical background and importance of the Nepalese bronze art.

Findings

1. The main technique of Nepalese bronze art applied by the Newar artists of Kathmandu Valley, especially of Patan, is Cire-Perdue or Lost Wax process following the very ancient technology of India known as *Madhuchhistavidhana.* This technology is still practised in Nepal.
2. The technique of Indian artists was and is applied by Newar artists, though they claim of having their own technology.
3. Unlike the solid casting of the south Indian artists, the Newar artists mostly produced hollow casting, which is the process mostly applied by the present eastern Indian artists. The Chinese visitor's surprising note that "there are sculptures to astonish you" might

indicate the repouse art and sculpture that covered the temples.

4. The technique applied to paste gold or gilding in the bronze image is purely Newar artists' own contribution. The ancient Indian artists used *astadhatu* (amalgam of eight metals) in scientific proportions, but the Nepalese artists hardly used *astadhatu*; Nepalese rather after cheselling the work they applied gold dust and gold by other technique. For the last few hundred years, they are using mercury.

5. The inlaying of semi-precious stones on the image was practised in Nepal only after development of trade-link with Tibet. Early images lack these precious stones, but those after eighth/ninth centuries have semi-precious stones like raw crystal, polished crystal, topaz, turquoise, raw ruby, quartz, etc.

6. Stylistic changes took place between the Lichhavi and Malla bronzes. During post Lichhavi period. Many artists from eastern India viz., Nalanda and Vikramshila Universities came to Kathmandu Valley as refugees after Muslim invasions. They brought with them contemporary Indian styles and gods; we can cite Vasudhara, Jambhala (a Buddhist term for Kuvera, god of wealth), Dipankara Buddha, the conception of Adi Buddha - Vajradhara, Prajna and so on. In the medieval period, because of tantric influence, male deities like Samvara, Cakra Samvara, Prajnaparamita, Heruka, Hevajra, Ganesh, etc. are seen placed together with their Shaktis (consorts),

7. The Nepalese artists introduced new characteristic features. They provided *yajnopavita* (sacred thread around body) even to Lokesvara and Boddhiosattvas.

8. N.R. Banerjee cited eight characteristic features of the Lichhavi art, viz., ornately elaborate hair style, proportionate limbs, plastic and mobile body, slenderness of waist, moderately exaggerated hips, restrained ornaments, not too plumb breasts and decorated and diaphanous drapery. The special features of both the ages may be enlisted as: religious in nature; slenderness of the waist; moderately exaggerated lower limbs; facial structure during the Lichhavi period is of the Gupta style, and the Pala style in the medieval period. There is simplicity in the Lichhavi bronzes against heavy ornamentation in the art objects of the medieval period. Lichhavi bronzes look like real, alive, lively, mobile and plastic in character.

9. Many devotee images of the medieval period found in and around Kathmandu Valley are portrayed in the *anjuli mudra* (devotional posture to deities); but this nature is not available in art works of the Lichhavi period. The devotee's images were depicted by the Lichhavis only in the form of the Garuda (kept kneeling down with folded hands above).

All the above factors enriched the Nepalese art both in theme and quality.

ii. **Problems**

The researcher had to face some problems during her study. Many images, referred to by scholars in their works, either from private or public places, could not be located. They are either stolen or destroyed. Many international institutions, including the cultural sections of UNESCO, government organizations like Interpol are working hard to stop the art theft, robbery and removal from one country to another.

It should also be noted that, though this work adequately covers various aspects of the bronze arts in Nepal, it was not possible to include its specimens, which exist and are on display outside the country.

Most of the art objects in Nepal are in private collections, placed in some *math / mandir* (monasteries/temples) and are not made available to anybody, other than the priests, even for the purpose of study. So the only way open is to rely on the priest's accounts, who are normally confined in their views.

In some instances inscriptions on or about bronze objects are near blurred because of constant use, leaving them undecipherable.

Same is the case with archaeological sites - some of them are not accessible. Available literary sources too are almost silent on many matters of the saved temples where these art treasures are housed. In some instances the *torana* (*tolan*), which is generally installed just above the gateway of the temples and which may carry some inscription - is found to be missing. At some places bronze idols too, are not original. Not only that, the Government of

Nepal does not have even proper catalogues of the art works of private collections. The aristocratic and priestly families of Bhaktapur and Lalitpur have thousands of pieces of art works - they are not properly studied. Our traditional Guthi system (guided by religious motives) allows only the most senior citizens known as *thakali* or a special priest, to worship and take care of those art works. The researcher found in many places that the *thakali* himself replaced the old statues by new ones and misused the old ones by selling or smuggling.

Thus, the socio-religious background of many undated bronze specimens remains unknown.

Another difficulty a researcher often faces is while identifying the cult ideology associated with particular specimens (Hinduism / Buddhism). Hence the classification based on the religious affiliation or a particular age of its ideology becomes very difficult. However, it was observed that there couldn't be any categorical solution for such classification.

The poverty and ignorance are the main factors that cause loss of hundreds of art objects almost every year. A few hundred dollars are regarded as a good amount of money and the owners sell the antiques.

iii. Suggestions

1. The Government, NGOs and INGOs have to work hard to increase the awareness of the people about the value of the centuries old art objects. The people should be properly educated to preserve their art objects. Once they understand how useful these things are to the country and to the future generations, they would stop selling or exchanging these art objects with modern electronics.
2. The government and other related organizations should convince the owners about need of photographs of every art object and preparing of proper catalogue of them, so that in case of theft and smuggling, necessary action can be taken.

3. If education and persuasion fail, there should be a strong law against art smuggling. Even though we have a law, it is not properly implemented. So the law should be strong and be properly implemented.
4. The donors should be encouraged to donate their valuable art objects to museums, universities and other institutions for safe stock and study. These donors have to be socially recognized for their donations.
5. The traditional technique is time consuming, sometimes not bringing enough rewards; so there must be some traditional schools to enroll apprentices with certain amount of scholarship for training, so that they would be interested to learn their inherited skill.
6. For bronze art objects, raw materials like wax, coal, charcoal, wood, metals and crucibles are needed; most of these materials have to be imported only against payment of heavy duties to customs authorities. Besides, prices too of these materials don't remain stationary. So it becomes difficult to manufacturers to meet consumers' demand. Also, there is no big market for their crafts at home. The manufacturers depend on foreign markets. What becomes clear is that the materials so needed be made available easily. Market facility both to procure raw materials and also to dispose of finished goods is equally needed. For promotion of sales at home and abroad, market, information customer choices are to be made available either by the government or by organizations like Chamber of Commerce and Federation of Nepalese Chamber of Commerce and Industries. For such an activity, Trade Production Centre, Overseas Trade Organization, Federation of Nepal's Industries and Commerce, etc., have come forward.
7. Occasionally, there should be an exhibition of traditional crafts; they should be properly judged; evaluated and best ones should be rewarded properly.

The above points in the opinion of the researcher would encourage traditional artists to produce high quality pieces and help the country to protect its cultural heritage.

References

Agrawal, V.S. 1950. *Greater India Archaeology in India*. Calcutta: Government of India.

Alsop, I. 1984. Problems in Dating Nepalese Metal Sculptures: Three Images of Visnu. *Contributions to Nepalese Studies* 12(1): 23-49.

Aryal, K.R. (tr.) 1967. *Kautilyako Arthasastra*. Kathmandu: Royal Nepal Academy.

Bangdel, L.S. 1970. Early Nepalese Bronzes, *Bulletin of NAFA Art Magazine*, pp. 1-11.

Bangdel, L.S. 1976. Nepali Dhatu Ka Murti (Vernacular), *Prajna* 1(4): 81-109.

Barrett, D. 1957. The Buddhist Art of Tibet and Nepal, *Oriental Art* 3(3): 91-95.

Bolon, C.R. 1991. Images of Agastya in Nepal, *Artibus Asiae* 51(1-2): 75-85.

Brown, P. 1912. *Picturesque Nepal*. London: Adam and Chales Black.

Chattopadhyaya, D.B. 1970. *Taranath's History of Buddhism In India*. Simla: Indian Institute of Advanced Study.

Chattopadhyaya, S. 1958. *Early History of North India*. Calcutta: Progressive Publishers.

Coomaraswamy, A.K. 1921. A Nepalese Tara, *Rupam* 6: 1-2.

Coomaraswamy, A.K. 1927. *History of Indian and Indonasian Art*. New York: Dover Publication.

Czuma, S. 1970. A Gupta Style Bronze Buddha, *Bulletin of Cleveland Museum of Art* 57(2): 55-56.

Darnal, P. 2002. Archaeological Activities in Nepal since 1983 A.D. to 2002 A.D, *Ancient Nepal* (Journal of the Department of Archaeology/HMG) 150: 39-48.

Dhungel, R. 1986. *Prachin Artha Vyavastha* (Vernacular). Kathmandu: Sharada Prasad Dhungel Publication.

Gairola, C.K. 1978. Nepalese Bronzes in Virginia Museum of Fine Arts, *Oriental Art* 29(3): 317-25.

Gautam, S.S. 1966. *Himavarsha aur Nepal*. Gorakhapur: Manava Jeevan Sansthan.

Gorakshkar, S. 1971. Two Nepali Bronzes in The Prince of Wales Museum, *Bulletin of Prince of Wales Museum of Western India* 11: 26-32.

Hagen, T. 1971. *Nepal*. New Delhi: Oxford and IBH Publishing Co.

Jayaswal, K.P. 1936. Cronology and History of Nepal, *Journal of Bihar and Orissa Research Society* 22(3): 161-264.

Jha, H.N. 1970. *The Lichhavis*. Varanashi: Chowkhamba Sanskrit Series Office.

Joshi, S.C. 1986. "Nepal Himalaya: A Physiographic Appraisal" (Extracted from *Nepal Himalaya Geo-Ecological Perspectives* edited by S.C. Joshi, co-edited by Martin J. Haigh, Y.P.S. Pangtey, D.R. Joshi and D.D. Dani). Naini Tal: Himalayan Research Group. Published in 1986.

Joshi, S.M. 1976. Nepali Dhatu Moortiko Vikashkrama (Vernacular), *Prajna* 5(4): 42-55.

Joshi, S.M. 1978. *Nepali Dhatu Moortikalako Vikashkram* (Vernacular). Kathmandu: Royal Nepal Academy.

Khanal, M.P. 1983. *Changu Narayana Ko Aitihashik Samagri* (Vernacular). Kathmandu: Research Centre for Nepal and Asian Studies.

Khandalavala, K. 1950. Masterpieces in South Indian and Nepalese Bronzes in the Collection of Mr. S.K. Bhedvar of Bombay, *Marga* 4(4): 8-27.

Kramrisch, S. 1964. *The Art of Nepal*. New York: Asia House Gallery Publications.

Krishnan, M.V. 1976. *Cire Perdue Casting in India*. New Delhi: Kanak Publications Book India.

Labriffe, M.C. 1973. Etude de La fabrication d'une statue au Nepal, *Kailash* 1(3): 185-92.

Lal, B.B. 1951. Further Copper Hoards from Gangetic Basin and Review of the problems, *Ancient India* 7: 37.

Levi, S. 1925. The Art of Nepal, *Indian Art and Letters* 1(2): 49-67.

Macdonald, A.W. and A.V. Stahl. 1979. *Newar Art*. New Delhi: Vikas Publishing House Pvt. Ltd.

Majumdar, R.C. (ed.) 1957. *The Struggle for Empire*. Bombay: Bharatiya Vidya Bhavan.

Marshall, J. 1931. *Mohenjo-daro and Indus Civilization*. London: Aurther Probsthain.

Mehta, R.J. 1971. *Masterpieces of Indian Bronzes and Metal Sculptures*. Bombay: D. B. Taraporevala Sons & Com. Pvt. Ltd.

Mishra, T.N. 1994. The Archaeological Research in the High Mountains of Mustang District, *Ancient Nepal* (Journal of the Department of Archaeology/HMG) 136: 141-61.

Mitra, D. 1972. *Excavation at Tilaurakot and Exploration in the Nepalese Tarai*. Kathmandu: Department of Archaeology / His Majesty's Government.

Pal, P. 1971-72. Three Dated Nepali Bronzes and Their Stylistic Significance, *Archives of Asian Art* 25: 58-66.

Pal, P. 1974. *The Art of Nepal Part I (Sculpture)*. Leiden/Koln: E.J. Brill.

Pal, P. 1975. *Nepal Where the Gods are Young*. New York: Asia House Gallery.

Pal, P. 1978. *The Ideal Image*. New York: Asia House Gallery.

Pandey, R. N. 1968. *A Brief Survey of the Nepalese Art Forms*. Kathmandu: Department of Culture / His Majesty's Government of Nepal.

Petech, L. 1958. *Medieval History of Nepal*. Roma: ISMEO.

Rajbanshi, S.M. (ed.). 1970. *Kantipur-Shilalekha-Suchi*. Kathmandu: Department of Archaeology / His Majesty's Government of Nepal.

Rajendra Ram 1978. *A History of Buddhism in Nepal A.D. 704-1396*. Delhi: Motilal Banarasidas.

Ray, A. 1973. *The Art of Nepal*. New Delhi: Indian Council for Cultural Relations.

Ray, N.R., K. Khandalavala and S. Gorakshkar. 1986. *Eastern Indian Bronzes*. India: Lalit-kala Academy.

Reeves, R. 1962. *Cire Perdue Casting In India*. New Delhi: Crafts Museum.

Regmi, D.C. 1992. Maligaon Ka Moortilekha (Vernacular), *Gorkhapatra* Dainik Supplementary, p. 1.

Regmi, D.R. 1965. *Medieval Nepal Part I.* Calcutta: Firma K.L. Mukhopadhyaya.

Regmi, D.R. 1966a. *Medieval Nepal Part II.* Calcutta: Firma K.L. Mukhopadhyaya.

Regmi, D.R. 1966b. *Medieval Nepal Part III.* Calcutta: Firma K.L. Mukhopadhya.

Regmi, D.R. 1966c. *Medieval Nepal Part IV.* Patna: The Auther.

Regmi, D.R. 1969. *Ancient Nepal.* Calcutta: Firma K.L. Mukhopadhyaya.

Regmi, J.C. 1968. *Lichhavi Sanskriti* (Vernacular). Kathmandu: Ratna Pustak Bhandar.

Rijal, B.K. 1979. *Archaeological Remains of Kapilvastu, Lumbini, and Devadaha.* Kathmandu: Education Enterprises (PVT) LTD.

Roerich, G. 1959. *Biography of Dharmasvamin.* Patna: K.P. Jayaswal Research Institute.

Sahai, B. 1981. "The Art of the Pala Period" (Extracted from the *Eastern Indian School of Medieval Sculpture* by R.D. Banerjee). New Delhi: Ramananda Vidya Bhavan. Published in 1981.

Schroeder, U.V. 1981. *Indo-Tibetan Bronzes.* Hong Kong: Visual Dharma Publications.

Schuh, D. 1992-93. Introduction, *Ancient Nepal* (Journal of the Department of Archaeology/HMG) 130-133: c-m.

Setencko, A.Y. 1978-79. The outcomes of the Scientific Mission to Nepal in Brief, *Ancient Nepal* 43-45: 1.

Sham Sastri, R. 1956. *Kautilya's Arthasastra.* Mysore: Printed at Sri Raghuveer Printing Press.

Sharma, J.L. 1982. *Hamro Samaj (Ek Adhyayan).* Kathmandu: Sajha Prakashan.

Sharma, P.R. 1967. Bronzes of Nepal, *Journal of Tribhuvan University* 3(1): 8-15.

Sharma, P.R. 1968. Introduction to Nepalese Art and Architecture, *Journal of Tribhuvan University* 4(1): 74-95.

Sharma, P.R. 1970. A Note on Some Bronzes at Vajrayogini, *Journal of Tribhuvan University* 5(1): 1-5.

Shrestha, S.S. 2002. Tukan Bahal Stupa, *Ancient Nepal* (Journal of the Department of Archaeology/HMG) 150: 20-38.

Simons, A. 1992-93. Trial Excavation of a Cave System in Muktinath Valley, *Ancient Nepal* (Journal of the Department of Archaeology/HMG) 130-133: 1-19.

Simons, A., W. Schon and S.S. Shrestha 1994. Preliminary Report on the 1992 camping of the Team of the Institute of Prehistory, University of Cologne, *Ancient Nepal* (Journal of the Department of Archaeology/HMG) 136: 51-75.

Slusser, M.S. 1975-76. On the Antiquities of Nepalese Metalcraft, *Archives of Asian Art* 29: 81-85.

Srivastava, B. 1967-68. Sankhu Buddha, *Puratattva* 1: 85-86.

Thapa, R.J. 1970. Nepali Murtikala (Vernacular), *Ramjham* 6(3): 8-31.

Tiwari, D.N. 1984-85. Burials from Western Nepal, Mustang, *Ancient Nepal* (Journal of the Department of Archaeology/HMG) 85:1-12.

Vajracharya, D. 1973. *Lichhavi Kalako Abhilekha* (Vernacular). Kathmandu: Research Centre for Nepal and Asian Studies.

Vajracharya, D. and K.P. Malla (eds.) 1985. *The Gopal Raj Vamsavali.* Kathmandu: Franz Steiner Verlog Wiesbaden GMBH.

Vajracharya, G. 1976. *Hanumanadhoka Rajdarbar* (Vernacular). Kathmandu: Researsh Centre for Nepal and Asian Studies.

Vajracharya, G. & M.R. Panta. 1961. *Abhilekha-Sangraha* Part III. Kathmandu: Samsodhan-Mandala.

Vats, M.S. 1940. *Excavations at Harappa Being an Account of Archaeological Excavations at Harappa Carried out In Between the Years 1920-21 and 1933-34.* Delhi: Published by Manager of Publications.

Walsh, E.H. 1973. *The Coinage of Nepal.* Delhi/Varanasi: Indological Book House.

Watters, T. 1904. reprint 1988. *On Yuan Chwang's Travels in India 629-645 AD Vols. I & II.* London: Royal Asiatic Society.

Wright, D. 1972. *History of Nepal* 3rd ed. Kathmandu: Nepal Antiquated Book Publishers.

Yogi, N.N., L.R. Satyal, B.C. Yogi and L. Chaulagai (eds.). 1956. *Himvatkhanda.* Kashi: Gorakshatilla Kashi Yogapracharini Mahasabha.

SOUTH ASIAN ARCHAEOLOGY SERIES

EDITED BY ALOK K. KANUNGO

SAA No 1.   Kanungo, Alok Kumar 2004 *Glass Beads in Ancient India: An Ethnoarchaeological Approach* (*British Archaeological Reports, International Series* S1242) Oxford. ISBN 1 84171 364 3.

SAA No 2.   Kanungo, Alok Kumar (Ed) 2005 *Gurudakshina: Facets of Indian Archaeology, Essays presented to Prof. V.N. Misra* (*British Archaeological Reports, International Series* S1433) Oxford. ISBN 1 84171 723 1.

SAA No 3.   Swayam, S. 2006 *Invisible People: Pastoral life in Proto-Historic Gujurat* (*British Archaeological Reports, International Series* S1464) Oxford. ISBN 1 84171 732 0.

SAA No 4.   Mushrif-Tripathy, Veena & Walimbe S.R. 2006 *Human Skeletal Remains from Chalcolithic Nevasa: Osteobiographic Analysis (British Archaeological Reports, International Series* S1476) Oxford. ISBN 1 84171 737 1.

SAA No 5.   Jahan, Shahnaj Husne 2006 *Excavating Waves and Winds of (Ex)change: A Study of Maritime Trade in Early Bengal (British Archaeological Reports, International Series* S1533) Oxford. ISBN 1 84171 753 3.

SAA No 6.   Pawankar, Seema J. 2007 *Man and Animal Relationship in Early Farming Communities of Western India, with Special Reference to Inamgaon (British Archaeological Reports, International Series* S1639) Oxford. ISBN 978 1 4073 0062 7.

SAA No 7.   Sharma, Sukanya 2007 *Celts, Flakes and Bifaces – The Garo Hills Story (British Archaeological Reports, International Series* S1664) Oxford. ISBN 978 1 4073 0068 9.

SAA No 8.   Kanungo, Alok Kumar (Ed) 2007 *Gurudakshina: Facets of Indian Archaeology, Essays presented to Prof. V.N. Misra* (Part II) (*British Archaeological Reports, International Series* S1665) Oxford. ISBN 978 1 4073 0069 6.

.

www.ingramcontent.com/pod-product-compliance
Lightning Source LLC
Chambersburg PA
CBHW051302270326
41926CB00030B/4695